Agnon's Tales
of the Land of Israel

YESHIVA UNIVERSITY CENTER FOR ISRAEL STUDIES SERIES

Yeshiva University Center for Israel Studies Publications
Academic Advisory Committee

Selma Botman
Shalom Carmy
Steven Fine
Joshua Karlip
Jill Katz
David Lavinsky
Zafrira Lidovsky Cohen
Ronnie Perelis
Jacob Wisse

Agnon's Tales of the Land of Israel

EDITED BY
JEFFREY SAKS AND SHALOM CARMY

FOREWORD BY
STEVEN FINE

☙PICKWICK *Publications* · Eugene, Oregon

AGNON'S TALES OF THE LAND OF ISRAEL
Yeshiva University Center for Israel Studies Series

Copyright © 2021 Yeshiva University. All rights reserved. Except for brief quotations in critical publications or reviews, no part of this book may be reproduced in any manner without prior written permission from the publisher. Write: Permissions, Wipf and Stock Publishers, 199 W. 8th Ave., Suite 3, Eugene, OR 97401.

Pickwick Publications
An Imprint of Wipf and Stock Publishers
199 W. 8th Ave., Suite 3
Eugene, OR 97401

www.wipfandstock.com

PAPERBACK ISBN: 978-1-7252-7887-5
HARDCOVER ISBN: 978-1-7252-7888-2
EBOOK ISBN: 978-1-7252-7889-9

Cataloguing-in-Publication data:

Names: Saks, Jeffrey, 1969-, editor ; Carmy, Shalom, editor ; Fine, Steven, foreword.

Title: Agnon's tales of the land of Israel / edited by Jeffrey Saks and Shalom Carmy ; foreword by Steven Fine.

Description: Eugene, OR : Pickwick Publications, 2021. | Yeshiva University Center for Israel Studies Series. | Includes bibliographical references and index.

Identifiers: ISBN: 978-1-7252-7887-5 (paperback). | ISBN: 978-1-7252-7888-2 (hardcover). | ISBN: 978-1-7252-7889-9 (ebook).

Subjects: LCSH: Agnon, Shmuel Yosef, 1887–1970—Criticism and interpretation. | Authors, Hebrew. | Hebrew literature, Modern—History and criticism.

Classification: PJ5053.A4 A25 2021 (print). | PJ5053 (epub).

Cover image information:
  Painting by Reuven Rubin
  Painting: New Colony (Tel Aviv), Reuven Rubin, 1929
  Reproduced with permission from Yeshiva University Museum

Scripture quotations in chapter 8 are taken from the Revised Standard Version of the Bible, copyright © 1946, 1952, and 1971 National Council of the Churches of Christ in the United States of America. Used by permission. All rights reserved worldwide.

Scripture quotations in chapters other than chapter 8 are the authors' own translations.

Contents

List of Illustrations | vii
Foreword | Steven Fine | ix
In Memoriam: Rabbi Ozer Glickman ז״ל | Selma Botman | xiii
Preface | Jeffrey Saks and Shalom Carmy | xv

1. Labyrinthine Quest: Agnon and Graham Greene as Resources for Religious Reflection | Shalom Carmy | 1

2. *Ge'ulah* in Zionist Ideology and Rhetoric and in Agnon's "Agunot" | Zafrira Lidovsky Cohen | 18

3. "Ma'aseh ha-Menorah": Agnon's "Tale of the Menorah" between Buczacz and Modern Israel | Steven Fine | 42

4. Reading Agnon's *Only Yesterday* Today | Hillel Halkin | 61

5. The Art of Agnon Annotation: Discussing Professor Avraham Holtz's Monumental Edition of Agnon's *T'mol Shilshom* | Avraham Holtz in conversation with Jeffrey Saks | 100

6. Hometown and Homeland: The Dialectic between *Eretz Yisrael* and Buczacz in Agnon's Late Works | Alan Mintz ז״ל | 114

7. "Always I Regarded Myself as One Who Was Born in Jerusalem": Agnon's Nobel Speech in Light of Psalm 137 | Jeffrey Saks | 125

CONTENTS

8. The Land of Israel for Its Own Sake: Agnon's "The Covenant of Love" | MOSHE SIMKOVICH | 135

9. Agnon's "Orange Peel": Word on the Street in the State Book Satires | LAURA WISEMAN | 151

10. From Hanye to Tehilla: The Righteous "Grandmother" as Personification of the Shtetl and Jerusalem in Baron and Agnon | WENDY ZIERLER | 166

11. "Savta Hanye" | DEVORA BARON, TRANSLATED BY WENDY ZIERLER | 189

12. Agnon at Yeshiva University | SHULAMITH Z. BERGER 197

List of Contributors 211
Index 215

Illustrations

Figure 3.1: Hanukkah Menorah, Poland, 18th century, North Carolina Museum of Art (photo: Steven Fine).

Figure 12.1: Certificate Presented to Agnon on the Occasion of His Nobel Prize Ceremony, Stockholm, Sweden, December 1966 (Yeshiva University Archives, Public Relations Events Collection, Box 5, Folder "Advertising—Obituary—S. Y. Agnon").

Figure 12.2: Agnon and Belkin at Yeshiva University convocation in Lamport Auditorium, June 7, 1967 (Yeshiva University Archives, Public Relations People Photo Collection, Box 1, Folder "Agnon, Shmuel Y)."

Figure 12.3: Esther Appelberg, Agnon's Niece (Yeshiva University Archives, Public Relations People Collection, Box 4, Folder "Appelberg, Esther").

Figure 12.4: "Yearning to breathe free," Yeshiva University 75th Anniversary. Advertisement, Supplement to the New York Times, September 10, 1961, Section 11, p. 8 (Copy in Yeshiva University Archives, Public Relations Events Collection, Box 32, Folder "Blueprint for the Sixties").

Figure 12.5: Agnon and Belkin Walking to Lamport Auditorium (Yeshiva University Archives, Public Relations Photo Collection, CPA Negatives, 22212_K19).

Figure 12.6: Yeshiva College Students of 1967 Watch Agnon's Academic Procession (Yeshiva University Archives, Public Relations Photo Collection, CPA Negatives, 22212_K21).

ILLUSTRATIONS

Figure 12.7: Agnon, Belkin, and Hartstein Walking on Amsterdam Avenue (Yeshiva University Archives, Public Relations Photo Collection, CPA Negatives, 22212_I3).

Figure 12.8: Agnon at the Podium Holding his Degree (Yeshiva University Archives, Public Relations People Photos, Box 1, Folder, "Agnon, Shmuel Y.").

Figure 12.9: Article on Agnon in the 1967 issue of the Nir (Yeshiva University Archives).

Figure 12.10: Letter of Thanks from Agnon to Belkin, July 6, 1967 (Yeshiva University Archives, Samuel Belkin Records, Cabinet A30, Drawer 4, Folder "Honorary Degrees to 1970").

Foreword

THE CENTER FOR ISRAEL Studies is dedicated to deepening Yeshiva University's relationship with the State of Israel. Our area studies approach to Israel, its land and peoples, brings together Yeshiva University's rich faculty, museum, and library resources to explore Israel in all of its complexities. Our work is expressed through diverse scholarship, publications, academic programs, museum exhibitions, public events, and educational opportunities.

I am most pleased to introduce *Agnon's Tales of the Land of Israel*, edited by Jeffrey Saks and Shalom Carmy. As one of the luminaries of contemporary Modern Orthodox thought, Shalom's broad knowledge of all things Jewish—and philosophical—is always astonishing to me. He is one of the true "holy men" of our community.

Jeffrey Saks is the acclaimed translator of Agnon into English, one of the foremost Agnon scholars today, and now editor of *Tradition* journal. His accomplishments are the pride of Yeshiva University, where he earned his BA in Yeshiva College, his MA in the Bernard Revel Graduate School of Judaic Studies, and his ordination at RIETS. We are honored to count him a Leon Charney Senior Fellow of the Center for Israel Studies.

This marvelous volume is the fruit of a conference organized by Carmy and Saks on our historic Washington Heights campus in 2016, under the auspices of the Center for Israel Studies. This was a magical event, bringing together both the most senior scholars in the field and the younger generation of Agnon lovers for an inspiring day of learning.

Alas, since that day our numbers have been depleted by two, with the passing of Prof. Alan Mintz ל״ז and of Rabbi Ozer Glickman ל״ז. The Jewish world is less for the loss of each of these amazing human beings, scholars, and leaders.

Foreword

For the Yeshiva University community, the loss of Rabbi Glickman is especially bitter. Ozer, my friend Tony, was a mainstay of YU and of our Modern Orthodox community. He was a founding member of the CIS board and eagerly joined the organizing committee for this conference. He was a *maayan ha-mitgaber,* an "ever flowing spring," of scholarship, civility, and kindness, of Torah, *derekh eretz, temimut,* smiles, and encouragement. A self-avowed amateur in Agnon studies, Ozer was anything but an amateur as he rattled off Agnon's rich Hebrew and revelled in each turn of metaphor.

We are most pleased to dedicate this volume in memory of our teacher and friend, Rabbi Ozer Glickman, secure that somewhere in a corner of the heavenly *beit midrash* he occasionally curls up with the writings of Agnon, on occasion basks in the *shiurim* of Reb Shmuel Yosef—and always radiates the light of the *Shekhinah.* יהי זכרו ברוך

We thank our partner and my academic home, the Bernard Revel Graduate School of Jewish Studies, for its support of this project, as well as the Agnon House of Jerusalem for its partnership in the conference. *Agnon's Tales of the Land of Israel* is a product of the academic and even spiritual depth of scholarship and teaching that flows from Yeshiva University in all its many parts, recently brought together under the rubric of *Judaic Studies @ YU.* CIS is a proud constituent of this exciting initiative.

Agnon's Tales of the Land of Israel, both the conference and this volume, was made possible by the Dr. Joseph and Faye Glatt Fund of the Center for Israel Studies. We especially thank President Richard Joel for his commitment to CIS from the very beginning and his family for facilitating this gift.

We thank our Provost, Vice President for Academic Affairs, and CIS board member Prof. Selma Botman, for her continuing commitment to CIS, and for sharing her memories of Rabbi Glickman. Dr. Ari Berman, our president, is a true friend of the Center for Israel Studies, of Revel, and of academic Judaic Studies at Yeshiva University. We thank Rabbi Berman for his support of all we do.

Steven Fine,
Dean Pinkhos Churgin Professor of Jewish History,
Director, Yeshiva University Center for Israel Studies
New York and Jerusalem

In Memoriam: Rabbi Ozer Glickman ז״ל

RABBI OZER GLICKMAN WAS a learned rabbi with a remarkable intellect and an inspirational dedication to his students, colleagues, and family. Equally comfortable dazzling a large audience with his wit and insights as offering quiet wisdom and guidance to a single individual, he modeled a spiritual life that combined his love of Jewish law and ethics, American legal theory, and business.

This volume is dedicated to his life and spirit. As his former colleagues, friends, and family remember so well, Ozer was philosophical, deeply reflective, and refined, combining a profound knowledge of Torah with the exquisite cultural sophistication of a widely honored scholar. Broadly well-read and multilingual, he could opine as comfortably on Victor Hugo and Alexandre Dumas as on the works of Rambam and Rashi. He was in every respect a vibrantly cultured citizen of the world.

Ozer and I conversed often on subjects as diverse as family business transfer in China, Egyptian politics, and American poetry and literature. A charming raconteur, he was always ready to recommend a new novel or share his opinions on contemporary political and social life in addition to his passion for transactional business practices. However, it was when he spoke about his students that his always animated face would light up even further. He would volunteer stories of regularly meeting students either on or off campus to advise them about their studies or the business world. He cared genuinely about their success and devoted himself to helping them secure internships and jobs after graduation.

Yeshiva University, together with his many friends and international business associates, will miss this thoughtful and compassionate man who contributed so much to our University and the world at large. I am most pleased that this volume dedicated to the writings of S.Y. Agnon is

In Memoriam: Rabbi Ozer Glickman

dedicated to the memory of my friend Ozer. Rabbi Glickman truly loved all things Hebrew, and Agnon was among his favorite authors. This is a truly fitting tribute by our Center for Israel Studies, on behalf of the entire Yeshiva University community.

May the memory of Rabbi Ozer Glickman ז״ל be a blessing to us all.

Selma Botman
Vice President and Provost
Yeshiva University

Preface

LATE IN T'MOL SHILSHOM, *Only Yesterday*, S. Y. Agnon's epic novel of the Second Aliyah, the decade of Jewish immigration leading up to World War I, readers are privy to a highly symbolic dream playing itself out in the unconscious of the tragic hero, Yitzḥak Kummer. A would-be pioneer, Kummer finds himself torn between secular Jaffa and ultra-Orthodox Jerusalem. One need not be Sigmund Freud to unpack the symbols in the dream in which he finds himself

> in the street barefoot without shoes, his head bare. He heard the sound of prayer and followed the sound. He came to a two-story house, the bottom story in ruins and you climbed a ladder to the top story where they were praying. And the ladder stood straight. He leaned the ladder and ascended. When he put his head in, the door closed on him from inside and his body was outside.[1]

The novel is replete with the symbols of hats and shoes, variably interpreted are clear indicators for "that which is above and that which is below" (cf. Mishnah Hagigah 2:1). Yitzḥak being barefoot and bareheaded in the dream telegraphs his disconnect from both Earthly and Heavenly "Jerusalems," as does his being suspended inside-outside, hanging off the second story of the building, unable to access the prayers being recited above. The dream is a symbol for the tragic vision of *T'mol Shilshom* (and the tragedy of so many young people of the Second Aliyah), the unsuccessful attempt to combine the thesis and antithesis of Judaism: traditional observance and Zionism.

And yet, the late Israeli novelist Aharon Appelfeld cautions us that the conventional reading of this novel—and so much of Agnon's writing—is

---

1. Agnon, *Only Yesterday*, 573.

Preface

misleading. It is too convenient to assume the great author set out the tensions in religious life with such neat symmetry. In fact, the binary reading of *T'mol Shilshom*'s symbols is suspicious:

> True, [such symmetry] may be found in nature, but things are different where the soul is concerned. [Here, in this novel as elsewhere,] it is an illusion. Jerusalem is a city of paupers, of fanatical traditionalists, and not at all a place of genuine faith ... There exist truly religious people in Jaffa as in Jerusalem. Indeed, Agnon did not divide people into religious and secular, but held that some Jews had a spiritual Jewish quality that others lacked.[2]

While balance is required, it is unclear what rests on each side of the scales. Yehuda Amichai captures something of this fraught balancing act in one stanza of his poem "Jerusalem, Jerusalem, Why Jerusalem?"

> Why is Jerusalem, Yerushalayim, always two,
>   the Heavenly and the Earthly?
> I want to live in an in-between Jerusalem,
> Without banging my head up above or gashing my feet down below.
> And why is Yerushalayim in the dual form like hands, *yadayim*,
> and feet, *raglayim*?
> I want to live in Jerusal, singular,
> Because I am just I, singular, not an I-im.[3]

Amichai's poem gives further lie to the naïve notion, exploded by Appelfeld, that Jerusalem (as distinct from Jaffa) is an island of equanimity and balance. Embedded in the holy city's very plural name is the tension of celestial, ideal Jerusalem, and very real, and imperfect, terrestrial Jerusalem. Instead of an oasis of tranquility he hopes to achieve, what Yitzḥak actually discovers through the bite of a dog that has become mad through his own paintbrush, is Jerusalem as the locus of the return of the repressed. When the narrator opens his tale with, "Like all our brethren of the Second Aliyah, the bearers of our Salvation, Yitzḥak Kummer left his land and his birthplace and his city and ascended to the Land of Israel to build it from its destruction and to be rebuilt by it," astute readers will hear echoes of the biblical command to Abraham: "Go forth from your land and from your birthplace and from your father's home, to the land that I will show you"

---

2. Appelfeld, "Between Shelter and Home," 9.
3. Amichai, *The Poetry of Yehuda Amichai*, 503. The poet plays off the grammatical fact that the name Jerusalem is in the plural form (in a way similar to certain English nouns which only exist in the plural form, pants or eyeglasses).

Preface

(Gen. 12:1). Unlike, Abraham, Yitzhak never leaves "father's home" behind, since it can never leave him. Like so much of Agnon's work, *T'mol Shilshom* is a study in how the past exerts its pull over the present and future.

If this theme is central to Agnon's magnum opus, it is no less present scattered throughout his sprawling canon of works whenever the Land of Israel is concerned. The desired land is meant to be a place which restores balance to the Jewish people after their long exile—but, like Amichai's plural "Jerusalems," the Holy City and Land (to say nothing of the later State) are two-faced. Depending on which side of the lens one views *Eretz Yisrael* through, the vision of what can be achieved there appears clearer or more distorted. This typically Agnonian dual vision of the Land of Israel is given its most celebrated treatment in his magisterial novella "In the Heart of the Seas." First published in 1934, it is a tale of the journey to the Land of Israel by a group setting out from Agnon's own hometown, Buczacz. Written in the style of nineteenth century hasidic tales, the novella's weaving of folklore and *aggadah,* lore, into modern literature helped cement Agnon's reputation as the greatest Hebrew author of his time. The story was singled out for praise for its idealization of the Love of Zion, at a time that the Yishuv was undergoing great struggles. Between 1933 and 1935 over one hundred and fifty thousand Jews had arrived in Palestine, more than all that had arrived in the years of the British mandate up until that point. It should be noted that Hitler's assumption of the Chancellorship of Germany in January 1933, led to a wave of German Jewish immigration. Contemporary critics were especially mindful that this was the background on which the novella was composed. Agnon's tale is a mélange of both a realistic as well as supernatural narrative of ascent to the Holy Land, and was interpreted as a cautionary statement to the immigrants and builders of the Jewish settlement in the Land of Israel: Zionism cannot only focus on the here-and-now, physical construction, but must recall the miraculous story that undergirds our work. It is a vision that emphasizes love of the land over labor, and the supernatural over nature. An attentive reader will notice the dual frequencies on which the story is broadcast and the contrast between the natural travel tale of the group versus the mysterious voyage of miracle-man Hananiah who floats along "in the heart of the sea" atop a magical kerchief.

It was precisely this ability, in this specific story, to relate the "two faces" of the Land of Israel which was singled out by the Nobel Committee in the prize citation of 1966: "Mr Agnon… In one of your stories ["In the

Preface

Heart of the Seas"] you say that some will no doubt read it as they read fairy tales, others will read it for edification. Your great chronicle of the Jewish people's spirit and life has therefore a manifold message."[4] It should not be surprising that Agnon chose to retroject himself as a character into "In the Heart of the Seas," despite its setting one hundred years before its composition—"Rabbi Shmuel Yosef, the son of Rabbi Shalom Mordechai ha-Levi of blessed memory, who was versed in the legends of the Land of Israel, those legends in which the name of the Holy One, blessed be He, is hallowed; and when he commenced lauding the Land, people could see as it were the name of the living God engraved on the tip of his tongue"[5]—for that was how he envisioned the purpose of his artistic output especially in his Land of Israel stories.

These themes wove themselves into the many varied presentations at a conference convened by the Yeshiva University Center for Israel Studies on October 31, 2016, in honor of the fiftieth anniversary of Agnon's Nobel Prize. Dedicated to the topic of "Agnon's Tales of the Land of Israel," the event brought together leading scholars of Hebrew literature from the United States, Canada, and Israel. It was co-sponsored by the Agnon House, Jerusalem, a National Heritage Site dedicated to the work of the S.Y. Agnon and the Bernard Revel Graduate School of Jewish Studies. This volume is based upon the lectures delivered at that conference, supplemented with essays contributed by scholars who were unable to be with us in New York.

Zafrira Lidovsky Cohen, Alan Mintz, Moshe Simkovich, and Wendy Zierler each present treatments of specific stories of the "old" Land of Israel, especially as it was depicted in relation to the lands of the exile. To our great sorrow, Professor Alan Mintz ז״ל died suddenly in May 2017. Alan was among the world's leading scholars of Hebrew literature and had renewed his sharp scholarly fascination with Agnon in his later years. We are grateful to his student, Dr. Beverly Bailis, for preparing his essay from the transcript of his conference presentation.

T'mol Shilshom, Agnon's epic depiction of Jaffa and Jerusalem of the Second Aliyah, is analyzed in essays by Shalom Carmy and Hillel Halkin, and discussed at length by Avraham Holtz, who shares insights from his multi-decade work on an annotated, scholarly edition of that novel, in conversation with Jeffrey Saks. Turning to more recent periods, Steven Fine,

---

4. "Nobel Prize Banquet Speech" in Agnon, *Forevermore & Other Stories*, 264.

5. Agnon, "In the Heart of the Seas," in *Two Scholars Who Were in Our Town and Other Novellas*, 74.

Preface

Jeffrey Saks, and Laura Wiseman present essays which explore some of the complexities of the Land of Israel in the period of the State of Israel and modern Jewish experience. Finally, Shulamith Z. Berger presents a documentary history of Agnon's relationship with Yeshiva University, uncovering pearls from the YU archives.

We are grateful to Yeshiva University, and especially to Professor Steven Fine, Director of the Yeshiva University Center for Israel Studies, for their ongoing commitment to bridging the distance between Israel and New York, to the benefit of both communities. Professor Fine's vision in convening the Agnon conference, along with his efforts to guarantee the dissemination of that day's teaching, study, and scholarship through this volume, are deeply appreciated as is his generous wisdom and enduring friendship. David Selis, a graduate student at the Bernard Revel School of Jewish Studies, and Center for Israel Studies associate, helped with copy editing. His sound advice and good judgement were most helpful. The people of Wipf and Stock publishers were most professional, and we appreciate their work in producing this volume, the second in the Yeshiva University Center for Israel Studies Publication Series. We especially thank the Leon Charney Legacy Fund of the Center for Israel Studies and the Michael Scharf Publication Trust of Yeshiva University Press for their support of this project.

Rabbi Ozer Glickman ז״ל, a founding member of the academic committee of the Center for Israel Studies, was an important partner in conceptualizing and planning the conference. Ozer had begun to draft a paper on Agnon's "In the Heart of the Seas" for this volume before his untimely loss. Those that knew him, and his love of Israel, can imagine how he would have analyzed the story whose plot is outlined above. He is sorely missed by his many colleagues and students, friends, and *talmidim*. We dedicate this volume in his memory.

Jeffrey Saks
Shalom Carmy
Jerusalem and New York

Preface

Bibliography

Agnon, S. Y. *Forevermore & Other Stories*. New Milford, CT: Toby, 2016.

———. *Only Yesterday*. Translated by Barbara Harshav. Princeton: Princeton University Press, 2000.

———. *Two Scholars Who Were in Our Town and Other Novellas*. New Milford, CT: Toby, 2014.

Amichai, Yehuda. *The Poetry of Yehuda Amichai*. Edited by Robert Alter. New York: Farrar, Straus & Giroux, 2015.

Appelfeld, Aharon. "Between Shelter and Home." *Modern Hebrew Literature* 14 (Summer 1995) 9–11.

1

Labyrinthine Quest
Agnon and Graham Greene as Resources for Religious Reflection

SHALOM CARMY

AGNON'S LONG CAREER COINCIDED with a golden age of powerful Catholic fiction and literature in English and French, among whom Mauriac, Bernanos, Graham Greene, and Flannery O'Connor continue to find readers. It is unlikely that Agnon knew their work or that they read his. I come to you as one who has always appreciated Agnon's prose and who, at a crucial point in my own development, contracted a debt to the work of his Catholic and Protestant contemporaries.

It is impossible to love the Hebrew language without loving Agnon as its extraordinary impresario. From high school on I was enchanted by the relaxed narration that seemingly without effort, and without straining for effect, drew on all layers of the Hebrew language, bringing to life a rich tapestry of Jewish life from the Middle Ages down to the mid-twentieth century. The Agnon who won me in adolescence, together with some of my classmates encountering him as an assigned text, was the realistic novelist of *Sippur Pashut, A Simple Story*. It was this Agnon, more than any of his predecessors or peers, who wielded the ironic and realistic pen of the great European novelists. He described his Jews and their society as they were, in their epic scope, accurate in his depiction of society, painfully precise in rendering the individual heart, equally free of the rebel's rancor and the nostalgic exile's romanticizing. The verisimilitude of his vision, no less than the sheer beauty of his narration, in my youthful eyes, conferred authority on Agnon's more fanciful writing, be it the short ironic pious tales whose allegorical interpretations didn't interest us much of the surreal productions of *Sefer HaMa'asim* and the enigmatic romantic tales I discovered on my own.

I knew that Agnon, unlike the other major Hebrew writers, was faithful to traditional religion and was commendable for the shrewdness and sympathy with which he presented its practitioners. In my teens and early adulthood, I was moving towards the general religious position I hold today, namely doctrinal and behavioral Orthodoxy. In this quest imaginative fiction played an ancillary but significant role.

Nonetheless, it was not Agnon, at that time, who served as the poetic Virgil who would chaperone me through hell and purgatory and point me towards paradise. Despite my respect and admiration for Agnon, he was not the spiritual artistic guide for me at that time. I looked at and to imaginative literature from the depths of religious crisis, and what I sought was not what I found in him but what I discovered in some of the aforementioned Christian novelists, in poets like T.S. Eliot and Auden and in prose writers like Kierkegaard and C.S. Lewis, to offer only a few examples. Forty and fifty years later Agnon has caught up with me: my mature pleasure in Agnon is linked to the religious themes he orchestrates. Recently, moreover, I have come to appreciate him as a possible resource for individuals seeking to deepen their connection to traditional Judaism.

Readers do not respond uniformly to art. As my own experience suggests, individual readers' responses frequently evolve in the course of a lifetime. So when I venture some generalizations about Agnon's subject matter and writing as they affect the questing religious reader, and contrast him with the influential Christian novelists of the time, in particular to Graham Greene, I open myself to the accusation of merely engaging in autobiography and that all this is of interest only to my friends. Yet I hope that my account, for all its particularities, will offer insight to readers and teachers, and a better grasp of Agnon's contribution to the reader preoccupied with religious truth and religious growth.

One reason for my youthful preference for the Christian masters over Agnon as resources for religious reflection is that despite, or precisely due to the integrity of Agnon's artistic vision, the focus of his account of religious wholesomeness was celebratory and backward-looking. Its force was evocative rather than inspiring. The world whose flaws and glories he depicted was in the process of dying. Outwardly Agnon looked past this by promising optimistic sequels about the hoped for future, most notably at the end of major works like *A Guest for the Night* and *Only Yesterday*, or he sweetened the plot by inserting a *deus ex machina* to supply an unearned happy ending as in *The Bridal Canopy*. The undisguised lameness of these attempts only served to underline that the new world was "powerless to be born."

There was surely a joy in Agnon's backward-looking accounts of time-honored religious practice. Traditional religion is steeped in time-sanctified rituals and texts that are studied and performed within the family and the broader community. This is even truer of the encompassing life of Judaism than it is for the majority of Christians. Furthermore, a happy religious consciousness (what William James would call "once born") exhibits continuity between early initiation in the religious world and religious maturity. This element in Agnon offers significant encouragement to individuals on the path to return. When those who have drifted away from religious practice and belief or rejected it prepare for reconciliation and return, they are often nourished on their journey by the good memories of childhood. The "second birth" draws on and may even be made possible by these resources.

But this advantage comes with a disadvantage. The contemporary religious writer who cherishes such experience at first or second hand and who desires not just to describe it but to communicate it must try to reach the reader for whom these resources are unfamiliar or in significant respects unattractive. And there are readers for whom the celebration of nostalgia, and in particular the cultivation of childhood experience, seems escapist and threatens to become a distraction from finding a way of existence for which one can live and die.

Precisely due to the thick social fabric of Judaism there is a danger, endemic to cultural Judaism, of allowing mores and social cohesion to substitute for divine truth. In the ubiquitous teachings of Ahad Ha'am and his disciples God is unceremoniously replaced by national consciousness. Genuine religious commitment is no less undermined when the trappings of traditional practice are maintained in the absence of theological conviction. For those seeking religious conviction the beautiful depictions of traditional religion are suspect because their probative philosophical value appears negligible and the authors come across as glibly oblivious to these questions. A kind of aesthetic Gresham's Law, in which a more valuable commodity is pushed out of circulation by its cheaper competitor, allows sentimental colporteurs, passing off heartwarming nostalgia as penetrating art, to cheapen even first rate works by association. The sentimentalism propagated by religious or cultural Zionist spokesmen is liable to provoke more distrust than identification. Let me phrase it differently: Gershom Scholem spoke of much in Agnon's production as "a kind of desperate incantation," pleading with new generations, saying: "Since you no longer accept the continuity of tradition and its language in their true context, at least take them in the transformation they have undergone in my work."[1] What I sought was a relationship to the "true context" or nothing at all. I could recognize Agnon's adherence to the faith and, as noted already, I could admire him as an honest craftsman, bent on giving rebellion and estrangement from faith both emotional force and formidable articulation, and I was gladly transported by his mastery of language. Yet the nostalgic and celebratory quality of his prose had something in it of the plaintive effort to supply tradition to an irreligious culture. This did not seem to be the tight-lipped hard edge I was looking for.

The Christian twentieth century masters had to work without the benefit of a happily shared cultural framework. Church liturgy may from time to time inspire and resonate with well-educated poets like Eliot and Auden, but neither they nor any of the English novelists grew up in a thick religious culture. Those like Greene who were Roman Catholics, mostly came to the church as adult converts joining a minority culture. In any event, characters ensnared in the desperate situations depicted in many realistic novels do not have at their disposal a worldview rooted in nostalgic recollections. These characters are authentic, sometimes to the point of grotesqueness, precisely because there is no tradition to mediate their encounter with God.

Greene's protagonists, for example, have no such thick Christian or Catholic identity. Some, like Sarah Miles and Bendrix in *End of the Affair*, are outsiders to the Church, but I include even the ones who are familiar with religious practice, like the psychopath Pinkie in *Brighton Rock* or Scobie in *The Heart of the Matter* or Querry in *A Burnt Out Case*, some of whom, like Scobie, are obsessed with theological doctrine, and who snatch at fragments of church doctrine and liturgy as they grapple with their salvation and damnation, and I am not sure one can make an absolute exception for his priests who are often trapped in seedy outposts far-removed from

---

[1] Scholem, "S.Y. Agnon—The Last Hebrew Classic," 96.

the intellectual and spiritual delicacies of the seminary. O'Connor, a cradle Catholic writing about the Bible Belt (and very Protestant) South, specializes in the invasion of the divine into the lives of uneducated people unprepared for it and educated but close-minded secularists determined to resist it. Think of the ignorant crazed religion-driven characters in *The Violent Bear It Away* and their shallow secularist counterparts in that novel. The point is that their familiarity with or ignorance of thick religious culture and the intellectual traditions associated with traditional religion give them no guidance in struggling with their personal dilemmas nor do its hallowed institutions and practices provide a secure framework for their lives.

One who comes to Agnon with a post-Orthodox sensibility, which includes many, perhaps most of his contemporary readers, is likely to get a message that resembles that of his cultural Zionist forebears in Modern Hebrew literature more than that of the major Christian men of letters. To a reader concerned about the vitality and viability of religious commitment, rather than cultural identification, Agnon seemed to be offering in effect something not much unlike Bialik's secularized Jewishness. The *Matmid* in Bialik's Lithuanian *beit midrash* engaged in heroic self-denying dedication to an outmoded ideal, his legacy to be cherished only as a model for more extroverted strivings better suited to the new enlightened age. For his part Agnon's "guest for the night" attempts to revive the *beit midrash* in his Galician town, not as an arena for intense intellectual conquest and self-mastery but rather as a place where the community can come together in worship and engage in a modicum of study. The guest fails—the old Study House no longer has a future in Europe and its eschatological transplantation to the Land of Israel is posited rather than shown. With my life ahead of me, I wanted a literature that made sense of the present in which I found myself. Whether I could find enjoyment and identity by forging links to the chain of Jewish generations was a secondary question.

This is not to imply that Agnon's people exhibit uniform religious literacy. Certainly, they vary in the nature of their religious commitment. Indeed, given Agnon's encyclopedic knowledge of his milieus it is not surprising that his vast host of characters portrays variations in personal piety and knowledge as wide as the societies he chronicled. Nonetheless, almost all of his substantial characters are rooted in Jewish life and lore. How much more so is the narrator who is his most ubiquitous invention. Even those who have withdrawn from the tradition are familiar with its thick practice and have some degree of formal or informal Jewish education. When any of these alienated characters considers reconnecting to the tradition it is not felt to be a revolution in one's existence but rather a reversion to one's past identity.

Agnon's drama rarely throws up the kind of crisis in which a lonely individual must choose unambiguously between faithfulness and betrayal. The figure of Yitzḥak Kummer in *T'mol Shilshom, Only Yesterday* offers such an opportunity but Agnon does not take it. Early in the novel the narrator's voice editorializes that Kummer's defection from Orthodox practice was entirely a matter of conformity to the behavior of his peer group. Later, after he enters the traditional community of Jerusalem, we arrive at the famous scene where he finds himself alone at sunset, it is time to pray *Minḥah*, and his decision to do so, in the absence of a peer group, in effect clinches his return to religious life. At this moment he thinks: "It is good for believers to pray, but what's the use of prayer for someone like me?" As he prays he asks himself whether he really wanted to pray, but verse follows verse and he finds himself praying with a "broken heart." Jacob Katz suggested that he is broken-hearted because he has no intellectual conviction to ground his decision. In any event, Yitzḥak's conversion seems to him a choice of the easier, more satisfying path.[2] Like the dog Balak, he seeks a life of meaning rather than life on the dangerous edge. No doubt many in Agnon's time, and many today, can identify with Yitzḥak's emotional situation. The Yitzḥak Kummers may be more prevalent than those who experience the challenge of religious commitment as an all-or-nothing decision which requires of the believer not so much a return to childhood harmony as an abandonment of one's earlier self and its attractions. Yitzḥak Kummer's story, as Agnon tells it over thirty years later is not one of religious triumph: his return to religion, from the Zionist perspective assumed in the novel and affirmed in its closing passage, amounts to an admission of failure. For instead of becoming the Zionist pioneer he dreamed of, working the land and building a worldly future, he retreats to the traditional old country ways of the old Yishuv in Jerusalem. The narrative arc of *T'mol Shilshom* is thus the same as that of the bitterly anti-religious Brenner's *Loss and Bereavement* depicting a similar regression. Like Agnon's masterpiece, the constraints of Brenner's story can end convincingly only in an undignified death.

One can thus contrast Yitzḥak Kummer's return with the many scenes in which Greene forces his characters to wager everything on a lonely decision of faithfulness or betrayal: Sarah Miles deciding to commit herself to

---

2. Katz, "*Agnon Mul HaMevukhah HaDatit,*" 163–77.

the god she doesn't believe in; Scobie deliberately damning himself by receiving communion is a state of mortal sin; the hunted priest in *The Power and the Glory*, reproaching himself bitterly for his failings, yet unable to abandon his lonely vocation. From one perspective, Agnon and Greene share an addiction to unhappy endings. Greene too is adept at creating insoluble predicaments for the heroes of his Catholic novels (and many of his other books), impossible situations that can end only in death. The difference is that Greene's destinies are driven by individual psychology—his characters cannot survive because they play out, in intolerably extreme form, conflicts endemic to the human condition, at least as experienced by certain religious types. The reason that Agnon's protagonists fail, in the fiction of social realism like *Only Yesterday* and *A Simple Story* that attracted me to him in my youth, is that they are products of a dead-end culture from which they are unable to find a creative escape.

The difference should not be attributed to religious factors alone. It is a commonplace of Agnon criticism to point out that his heroes, certainly the men, are passive. It is not Agnon's custom to fully inhabit, from within their own subjectivity, individuals who put their lives on the line through a stark irreversible act of choice like Greene's religious or political characters. They are more acted upon than acting. This limitation may be a matter of choice or temperament. Either way, it narrows the range of Agnon's religious appeal.

II

So far, we have discussed social factors that separate Agnon from my roster of Christian authors. There is also a crucial difference regarding their attitudes to evil. I do not mean the philosophical or existential challenge of squaring divine omnipotence and benevolence with the conspicuous presence of evil in the world. As a novelist who deals with ideas, Agnon certainly does not shy away from confronting these matters: Daniel Bach, in *A Guest for the Night* is an especially eloquent spokesman for those alienated from God because the universe seems careless of human fate. But there is another kind of evil, not outside of us, but within us, at the heart of theological anthropology. This is the experience of sin. The Christian writers were preoccupied with human evil and rebelliousness. I didn't find Agnon equally helpful in this area though with time my thinking has changed for reasons we will consider.

Greene is fond of the nineteenth-century poem "The Hound of Heaven" where God pursues the fleeing, resisting sinner down the labyrinthine streets of corruption: the American title of *The Power and the Glory* was *The Labyrinthine Ways*. Agnon's funniest and perhaps greatest invention is the dog Balak, with whom Yitzḥak Kummer's fate is inextricably interwoven, who wanders the back alleys of Jerusalem struggling to understand his tragic lot. To use William James' phrase, Greene's religion is tough-minded. Agnon's honesty is mediated through irony.

How do Agnon and Greene typically differ in their artistic presentation of sin and remorse?

The chagrin, the overwhelming sense of missed opportunities, that pervades many of the stories in *Sefer HaMa'asim* are representative of Agnon's sense of sin: not refusal of one's prior way of life but confusion and regret at failing to live up to its standards. Think for example of the narrator's failure to mail the letter entrusted to him by Dr. Yekutiel Neeman in the short story "A Whole Loaf." It is not as if the narrator, for some perverse or malignant reason, rejects his mission. He has no desire to defy Dr. Neeman (a coded reference to Moses and his Torah) or God. Instead the hapless, famished narrator is waylaid by Mr. Gressler, understood as Satan or merely the narrator's sinful alter-ego, and ends up locked overnight in a restaurant, totally frustrated in his efforts to achieve his goal of a good meal.

As we have seen, Agnon's sense of religious wholesomeness is understood in terms of return to tradition rather than the leap into a dangerous almost inconceivable future. Hence it is not surprising that his carefully parceled out recollections of childhood provide a faithful reservoir of religious warmth and authenticity. The observance of Yom Kippur carries special weight in Agnon's universe. Kurzweil, who wrote about the image of Yom Kippur in Agnon, most strongly commended the preface to his anthology *Yamim Noraim* in which Agnon attempts to communicate what Yom Kippur can be by recalling his early childhood experiences on that high holy days in his grandfather's synagogue.[3] Yom Kippur is likewise fraught with ominous meaning in Agnon's anxious and nightmarish tales of spiritual failure. In "Another Tallit" impediments and delays prevent the adult narrator from praying properly with that imagined grandfather on Yom Kippur. Eventually he is filled with an overwhelming mood of *agmat*

---

3. Kurzweil, *Masot al Sippurei Shai Agnon*, chap. 20, 269–282. Oddly, in the preface Kurzweil draws the reader's attention to was left untranslated and not included in the English edition, *Days of Awe*. For a different survey of Agnon's Yom Kippur, see Nash, "Two Poles of the Yom Kippur Experience in Agnon," pp. 297–302.

nefesh (consternation and chagrin), not simply because he has donned an invalid tallit, but because he has frittered away the precious hours of the holy day "without prayer and without anything."

When we turn to Greene or his confreres, their world of childhood is harsh, brutish and blighted from the cradle. In "A Parable and Its Lesson" Agnon sends his emissaries to literal hell, but on tourist visas, as it were. Many of Greene's most striking characters by contrast seem to have been born with the taste of sulfur in their mouths. It is not merely that they lack the primeval sustaining experience of God we find in Agnon. They belong to different universes. In Agnon, God is in His heaven: skepticism and backsliding and spiritual failure come later, with the hard knocks of life. For Greene, evil is firmly in the saddle and only spiritual struggle and suffering point to a world animated by an astringent divine love. For the Christian novelists I am thinking of, neither the substance of religious tradition nor the happy memories of childhood can provide the basis for mature religious flourishing. For Agnon's characters and their creator, tradition is the substance of religious life and childhood again and again incubates faith.

If Greene depicts fiery and desperate rebellion, from the inside, even in his attractive characters, Agnon fails to express the anatomy of evil even among his most devilish. Let us contrast the atheist baker in Greene's story "A Hint of an Explanation" with Mr. Gressler. The baker tempts the narrator as a child to desecrate the Host. He is presented convincingly as an unhappy, lonely individual driven by hatred and envy and the child is paradoxically mystified by the energy with which he hates something that, in his opinion, doesn't exist. Such defiant self-damnation occurs elsewhere in Greene and even in C.S. Lewis. What I want to emphasize is that Greene undertakes to display his perverse motives as he would any other character.

Now consider Mr. Gressler. There can be little doubt that Agnon introduces him as an emblem of evil temptation. The narrator has experienced him repeatedly and always with the most baleful results. But Gressler always sweeps him away because he is magnetic and extroverted—it seems impossible to say no to him. He knows Gressler long and well. But what motivates Gressler, what makes him tick, why he always lures the narrator to dereliction, why he is an inevitable engine of misfortune, what underlies his demonic opaque psyche—this the narrator makes no attempt to probe.[4]

---

4. One may be tempted, following Kurzweil, to think of Balak as such a character. If there is validity to this approach, it is surely germane that Agnon uses the consciousness of a dog rather than a human being to make this investigation; see Kurzweil, *Masot al Sippurei Shai Agnon*, chap. 10, 104-115. It may be instructive to think of the psychotherapist

One is tempted to ask whether the differences I delineate define Agnon in some way as a Jewish writer as opposed to Christians like Greene, O'Connor, etc. This question can be raised at the social plane: was the Jewish society of Eastern Europe that provided Agnon with his literary capital different from that of Western Christians in a way that determined a very different aesthetic outlook?[5] Or it may be presented as a theological hypothesis, according to which the authentic doctrines and practices of Judaism shape a worldview at variance with that nurtured by the teachings and practices of Christianity. It is foolhardy to reduce a great writer to a particular message, be it religious, ethical or psychological. A writer has his or her individual, often idiosyncratic range of subject matter and aesthetic orientation that cannot be boiled down to a bottom-line philosophy. The spiritual questions reflected in their work and often driving their work should not schematically be treated as mere reflections of the faith they subscribe to. When generalizing about literature, this is a risky maneuver at best.

Nonetheless, I want to bring to bear Rabbi Joseph B. Soloveitchik's remarks about paradigms of sinfulness and the theological dynamics of evil

---

Dr. Tamkin in Saul Bellow's novella "Seize the Day," also an almost allegorical figure who virtually hypnotizes Tommy Wilhelm into destruction. Wilhelm, however, unlike the narrator of "A Whole Loaf," makes fitful attempts to learn something about his nemesis's background and possible motivation. Though Agnon's narrator has a long history with Gressler, he is not curious about his motivations.

5. In Agnon's case, the realistic depiction of demonic evil is limited by his inability or disinclination, in the major texts published during his lifetime, to enter into the consciousness of evil Gentiles. His two "Lamia" stories, "The Lady and the Peddler" and "Disappeared" focus on the Jew entrapped by the demonic figure. "Disappeared" contains the diary of the noblewoman, probably to demonstrate that the Jewish soldier Dan remained chaste to the end. The story she tells provides plausible motivation for her monstrous behavior, partly by testifying to comparable abuse of her mother, partly by indicating that she never quite decided with full deliberation to hold Dan prisoner. Like a typical male character in Agnon's writing she sees herself as passive: she becomes entangled in evil rather than defiantly choosing it and once the horrible episode comes to an end, she retires to a nunnery. In this respect her story does not deviate from the approach to moral evil I have described as characteristic of Agnon. One wonders whether Agnon's late project of resurrecting *The City in Its Fullness* inclined him to devote fuller attention to Jewish interactions with the Gentile environment. Among earlier stories "In the Forest and in the City" purports to present a meeting of the minds between the adolescent Jewish narrator and an escaped, Gentile murderer. Given the language barrier to which the story calls attention and other clues in the story, I read it as a parody of youthful, romantic naïveté that underlines Agnon's awareness of the treacherousness of such assumed understanding.

in his *Emergence of Ethical Man*. The manuscript of this book was drafted in the 1950s and published posthumously. I believe his account of the respective Jewish and Christian depictions of human corruption sheds light on the paradigmatic examples we have looked at in Greene and Agnon.[6]

Early in the book Rabbi Soloveitchik discovers two models for understanding the human being. The model he associates with Judaism views man as a naturalistic being, subject to natural corruption. The New Testament, by contrast, "drawing on the idea of individual *het*, sin, which found its full formulation in Ezekiel, shifted man to a different plane ... Man is not any longer the pendulum that swings between birth and decay, but the being who is torn by satanic revolt, sin and obedience, between living and falling from his God-Father . . ."[7] He goes on to distinguish between the sin of pride in its Christian and Jewish forms. In spite of the typological opposition between Judaism and Christianity he recognizes that the Christian conception draws on passages in the Hebrew Bible. Perhaps if R. Soloveitchik had revised the manuscript he would have referred explicitly to Isaiah 14—the prophecy about Helel ben Shahar, or to the notion of fallen angels that played an occasional role in Second Temple Judaism. He might have illustrated this orientation to the perversity of evil by mentioning Augustine's *Confessions* or the novels of Dostoevsky.

Later in the book, when Rabbi Soloveitchik offers his interpretation of the original sin in the Garden of Eden, the psychology of the first couple (as opposed to the demonic serpent) is rooted in the Jewish model. Unlike the New Testament paradigm, Eve and Adam's sin is not a matter of diabolical defiance, emanating from pride and lust for power, which would be the case if sin were conceived as the rebellion of a spiritual being against God. Nor is it merely the consequence of material weakness where recognition of the good is overwhelmed by desire for what is prohibited. On Rabbi Soloveitchik's reading, Eve is seduced by the serpent, hypnotized and distracted from the good. There is something of Mr. Gressler in the serpent.

This thesis is worthy of analysis. At the risk of simplification, let me derive a lesson for our present discussion. There is an "everyday" perspective on sin. According to this conception, sin does not arise from premeditated malice on the part of man, but from human weakness, albeit the kind

---

6. Soloveitchik, *The Emergence of Ethical Man*. For a preliminary analysis of this book, see Carmy, "In Many Respects God was Closer to Abraham Than He Was to Moses" 11–26.

7. Soloveitchik, *Emergence of Ethical Man*, 7–9.

of weakness for which human beings bear responsibility. There is a more dramatic "Promethean" conception of sin, which is less prevalent, but which highlights a more exciting and perverse psychology, one which recognizes the good and in full consciousness, defies it. Whatever the respective values of each perspective for an overall understanding of the perennial human condition, it may be that the latter idea, apart from its incandescent dramatic potential, is especially expressive of the crisis of modernity, be it the nihilistic projection characteristic of political extremism or the defiant despair of radically humanistic social ethics or the despair of the individual cast adrift in a world without stable values. Agnon's narrator led astray by Gressler, the narrator who is situated in a divinely oriented world but chronically gets sidetracked, may be a bit too prosaic and homely for the reader who is struggling to make sense of the explicit rejection of the divine order and the divine command in the name of pride and self-will. It may of course be the case that such a reader may, in the course of a lifetime, come to be attracted to a more balanced psychology.

I am not implying that Agnon or the Christian authors with whom I contrast him write to instantiate a philosophical formula. Presumably it is the case that Agnon's experience of human nature, in himself and in others, guided his pen and informed the kind of story he chose to tell. In other words, it is a biographical fact that Agnon and the people to whom he devoted his writing career lived with a certain kind of harmonious relation to tradition and to a divinely ordered world that is constantly challenged and undermined in his work but nevertheless subsists in it, whereas this sense is absent from the Christian writers. Apart from religious background, it also seems that Agnon, whether for psychological or aesthetic reasons, had a predilection for passive protagonists, although this may apply less to his female characters, which is why stories like "Tehilla" have become touchstones for critics assessing his religious dimension. Writers like Greene and O'Connor, to the contrary, are attracted to the melodrama of desperate risk. Agnon's experience or recollection of his childhood and of childhood as a literary theme may have been happy, while his Christian counterparts refuse the romantic image of childhood associated with Victorian liberalism and the confident liberal image of man that it supported, a cheerfulness that Agnon may not have found obtrusive or pernicious.

For those who seek in literature a mirror to life, both orientations have credibility though readers may be more interested in and enlightened by one vision than the other. In the secular liberal world of the 1960s my moral and religious growth was probably better provoked by the stark crises of Greene's sinners than by the indolent confusions of Agnon's. My appreciation of Agnon today is affected by the knowledge that the psychology he explored is no less important for the moral-religious work of self-understanding and self-improvement than the dramas that occupied me then. I am also more attentive to, and grateful for, the enormous creative efforts that go into communicating authentically the positive constructive experiences of childhood.

III

I would like to say something on behalf of the more obvious ingredients in Agnon's religious contribution that I was always aware of but that meant less to me then than now.

One is the strong element of gratitude in his writing, gratitude for natural enjoyments and appreciation of the good in Jewish life. Let us examine one passage fairly early in *A Guest for the Night*. What strikes me now is not only the content of the Guest's musing but the placement of the passage in the novel, an awareness that is strengthened by repeated reading.

By chapter 7 the Guest has had an opportunity to survey the poverty and destruction wreaked by World War I on his town. The one untroubled place is the House of Study which he begins to visit for several hours a day. Of his motivation to study he writes:

> I do not study to enlarge my mind or to become wise and know the works of the Lord. I am like a man who walks by the wayside—the sun beats on his head, the stones bruise his feet, the dust blinds his eyes, and all his body is weary. Then he sees a booth and enters—and the sun no longer beats on his head, nor do the stones bruise his feet or the dust blind his eyes. As he is weary, he wishes to rest, and pays no attention to anything. After he has recovered, he notices the booth and its furnishings. And if he is not ungrateful he gives praise and thanks to Him who made a booth for him and prepared everything in it to supply his needs. I am that man, and that booth is our old Beit Midrash.[8]

The manifest religious content of this paragraph is the movement from enjoyment to gratitude to God who has provided the respite. The context of the chapter puts the narrator's serenity in question: is it indeed justifiable to

8. Agnon, *A Guest for the Night*, 34.

give thanks for one's fortunate lot when one's neighbors are burdened and oppressed? To some degree the Guest attempts to disarm such criticism by stressing the ordinariness of his pleasure: he does not present himself as the religious idealist engaged in an elitist quest but as everyman chancing upon the kind of satisfactions available in principle to all.

This chapter leads into chapter 8 which culminates in Daniel Bach's account of his horrifying experience in the trenches of World War I which led to his loss of religious faith. To this the Guest can only respond by recounting an anecdote from the old *Shevet Yehudah* chronicle he once read about a Jew whose family starves to death and who nevertheless does not abandon his devotion to God. The Guest speculates about his fate, whether he had the opportunity to rebuild his life, but remains dubious as to whether such recovery can bring comfort. Here again the intellectual self-confidence of the Guest is undercut by the awareness that he can only comment second-hand on the trauma of others.[9] In the next chapter he goes to sleep, knowing the night will not pass without dreams. In his dream he finds himself on a boat of joyous Jews bound for Israel. The time comes for prayer and, as is common in the Agnonian nightmare, the ritual ends in disaster—his prayer shawl catches flame; instead of casting it off he jumps into the sea where his cries for help are ignored and finally he is borne off by the waves in the direction of the light ... which turns out to be his bedside lamp. The dream clearly replays Bach's scene of horror and articulates the narrator's sense of helplessness in catastrophe. In chapter 10 the Guest, having stayed into the cold season, realizes that he needs a winter coat. He is somewhat embarrassed to acquire a new distinctive wardrobe and a bit ashamed of the fact that he can afford to be comfortably dressed while his fellow Jews are insufficiently clad. Preoccupied with other people's clothing his regular visit to the House of Study does not go well.[10]

The sense of gratitude expressed by the Guest conveys an important, perhaps a perennial element in religious experience. Agnon's narration stands out insofar as it is not only an account that is true to the quotidian

---

9. See my comments in "Job's Children," *First Things*. Agnon spent the years of the Great War in Germany. His fiction about that period, especially *To This Day*, which was written over thirty years later, also reflects the experience of one who was not conscripted but who observed the anxiety of those who were.

10. It is noteworthy that both the House of Study scene in chapter 7 and the dream in chapter 9 evoke Jonah's tense confrontation with God. The visitor is refreshed by a booth (*sukkah*) that has been provided for him. The dreamer's imminent drowning is avoided when the waves carry him away.

world of the individual who is not a religious virtuoso. Even more so, he acknowledges subtly, in a manner that is psychologically realistic, the uneasiness felt by such an individual given the contrast between his own good fortune and the dismal state of so many others in this difficult world, an uneasiness that is often felt and frequently repressed, especially in the post-Holocaust age. In this respect, Agnon performs theological work that is not done by great medieval Jewish philosophers like Sa'adia Gaon and R. Bahya ibn Paquda, who make gratitude the foundation of their theological system without confronting its problematic nature. Imaginative recreation of an emotion or an experience often yields insight that escapes pure analysis.

I was always attracted to Agnon's stories about religious poets caught between the desire to create art and the task of fulfilling their religious vocation. Let us examine one of the most suggestive of these—"HaSiman" ("The Sign"). In the first, brief version, the story presents a narrator uncertain about the fate of his town under Nazi occupation who has a vision of the medieval poet-philosopher Shlomo Ibn Gabirol. In the revised version, written in 1945, "Agnon" has just learned that nothing at all remained of his hometown. It is the eve of Shavuot and Jewish law enjoins him from mourning on the holy day. Fortified by the mandates of *halakhah* and his awareness that, despite all the dangers awaiting the Jews in the Land of Israel, that community can at least defend itself, the narrator resolves to meet his obligations. He welcomes the holiday with sober outward joy—he does not divulge to his wife and children the terrible news he is in possession of. He goes to the Synagogue to spend the night in study. While reciting Ibn Gabirol's versification of the 613 commandments, he encounters the poet.

At one level, this story partakes of the dreamlike atmosphere of *Sefer HaMa'asim* which only highlights the sharp differences. Nowhere in sight is the flustered, distracted, frustrated accident-prone first-person narrator of *Sefer HaMa'asim* who chronically fails to keep faith with the letter and spirit of the commandment. Here the narrator conducts the festive meal at home, recounts stories of his town at length and with even temper before repairing to the Synagogue. In *Sefer HaMa'asim* the frequent dislocations of time and space resemble those of a dream or a nightmare, perhaps intensified by the geographical distance between the narrator's present and the irrecoverable past. In *HaSiman* the narrator knows exactly where he is and where he belongs. He deliberately shifts from Europe to Jerusalem and back. He reminisces in a fully conscious mode about his hometown and the differences between its ancient synagogues and the new sanctuaries of his young Jerusalem neighborhood with its unformed customs. It is as if the very severity of his grief demands composure in accordance with the *halakhah* and strictly prohibits the anti-heroic and somewhat self-indulgent pose of his other tales.

What fascinated the narrator about Ibn Gabirol from childhood on, he recounts, is, first, his religious passion, specifically the tough edge of his experience, the painful search for God and the sense of recoil and inadequacy when he finds God. Second, he discovers that the same poet, already burdened by his individual quest, takes upon himself, in his liturgical poetry, the communal pain of captive Israel. As in the short original version of the story, Ibn Gabirol appears to him and improvises an acrostic poem on the name of Agnon's town. Only at this point, in silent communion with his great predecessor, is the narrator overcome by his grief and collapses in tears. And although he does not recall the lines of the poem, its very existence is the comfort he seeks that the men and women of Buczacz are not erased from the book of this world.

IV

Here then are four directions for those who would read and teach the literary master Agnon as a religious writer:

As a chronicler, he brings to life a wide variety of characters representing the Jewish people in several societies. He shows us models of authentic religious life, and models of its weakness, loss, breakdown and ruination. As a moral psychologist, he offers profound and dramatic insight into a particular character type. As I stated above, I did not find the characteristic Agnonian hero an inspiring model for my religious quest. I sought a more tough-minded religious framework. Nonetheless, the plight of the typical Agnon protagonist is, to some extent, pertinent to all of us.

Moreover, Agnon's storytelling, and especially the narrative persona, captures important everyday qualities of religious experience: I discussed the sense of gratitude in particular. While these reflections lack the elements of melodrama and risk often intertwined with the religious quest, they may be even more significant to a steady life lived in God's presence and they require re-articulation for the contemporary spirit. Lastly, and least ambiguously, Agnon achieved the status of a committed Jewish artist, who both deepens religious insight and commemorates the Jewish people. What Kurzweil once said—that the true hero of Agnon's work is not any individual but the Jewish people as an organism—is even more fittingly said of him today, with the huge addition of his posthumous writings above and beyond what was available to us fifty years ago. To me as I am now, it is an inspiring example.

Bibliography

Agnon, S.Y. *A Guest for the Night*. New Milford, CT: Toby, 2014.
Carmy, Shalom. "In Many Respects God Was Closer to Abraham Than He Was to Moses." In *Scholarly Man of Faith*, edited by E. Kanarfogel and D. Schwartz, 11–26. Jerusalem: Ktav, 2017.
———. "Job's Children." *First Things* (April 2018).
Katz, Yaakov. "*Agnon Mul haMevukhah haDatit.*" In *L'Agnon Shai*, edited by D. Sadan and E. E. Urbach, 163–77. Jerusalem: Jewish Agency, 1966.
Kurzweil, Baruch. *Masot al Sippurei Shai Agnon*. Jerusalem: Schocken, 1976.
Nash, Stanley. "Two Poles of the Yom Kippur Experience in Agnon." *Prooftexts* 11/3 (1991) 297–302.
Scholem, Gershom. "S.Y. Agnon—The Last Hebrew Classic." In *On Jews and Judaism in Crisis*. New York: Schocken, 1976.
Soloveitchik, Joseph B. *The Emergence of Ethical Man*. Jersey City, NJ: Ktav, 2005.

2

Ge'ulah in Zionist Ideology and Rhetoric and in Agnon's "Agunot"

ZAFRIRA LIDOVSKY COHEN

SINCE TALMUDIC TIMES THE Hebrew term *ge'ulah*, redemption, signifies the end of exile and a return to independent Jewish life in the Land of Israel. During ages of diaspora living, it was predominantly a subject of countless legends, dreams, and prayers conveying an unyielding desire for a better future in the Land of Israel and the return of the glorious days of old. These yearnings remained essentially a phantasm even after the establishment of political Zionism at the end of the nineteenth century and the many plans, often conflicting ones, to settle the land that ensued. This all changed from language to deeds only when young Jewish men and women decided in the early years of the twentieth century that "[I]t's not enough to *talk* about Zion and forefathers' land." Determined to replace talk with deeds, they left their homes, moved to a "land swamps and boondocks," and began to "remove stones, dig wells, plough and sow."[1] These Jewish pioneers, known as

---

1. The citations are from Nathan Alterman, "The People of the Second Aliyah" [Hebrew]—an epic poem narrating the history and ideology of the first pioneers in the Land of Israel (1904–1914). It was published in 1958, ten years after the establishment of the State of Israel in a book for children titled *The Book of the Singing Box*. The poem was designed as a lesson in Zionist ideals at a time of erosion of Zionist values.

the people of the Second Aliyah, or *halutzim* (pioneers), believed that turning the dreams of *ge'ulah* into a reality required a personal commitment to actually settle the land and build all of its corners with Jewish hands, sweat and blood; to build it for future generations to inherit happily ever after so that "every man [will be able sit] under his vine and under his fig-tree; and none shall make them afraid" (Micah 4:4).[2] Most of the *halutzim* came from heavily populated, deeply religious, and poverty-ridden shtetls—Jewish enclaves in Eastern Europe. Eager to escape abject life conditions, they were swept by ideals of the socialist revolution in Russia, and their desire for national redemption in the Land of Israel became intertwined with a desire to repair a world gone astray. They saw in well-established rigid old Jewish customs and traditions an obstacle to their progressive undertakings, and they were looking to reinvent a new Jewish existence based on values of human dignity and social justice.

Albeit progressive thinkers, nonconformists, and nonobservant by Jewish law, the intention of the *halutzim* was nevertheless not to destroy Judaism but deconstruct it, in the postmodern sense of the word. They believed that to save Judaism from continued decay—weakening, decline, humiliation, rejection and dejection—firmly held human interpretations of Jewish sanctified texts must be challenged to begin to heal the nation and change its destiny. The Hebrew Scriptures were their guide to rejecting the customary, unmitigated pursuit of a divine solution to the misery of diaspora living. Time and again one hears them argue against Jewish customary practices that have become all but futile routines fostering the veneration of elusive concepts. Time and again one hears *halutzim* repudiating representational objects that have become the essence of Jewish faith and Jewish desire. Observing customs and performing rituals, all symbolic representations, they argue, became the highest manifestation of faith in God. The symbol in-and-of-itself—the prayer, the prayer book, the ritual—were deemed sacred and the object of one's desire, whereas what it symbolizes was no more than a distant memory, words, lines, stories. Their belief was this: There will be no progress without a *radical* change. For a nation submersed in customs and traditions to be redeemed, it has to be reborn. And it has to be rebuilt on solid foundations that are Jewish at core but pertain to Jewish life in the Land of Israel as a model community and a polity that biblical prophets imagined. It can no longer bear any resemblance

---

2. For a study of the signification of *ge'ulah* in Zionism, see Almog, "Ge'ulah in Zionist Rhetoric," 65–82.

to diaspora living and to the substitute Jewish lifestyle that were established there for the sake of evoking the land's memory and/or grieving over its absence. The radical change in traditional Jewish life they introduced was for the sake of a better future they imagined. They believed that the necessary change would come only by breaking all barriers, burning all bridges to past impediments, and reinventing a new way of Jewish existence, or else the fate of the forlorn nation will forever remain unresolved.[3]

Born in Galicia, Shmuel Yosef Agnon, Czaczkes back then, arrived in Ottoman ruled Palestine, or *Eretz Yisrael*, for the first time in 1908 during the high days of the Second Aliyah.[4] He was twenty years old. Like most of the young people who came during those years, he was inspired by practical Zionism as well as by romantic fantasies about a renewed Jewish life in the Holy Land.[5] He settled in Jaffa, back then a vibrant secular city and the epicenter of Hebraic cultural activities. The literary circles he encountered contained progressive thinkers enthusiastically adopting what the foremost author of the era, Yosef Haim Brenner, derisively termed sometime later "the *Eretz Yisrael* genre and its accessories"—describing the young men and women of the Second Aliyah discarding their past and being born anew as "high priests of the land."[6] Brenner was celebrated for presenting a more scrappy view of the land, its struggles, challenges, as well as misgivings of young ḥalutzim in adjusting to the harsh realities they faced which he began to publish upon his arrival.[7] A similar portrayal, only in Agnon's surreal style, was eventually featured in a monumental novel he wrote, *Only Yesterday*, but not before 1945.[8] The first story Agnon published in the

---

3. These assertions are based on my current study of the literary works of people of the Second Aliyah, mostly works of poetry that were never investigated before and mostly forgotten poets such as Mordechai Temkin, Avraham Solodar, and Noah Naftulsky. The lives and ideas of the people of the Second Aliyah are inscribed in a wonderful memoir by Shimon Kushnir (a member of the Second Aliyah himself), *Anshe Nevo: Pirke 'Alilah shel Anshe ha-'Aliyah ha-Sheniyah*.

4. In the history of the Jewish settlement of the Land of Israel in modern times, the term "Second Aliyah" refers to approximately 35,000 young men and women that arrived in the years 1904–1914. For an historical background for the Second Aliyah in English see: Halpern, "The Cultural and Social Background of the Second Aliyah," 487–517.

5. See Ben-Dov, "The Raven's Message of Return," 95–112.

6. The term is adopted from G. Gressel's eulogy of Meir Vilkansky, a well-known member of the Second Aliyah, *Davar*, October 23, 1959.

7. E.g., "Nerves," 1910; "From Here and from There," 1911; *Breakdown and Bereavement*, 1920. The essay "The Eretz Israel Genre and Its Accessories" was published in 1910.

8. Some stories integrated into the novel were published earlier in different venues,

Ge'ulah in Zionist Ideology and Agnon's "Agunot"

Land of Israel was "Agunot," in the year of his arrival, 1908.⁹ Soon after the publication of the story, Czaczkes changed his surname to Agnon, first as a pen name, and after 1924 it became his only name. "Agunot" evidently was an important story for the author's identity as a Jewish man born in the diaspora due to a "Jewish catastrophe," and who went to the Land of Israel at age twenty to "work it and eat from the fruits of his labor," as Agnon stated in his Nobel Prize acceptance speech in 1966.¹⁰ Only the story has nothing to do with the new life the young author allegedly sought in the Land of Israel.

It is hard enough to explain the detachment of "Agunot" from the ideological drive that pushed the twenty-year-old author to depart from his home in Europe. It is harder yet to grasp why the very first story Agnon published in the "land of his dreams" takes place in the old city of Jerusalem featuring a community mired in old Jewish traditions much like the one he left behind. Intrigued by the fable-like structures of "Agunot" scholars wonder whether the story is no more than a "parodic game or a masterful production by an author of remarkable stylistic virtues," as Yitzhak Bakon for example asserts. Relating to the various plots of love, loss, and existential dislocation that the story presents, Bakon proceeds to suggest that Jewish rootlessness is the main theme of "Agunot" and that young Agnon was quick to realize that a resettlement in the Land of Israel would not resolve this problem.¹¹ Other studies assert that the story's plot of failed unions is an allegory expressing Agnon's angst regarding the lifestyle of the *halutzim* he discovered upon arriving in the land, and the hazards of their detachment from God and religiosity.¹² A more recent study goes even further suggesting that "Agunot" is a veiled satire of secular Zionism.¹³ These

---

mostly during the 1930s.

9. According to David Knaani, a Hebrew author and essayist, Agnon wrote "Agunot" in a span of 24 hours after a day's work as an administrator at the periodical "*HaOmer*." See also, Be'er, *Gam Ahavatam, Gam Sin'atam:*, 30. "Agunot" is available in Hebrew in *Elu veElu*, 329–37; in English translation under the transliterated title "Agunot" in *A Book That Was Lost*, 39–51. In Hebrew the word *agunot* whose folk etymology means "enchained women," signifies a halakhic term relating to the status of Jewish women who are chained by a marriage to a husband who has disappeared or merely refuses to grant his wife a Jewish divorce.

10. Agnon's Nobel Prize acceptance speech is available in *Forevermore & Other Stories*, 264–69, and on the website of the Nobel Prize (www.nobelprize.org).

11. Bakon, "On 'Agunot,'" 67–179.

12. Golan, "The Story 'Agunot' and the Second Aliyah," 215–23.

13. Stern, *Agnon Hamekhuseh min HaAyin*.

assertions rely on the wealth of Jewish sources that Agnon interweaves into this story, and the many revisions the story underwent.[14] What all previous studies seem to overlook is the very close proximity of the publication of "Agunot" to Agnon's arrival in the Land of Israel, the Zionist ideology that drove him there, the progressive community he joined, and the traditionally nonobservant lifestyle he embraced at the time.[15] This study offers an alternative interpretation of the story based on the zeitgeist of the people of the Second Aliyah of whom young Agnon was a member. It reflects his critical view of the state of Judaism not only during his "irreligious" years but also soon after he returned to a religious way of life in 1924. His opposition is not to Judaism in-and-of-itself, but to well-established social structures, habits, and norms within deeply religious communities in the diaspora, and in several communities in the Land of Israel at the turn of the twentieth century. These are deemed obsolete and an obstacle to the quest for national revival in the pioneering era.[16]

Agnon's story "Fable of the Goat" provides an illuminating background to this assertion. It is a short tale Agnon published in 1925, thirteen years after the publication of "Agunot," one year after his return to the Land of Israel from a twelve-year sojourn in Germany, and his return to a religious lifestyle. "Fable of the Goat" is a simple tale of a father somewhere in the diaspora who squanders the possibility of ridding himself of a mysterious ailment and joining his son in the blessed Land of Israel. The son took a huge risk and went on a frightening long journey to the unknown so as to pursue the source of a miraculous remedy his ailing father received in the form of a goat's milk his doctors recommended. The goat kept disappearing from the yard and reappearing with her udder filled with the remedial milk. Curious to learn where the goat goes, but reluctant to take the journey

---

14. "Agunot" underwent 4 revisions between 1908 and 1953. For studies on the implications of the revisions see Weiss, *Agnon—Agunot, Ido veEnam*; Katznelson, "*Agunot shel Agnon*," 163–73.

15. Upon his arrival young Agnon became an assistant to the editor of *HaOmer*, a periodical dedicated to current affairs. The founder of the periodical, Sh. Ben-Zion, arrived in the Land of Israel a few years earlier determined to move the Hebrew literary center from the diaspora to the Land of Israel, strengthen the Zionist pioneers, and spread Zionist ideology around the world. Govrin, *HaOmer*, 20. "Agunot" was published in *HaOmer* 2:3.

16. The relation between Zionism and Judaism has been widely investigated. See, for example, Knaani, *HaAliyah ha-Shniyah*; Almog, *Tzionut vaDat*; Zeira, *Keruʻim Anu*. These studies commonly highlight the complex relationship of Zionism with traditional Judaism in its quest to revive Jewish life in the Land of Israel.

himself, the old man allows his son to follow the goat, and the frightening journey in a long dark cave brings him to the Land of Israel, which is of course the best cure to his father's otherwise incurable ailments. The story comes to a tragic end when the goat returns to the father's yard but without the son. In his anguish the father slaughters the goat, and so deprives himself of his own remedy, and consequently will perish in the diaspora. But the son, we are told by the omniscient narrator, has a good chance to live and "bear fruit in his old age, full of sap and richness, calm and peaceful in the land of the living."[17]

The reason the father will not be able to reach the Land of Israel and must suffer the rest of his life in the "dreadful diaspora" is twofold. The first one has to do with observing Jewish laws. Arriving in the Land of Israel just before the onset of the Sabbath the son was prohibited from making the journey back to fetch his father immediately. However, obeying a sacred law brought about the father's demise. The other reason has to do with Jewish temperament and a stereotypical bleak outlook. The son was unable to return immediately, but he did sent the goat back to the father with a message tucked in her ear thinking that the father will welcome her with a caress, she will then shake her head with delight, and the note will fall out. But when the goat returned alone, the old man instantly imagines the worst scenario. An obvious intertextual reference to the biblical Jacob's reaction to the loss of his beloved son Joseph implies that the old man featured in "Fable of the Goat" assumes the son has been devoured by evil beasts.[18] And so as to never be reminded of the pain, the guilt, and the loss, he orders the goat slaughtered. The old man's reaction is inherently bleak, panicky and rash. Biblical literature is his only guide to life, and he lacks rational thinking processes that might direct him to a concealed message of redemption that has come his way. As a result, he ends up killing the messenger and so, by his own doing, robs himself of the opportunity to heal, reunite with his son, and live happily ever after in the Land of Israel.

The main question that hovers over "Fable of the Goat" is why? Why does Agnon put forth a story that forever closes the path of the father to reach the Holy Land and enjoy the paradise his son discovered? There must be a reason Agnon decided to leave the old man behind to languish in the horrible diaspora. And so, the message of the story could be that for the son

---

17. Agnon, "Fable of the Goat," in *A Book That Was Lost*, 199–202; in Hebrew as "Ma'aseh HaEz," *Elu veElu*, 303–5.

18. Genesis 37:33.

to thrive in the Land of Israel, the old man with his old traits, old customs, old traditions, and old habits—must stay behind.

The negation of diaspora Agnon renders in "Fable of the Goat" is a well-known tenet of Zionism since its inception.[19] It has been a leading principle of Zionist settlers in the Land of Israel since the Second Aliyah and has been widely expressed in Hebrew literary works of the pioneering era. Many writers of the era, much like Agnon, similarly assert that the fathers' generation must be overlooked for young daring sons to have a promising future in the Land of Israel.[20] The Jewish Zionist pioneers' negation of the diaspora was material as well as spiritual. Pointing to the many moral shortcomings of diaspora living, much of the criticism was directed inward, toward the Jews themselves, and the choices they have made. Chief among them was Y. H. Brenner, who in a long article titled "Our Self-Evaluation in Three Volumes" (1916) proceeds to brazenly denigrate the "diasporic character" portraying it as abject, deplorable, and immoral. A similar argument was published in 1907 in the journal *Hashkafah* by Itamar Ben-Avi (the son of Eliezer Ben-Yehuda) seeking to underscore "what the Land of Israel has given us" to fix the diasporic disorders.[21] Agnon's rejection of diasporic mentality and its detriment to the Jewish revival endeavor, as we have seen in "Fable of the Goat," is far more subtle than Brenner's, but not less unequivocal. It is far more veiled in "Agunot," but also far more unforgiving.

"Agunot" is a more enigmatic story than "Fable of the Goat" and contains many more characters and a more complex plot. And yet the key question that hovers over the various schemes of love and loss, of abandoned women, as well as well-intended men who end up either punished or banished, is once again: why? Why did the young Agnon, upon arriving in Jaffa during the heyday of the Second Aliyah make his debut with a story that takes place in old Jerusalem and not in the wasteland which young, idealistic pioneers longed to conquer. Why would an author who decided to settle not in Orthodox Jerusalem but in Jaffa, the epicenter of progressive

---

19. On the evolution of "new Jews" in the Land of Israel in the early twentieth century, their rejection of traditional Judaism, "negation of the diaspora," and the repudiation of the social structures of traditional Jewish communities, see Shapira, "HaMitos shel haYehudi heḤadash," 155–74; Schweid, "The Rejection of the Diaspora in Zionist Thought," 43–70.

20. E.g., David Shimoni's famous poem stating defiantly "Son, don't listen to the teachings of your father . . . man, listen to the song of the son."

21. *Hashkafah*, Friday, November 22, 1907, 3.

and mostly secular young Zionists, tell a story detached from major events of the time and from the many emotional and physical struggles they faced. Why, in times of progress and change, present an old-fashioned fabulous tale of passionate love affairs all ending in heartbreaking losses?

Considering the time of its publication, the main impetus for Agnon's decision to move to the Land of Israel, and the community he joined when he first arrived, it is plausible to presume that it was too early for this author to confront the ideology of the people of the Second Aliyah, their lifestyle, as well as the difficulties they faced. These, as mentioned above, did take a center stage in his work but not much before the 1940s. In 1908 however it was not too early, and indeed not exceptional, for a young Zionist immigrant to view and review the state of traditional Judaism and earlier endeavors to settle the Land of Israel prior to the Zionist settlers' undertaking.

The community Agnon features in "Agunot" is known as the "Old Yishuv"—a community of deeply religious Jewish settlers that arrived in the Land of Israel mostly during the nineteenth century and settled for the most part in Jerusalem, or in the three other cities Jews considered "holy": Hebron, Tzefat, and Tiberias.[22] Members of the Old Yishuv were Jewish immigrants who were praised and financially supported by fellowmen in the diaspora for fulfilling the *mitzvah* of settling the land. Their mere dwelling in the land was their virtue, no less their commitment to a deeply religious way of life centered on observing Jewish laws and rituals, on the study of the Torah and daily prayer. Duplicating the deeply religious way of life in the diaspora, only in Zion, was to open the gates of heaven and bring *ge'ulah* to them and to the entire Jewish nation. The objection to the "Old Yishuv" by members the "New Yishuv"—Zionist settlers—was ideological, social, and economic. The new settlers' pursuit of social and national revolution was as zealous as the old community leaders' quest for religious preservation. They objected to the community's reliance on financial aid from abroad arguing that this would leave its members in a perpetual state of ignominy, dependency, and destitution. In their pursuit of a world built on kindness, compassion, goodness, charity, and grace—the Hebrew *tzedakah va-ḥesed*—they abhorred the leaders of the old community, blaming

---

22. The title "Old Yishuv" was coined by members of the first Zionist settler ("First Aliyah") who arrived in the Land of Israel in 1881–1904 and established new farming communities in forsaken parts of the land. Note that the Hebrew word for "old," *yashan*, signifies old-fashion, outdated, obsolete.

them for imprudence, corruption, and more—all for the sake of their own self-interest.[23]

Young Agnon's criticism of the Old Yishuv and what it stood for is equally uncompromising. "Agunot" is told by an omniscient narrator who begins the story by telling us a pseudo-midrashic tale. Once he completes this prefatory tale the narrator informs the readers—directly and unequivocally—that the moral lesson of this pseudo-midrash is the very theme of "Agunot." The introductory midrash of "Agunot" is filled with intertextual references that exploit the meaning of *agunot* in Jewish life, namely, the condition of married women whose husbands vanished without giving them a *get* (a Jewish divorce) thus condemning them to a life devoid of love and protection. In the midrashic tradition however the state of these women is commonly used as a metaphor for the estrangement of the Jewish people in exile from the love and protection of God.[24]

The pseudo-midrash which Agnon formulates in the introduction to "Agunot" argues the following: There is an eternal bond between God and the Jewish nation, but His support, love, and protection are not unconditional. It all depends on one thing and one thing only: good deeds, "even in exile," and only as long as the congregation has not "corrupted her God-given beauty or defiled herself *also* in the land of her adversaries."[25] In other words, inhabiting the Land of Israel in-and-of-itself does not merit the grace of God, His love and caring. The glorious days of the nation, either in the Land of Israel or in foreign lands, come with changing habits and choosing the "right path of good deeds that are honorable to the doers and will honor and be honored by others," in the words of the distinguished Rabbi Yehuda Hanasi in *Pirkei Avot* (2:1). Dreadful days come when the congregation stumbles morally. Then God's tender embrace disappears, and the forsaken congregation is torn apart sinking into utter despondency. This melancholy persists until God is finally appeased and proceeds to breathe a new spirit of good deeds into them.

The midrashic introduction of "Agunot" foreshadows the events of the saga to come and their aftermath. Social corruption and moral defilement permeates the Jewish community in the holy city Jerusalem. The tale

---

23. See Kaniel, *Hemshekh uTmurah*; Arieh Morgenstern, *Meshiḥiyut veYishuv*.

24. On Agnon's affinity for Jewish sources and their effect on his work in general and "Agunot" in particular see Shaked, "Midrash and Narrative: Agnon's Agunot," in *The New Tradition*, 244–61.

25. The translation from the original Hebrew is mine. Emphasis added.

Ge'ulah in Zionist Ideology and Agnon's "Agunot"

of separations and heartbreaks is an allegory designed to show that *this* community of settlers in the Holy Land does not merit God's love, grace, and protection; that it will suffer immensely for depraved conducts and consequently will fail to provide the redemptive "anchor" for the drifting nation.[26]

The deconstructive plot of "Agunot" begins with a wealthy communal leader named Aḥiezer, "who set his heart on going up from the diaspora to the holy city Jerusalem [. . .] to work great wonders of restoration in the midst of her ruins, and in this way to resource at least a corner of the anteroom which will be transformed into a mansion of glory on the day when the Holy One, blessed be He, restores His presence to Zion."[27] In other words, the story introduces us to a man acting as a *"mitzvah* emissary" who takes upon himself the task of restoring Jerusalem and readying it for complete *ge'ulah*. His distinctive name, Aḥiezer, signifies brotherhood and public service, and alludes to a prominent leader of the Dan tribe in Moses' times who was among the leaders charged with the festivities of inaugurating the nation's first Tabernacle (Numbers 1:12). The Talmud famously praises *mitzvah* emissaries for their grace and righteousness and assures them no harm will come their way (Pesaḥim 8a).

So, what went so terribly wrong in a story that begins with an honorable man's decision to act upon a desire to restore Jewish life in Zion?

Aḥiezer's transgressions begin with his leadership credentials, his objectives, his priorities, as well as his plan of action. He is a typical Jewish rich man, known in the impoverished shtetel as *gvir*, who gained power and prominence within the community due to his wealth alone. Marrying into the *gvir* family was a badge of honor and a promise of prosperity and prominence. Yet in many of Agnon's stories rendering Jewish life in pre–World War II Eastern European shtetels, the *gvir* is all but a reviled figure, hunting for glory and fame, and lacking human compassion.[28] Aḥiezer of "Agunot" is not presented as a villain. Affluence alone is under scrutiny; affluence as an attribute that qualifies a "chief" (*katzin*) of a congregation somewhere in the diaspora to show up in the holy city of Jerusalem and crown himself the king of the city and the harbinger of redemption in Zion.

---

26. Note that in Hebrew the word for anchor, *ogen*, and the word *agunot* (*agunah*), derive from the same root.

27. Translated by Hochman, in Agnon, *A Book That Was Lost*.

28. See for example Agnon's 1912 novella *And the Crooked Shall Be Made Straight* as well as "Rothschild's Luck" in *The Outcast and Other Tales*.

Agnon does not render the historical timeframe of the story overtly. A reference to the Old Yishuv is provided subtly in Aḥiezer's objective to "set regulations" as means of achieving complete *ge'ulah* graced by God. The Hebrew term for regulations, *takanot*, relates mostly to rabbinical legislation regarding religious matters, known as *takanot ḥakhamim*, Talmudic sage's regulations. In the course of diaspora living another type of regulations became widespread, "congregational regulations," *takanot ha-kehilah*. These refer to communal rules that were instituted within Jewish congregations in the diaspora, relating mostly to social administration. In these communal structures, the leadership grew out of community members who had assumed immense powers over the congregation. Community leaders were chosen for distinguished and distinguishing qualities such as education and wealth. Many of the regulations controlled civil conduct, but they were never too far from overseeing the community's religious life.[29] This governance style persisted for generations and allowed the insular congregations of the diaspora to sustain a civic *and* Jewish way of life in foreign and often hostile lands. It was then transported to Jerusalem in an attempt to fix the many social and economic problems that plagued the Jews of the Old Yishuv. These were known as *takanot Yerushalaim*, the Jerusalem regulations, implying corrections or repairs—and were to improve the lives of the indigent Jewish inhabitants of the city. Except that they never did. The Jerusalem Agnon and other members of the Second Aliyah encountered upon their arrival in the Land of Israel in the early 1900s was, in Brenner's blunt language, an "abject, lifeless" city filled with indolent and sickly human beings manipulated by "dealers," *'askanim*, caring for nothing but their own eminence.[30] Agnon's approach to the social blunder he witnesses in Jerusalem of 1908 is as political as it is theological. In the scheme of "Agunot" the idea of an affluent man arriving in Jerusalem from the diaspora with old fashion communal practices in tow is a very bad omen and foreshadows a chain of misdeeds with heart-rending consequences.

There are additional clues in the rendering of Aḥiezer's life that suggest the breakdown to come. Surrounded by abject poverty, the "brother" who came to help the hapless congregation of Jerusalem resides in a secluded

---

29. Note that affluent leaders like the fictional character of Aḥiezer were commonly addressed as "Rabbi Aḥiezer" even though they were not scholars and had no rabbinical credentials. When Agnon first introduces the character he refers to him as an honorable "chief" (*qatzin*) and "minister" (*sar*) but then mostly as Rabbi Aḥiezer or in the Hebrew abbreviated form R. Aḥiezer.

30. Brenner, "MeḤaye Yerushalaim."

palace with his precious only daughter who is treated like a delicate princess.[31] She is kept away from the masses, and surrounded by maids and servants making sure every wish of hers is honored. Another hint is the daughter's name, Dina, a subtle reference to an enigmatic heart-wrenching biblical story of an illicit love, of defilement, and rage, as well as of an imprudent reaction that results in tragically unforeseen consequences (Genesis 34).

The snag begins when the time arrives to marry-off Dina, and despite the presence of eligible, brilliant grooms within the local *yeshivot*, Aḥiezer rejects them all as being unworthy. The perfect match for a nobleman's precious daughter can only be found in "the exile abroad." And that is when "the Satan intervened," we are informed by the omniscient narrator, and the people of Jerusalem rightly began to voice their discontentment, albeit behind the mighty Aḥiezer's back. Needless to say, as is customary in this community, the girl is not asked, and she would never dare to share her passion for another young man with her father. The appearance of the Satan not only foreshadows the story's bitter end but also sends us back to rethink the implications of its introductory allegory: When the Satan shows up things fall apart. And things fall apart on account of bad deeds. Deciding on a groom from the diaspora is the transgression, and so once again the inevitable moral lesson is that for a revival of Jewish life in the Land of Israel to succeed and for the young generation to thrive, the gates to anything that smacks of the diaspora must be tightly shut.

The underlining rejection of the diaspora is well explained within the narrative structures of "Agunot."

Once a "wondrous lad" is found somewhere in Poland, Aḥiezer decides to build a palatial yeshiva with an ornate synagogue worthy of a distinguished rabbinic prodigy. He then hires an equally prodigious artist to craft a Holy Ark extraordinaire, a man that stood out from other artists by the "extraordinary spirit that flashed from his glance and the work of his hands." It is not all clear where the artist comes from, but he was noticeably not part of the congregation and very different from them. He was a "quiet and modest man" pursuing his undertaking at once with enthusiasm and vigor, with an immensely creative energy, and delight. The implicit description of an enigmatic young man whose ingenious soul is ignited by a divine spark echoes the legend of the pioneers' character that was celebrated

---

31. It is important to note that Aḥiezer is a widower.

when Agnon arrived in the land of Israel in 1908.[32] His unusual name, Ben Uri, signifying literally "son of light." It echoes the new energy of life that motivated members of the new community in the Land of Israel and also ever so subtly alludes to the battle against the "dark" forces of gloom and doom they were determined to fight akin to the brave Jews during the glorious Hasmonean era.[33] The name Ben Uri is mostly an obvious allusion to the biblical Bezalel Ben Uri who God named to build the tabernacle and "filled him with the spirit of God, in wisdom, and in understanding, and in knowledge, and in all manner of workmanship" (Exodus 31:1–5). Bezalel became the namesake of the art school the Jewish artist Boris Schatz established in Jerusalem in 1906. Schatz and his disciples in Jerusalem were Zionist artists and craftsmen who were convinced that the national revival in Zion could not be accomplished by cultivating the barren land alone, but must be accompanied by the creation of a national style of progressive art, blending classical Jewish traditions of all communities and times.[34] Opening the school in the heart of Jerusalem was intended to breathe new life into a stagnant city mismanaged by the leaders of the Old Yishuv and was also motivated by an unmitigated faith in Jerusalem as the historical and spiritual eternal epicenter of Judaism and the Jewish future. In 1908 Bezalel was bustling with creativity and sporting major artistic talents. And yet the school, its founder and students, were fiercely castigated by the religious establishment of the Old Yishuv disparaging them for a non-Orthodox, if not profane, way of life. At the same time however, Bezalel was highly praised by proponents of the Second Aliyah, including the literary periodical that hired Agnon as soon as he arrived in the land of Israel and also published

---

32. See Kushnir, *Anshe Nevo*. In a seven-part epic poem titled "From Midnight to Midnight," Noah Naftulsky, a prominent figure of the Second Aliyah writes: "Devoted to an inner command,—to a wondrous counselor, /we rushed forward to hasten the end. / We relied on wonders, on the rock of Israel [. . .] he was with us a foster and assessor / we espoused our hands to redeem the wilderness [. . .] we brought with us a will of action / and our two hands and a vision of redemption / these two a gift and a giving / didn't ask for a prize, done their duty." The historian Muki Tsur highlights the muted devotion of the pioneers to rebuilding the Land of Israel, adding that many of the young pioneers of the early twentieth century were affected by various progressive ideologies of their time, including the Mussar Movement, founded mid-nineteenth century by Rabbi Israel Salanter, with its focus on human morality based on generosity of the spirit, humility, and uncompromising self-criticism, Tsur, "HeḤalutz, haTipus, haDerekh."

33. See Yadin, *Megilat Milḥemet Bene Or biVene Ḥoshekh*.

34. Note that a similar ideology pertaining to Hebrew literature was the strong motivation of the authors that Agnon joined in Jaffa during those years.

his story "Agunot."³⁵ Where Agnon stands in this debate is unequivocal: Ben Uri by name and deeds is the only character in the story that in the words of the opening midrash "radiates in the light of beauty of the days of old in the city of sovereignty," and so the only character that "has neither been sullied not defiled even in the diaspora" where he purportedly came from and has worked before. And yet, these impressions, we should note, are rendered by the narrator, not by Aḥiezer. The haughty sire's sole reason for hiring this man was none other than Ben Uri's promise to produce an "astonishingly beautiful ark such as *no eye has ever seen before*."³⁶

When Aḥiezer decides to hire the "alien" Ben Uri for the holy task of building the ark, the people of the community were certainly unhappy, but no one dared to protest the chief's choice. Tucked away in the basement of the house, Ben Uri became at once consumed with crafting the ark but also romantically involved with Dina, who was bewitched by the song "his lips uttered all day long." Unable to withstand the lure of the man and the melodic voice she kept hearing through the open window of her room, she came down to examine Ben Uri's work and a romantic spark was ignited between the two.³⁷ Unfortunately, the more he worked, the more Ben Uri became bewitched, only not by the beautiful maiden, but by the ark, and so in no time he "forgot her altogether." Working on the ark filled Ben Uri with a unique sense of "awakening" he never experienced before in the many lands he worked prior to this job, and he begins to believe that biblical prophecies of redemption are coming to life by the labor of his two hands. In his ingenious mastery of Hebrew and Jewish sources, Agnon meticulously describes Ben Uri's feeling as if he is breathing life into the decorative forms he shapes upon the ark, the lions and the eagles that are to house the Torah scrolls. Infusing old Jewish motifs with a new life was what he, akin to the real young artists of Jerusalem in the early twentieth century, was inspired to produce. Furthermore, the sense of spiritual ascent accompanying industrious endeavors is often heard not only from artists but also from many members of the Second Aliyah, authors and workers alike. Biblical images, words, visions, and prophecies were never far from

35. On the beginning of Bezalel see Biber, "Betzalel: Teḥilatah shel 'Amanut Eretz Yisrael," 24–26; Shalev-Khalifa, "Yerushalaim haḤadashah," 1–5; Werses, *Agnon ki-Feshuto*, 264–90.

36. Emphasis added.

37. In a subtle inverted allusion to the sirens in Greek mythology Agnon renders Ben Uri as a mysteriously dangerous creature with a sweet singing voice that will lure Dina and end up wrecking her life.

young Jews that settled the land during those years and worked to reestablish it as a modern advanced community rooted in and inspired by the old days of glory of biblical times.[38] That the pursuit of love was secondary to the mission at hand is also one of the myths accompanying the young men that arrived in the Land of Israel at that time, as Muki Tsur notes.[39] Ben Uri is a conspicuous image of this mythological figure. Yet, in the Old Yishuv he is seen as a menacing heretic and therefore treated with suspicion and loathing even though he did produce the "astonishingly beautiful ark" he was hired to construct.

The real surprise, however, is Ben Uri's own state of mind upon the completion of his finest artistic creation. When he finally sees the ark "alive and standing," Ben Uri turns at once miserable like a depleted "empty vessel." Feeling appalled, horrified, and distressed, "his grief-stricken soul" suggests not only a sense of loss, but also deep regret, and so he begins to cry. One can argue, and many do, that Ben Uri's despondency reflects an artist who is afraid that his vision and creativity have been exhausted. Only this does not explain the guilt. An intertextual reference that Agnon subtly inserts into the narrative brings us to the grief-stricken soul of the biblical Job, expressing remorse for not having "wept for him that was in trouble ... [and whose] soul has not grieved for the needy" (Job 30:25). In "Agunot" the paragraph rendering Ben Uri's distress follows a scene in which the narrator informs us what is to occur upon the completion of the ark: "already the worthies of Jerusalem awaited the day the ark would be borne up to the house of the Lord the hands of the grandee had built." Notably "the hands of the grandee" are credited for the ark, not the hands of Ben Uri. The worker is not worthy of any praise, nor is he seeking one. However, when the artist looks at the "work of his hands" in the very next paragraph, the sense of emptiness, estrangement, and self-loathing appears to signify a sober realization that the ark he has built will not result in the return of the divine presence to grace Jerusalem as he imagined, only further venerate Aḥiezer and the cronies of Jerusalem. Ben Uri then vanishes into thin air, but he is not forgotten. His spirit continues to haunt the saga up to its bitter end.

---

38. For example, in a moving paragraph in her autobiography *Anu Olim*, Rachel Yanait Ben Zvi, a prominent member of the Second Aliyah, while looking at the Judean Desert marvels about the spirit of the biblical prophets entering into the soul of the young pioneers.

39. Tsur, "*Anshe haAliyah haSheniyah*," 286–93.

Just as soon as Ben Uri disappears the Satan returns and with him the winds of destruction that will tear Aḥiezer's plan into pieces. The great surprise is that the destructive spell does not strike Aḥiezer directly but rather his "virtuous," "modest," and "gentle" daughter Dina. When Dina ceases to hear Ben Uri's voice and is unable to find him the Satan entered her soul and " put jealousy in her heart." The Satan blamed the ark for Ben Uri's desertion and so she impulsively pushed her "rival" and the ark fell out of the window. Miraculously the ark was not damaged one bit, and yet "all Jewish people of Jerusalem" react to the event hastily and irrationally just like the father in "Fable of the Goat." They did not try to inquire what happened or why. Their narrow minds led them to the only conclusion imaginable to them: "the ark was pushed by Heaven." And why would God want to push the ark? Because Ben Uri was a "good-for-nothing man, for sure a villain, and not fit for the hollowed work of the ark, and so now that it has been done it had been shunned by Heaven." In comes the rabbi, and with no contemplation or hesitation condemns the ark to banishment even though it was lying there out of the window wholly intact.

From this point on the plot of "Agunot" renders meticulously the total destruction of Aḥiezer's plan. Another ark was immediately ordered to replace Ben Uri's creation but it stood there "like a commemoration of destruction." Dina's impending marriage is to take place but will never be consummated, and the reluctant groom from Poland will lose his chance for bliss in the diaspora where the love of his life was made to marry someone else. More importantly, all leading characters, including the community rabbi, will end up displaced somewhere back in the diaspora.

There is a noticeable resemblance between the son in "Fable of the Goat" and Dina in "Agunot." They are both curious young people who dare to venture out of the comfort and safety of their fathers' home and become captivated by a world they find beyond their hermetically sealed milieu. But contrary to the son's blissful fate, Dina's life turns into hell on earth and she ends up returning to the "dreadful diaspora" with her father. Clearly, Dina's plight appears at first sight a result of her own recklessness. Her transgressions begin by "going out" of the secure confines of her home to explore an unfamiliar territory of strangers whose morals, traditions, and culture are so different from her own, much like her biblical namesake, Dina, the only daughter of Jacob. In his commentary to the biblical story known as "The Rape of Dina," the eminent medieval commentator Rashi relates Dina's violation by a Hivite prince of the land to her own misdeed:

"going out to see the daughters of the land" (Genesis 34:1). Rashi's focus on Dina's "going out" subtly suggests an unrestrained conduct unsuitable for an honorable, unwed young girl who is expected to remain within the "confines of the palace" (Psalms 45:14). Another midrash proposes further that the biblical Dina went out to pursue the Hivite prince not realizing that her attraction to a man not of her own moral kind will result in her "humbling" (Genesis 34:2).[40] And yet, from the very beginning of "Agunot" it appears that the leading culprit is the father, his unhallowed deeds, as well as a simpleminded community led by self-absorbed cronies, so why does the blame shift to his innocent daughter and why is she made to bear the main burden? Furthermore, why is she punished even after she confesses to the rabbi, asks for forgiveness, is fully absolved by him, and meticulously follows his counsel? Have we not learned from our great sages that the virtue of repenting sinners is greater than those of perfectly righteous people who have never sinned?[41]

Dina's fate and the burdens she is made to bear in "Agunot" are not the first time a literary masterpiece puts a young woman in the center of a story that comes to shed light on the moral shortcomings of traditional Jewish communities. In a cultural bombshell published in 1876, the *Haskalah* poet Judah Leib Gordon shocked the Jewish world with a tragic epic poem "Kotzo shel Yud" ("A Tiny Letter Yud"). Using Talmudic sages' misogynistic maxims, Gordon exposes the lot of women in Jewish society and condemns their fathers and an obtuse rabbinical authority for heartlessly wrecking their lives in the name of archaic Jewish laws and obsolete communal codes. The violation of women's rights nevertheless is not the main theme of "Kotzo shel Yud." The poem is mostly a critical commentary lamenting, as Ziva Shamir asserts, the nation's inability to break out of a "bewitched cycle" of a wholly failed, yet unbreakable "marital commitment" to a culture centered on unbending religious rules, and unwillingness to amend obsolete communal traditions unsuited for modern times.[42] With the fate of women dominating their narratives, prominent Hebrew writers that followed Gordon, like Jacob Steinberg and Devorah Baron as well as the eminent poet H.N. Bialik, similarly denounce a merciless, inequitable Jewish

---

40. Genesis Rabbah, 3, ed. Vilna, *Vayishlaḥ* 8:11.
41. BT Berakhot 34b.
42. See Shamir, *HaKol biGelal Kotso shel Yod*, 7–8, 23.

world incapable of divorcing itself from old customs and stringent laws that deprive young girls of a life of true love and everlasting happiness.[43]

Soon after she surrenders to forces that call upon her to conform and marry the foreign man her father chose for her, the guilt-ridden Dina lies in bed pondering the virtues of her "righteous," that is to say obedient, mother, whose memory she has disgraced. But much as she tries to suppress her feelings, her desire for Ben Uri is far stronger than any compunction she may sense. Restless she rises and goes over to the very same window through which she heard Ben Uri's voice for the very first time. The void that his absence created is then filled with a blowing wind:

> Dinah rose and crossed to the window; she rested her chin on her hands and looked out. Jerusalem is cradled in mountains. The wind swept down and entered her chamber, extinguishing the light, as in a sickroom where some invalid sleeps. It played around her hair and through her ears, whispering sweet melodies, like the songs Ben Uri had sung. Where, oh where, is he now?

Unlike the Talmudic position Agnon interweaves into this narrative, for Dina the natural hum of Jerusalem's airstream does not suggest a remedy against pagans and/or evil forces. Instead, it carries an invigorating force and a promising relief from the airtight, smothering environment that suffocates her in her father's palace, akin to the life-force the sound of Ben Uri's tunes brought to her oppressive environment, shaking it from the bottom up. Her longing for him is then summed up in the simple phrase: "Where, oh where, is he now?" Ben Uri was Dina's glimmer of light in an insulated dark and joyless existence she was trained to accept as reality itself. His presence allowed her to sense the possibility of an entirely different life beyond the walls of the palace where she is hopelessly trapped.

The bride's distress and the air of melancholy hovering over the entire community following the fall of the ark notwithstanding, preparations for the wedding of Dina to the imported groom, Ezekiel, proceed and consume Aḥiezer's household.[44] Once a date is set and the groom arrives, the

---

43. The assault on marriage customs and women's victimization begins in the Middle Ages in a fable titled "The Riddle of Efer and Dina," by Don Vidal Benveniste, a Spanish Jew who belonged to a distinguished group of Hebrew writers in Spain of the Middle Ages.

44. Note that the biblical prophet Ezekiel is known for challenging the perception that "The fathers have eaten sour grapes, and the children's teeth are set on edge" (Ezek 18:1). In the scheme of "Agunot" both Dina and Ezekiel are purportedly victims of their fathers' grand schemes as well as of traditions and customs that ignore the winds of

dreary mood in Jerusalem turns at once jolly, everyone eagerly preparing for "festivals Jerusalem has not seen the likes of since her sons were driven into exile." Aḥiezer's plan is working out after all. "The voice of joy and the voice of gladness, the voice of the bridegroom and the voice of the bride" that are about to be heard in the streets of Jerusalem are a sure sign that the promised *ge'ulah* is coming true (Jeremiah 33:10–11). As customary on a wedding day, the bride is brought to the rabbi to receive his blessing, and that is when Dina finally breaks down and tells the rabbi "all that tale of how the ark has dropped and fell down." Her unrelenting desire for another man must have been the main topic of the bride's tearful confession and her last chance to avoid marrying a man that was chosen for her without ever "inquiring her mouth" (Genesis 24:57). And yet in spite of his utter bewilderment, the rabbi feels compelled to exploit his eminence, force the marriage, and keep the community's traditions together with Aḥiezer's plans alive and well. Resorting to old customs and well-established credos, he reminds Dina that a wedding day is a day of grace and forgiveness. He appeases her with words of consolation that promise to dissolve past culpability, assuring her of a hallowed new life that a marriage embodies. The rabbi also suggests that Dina's involvement with the fall of the ark remain forever unspoken, and that God will forgive her. And so, like all women that preceded her, Dina submits, perhaps realizing she has no way out, perhaps trusting the rabbi and his assurance that marriage, a distinguished husband, and raising a family will resolve all of her qualms. And yet none of the rabbi's promises are attainable, and a wedding contract can appease neither the sad bride nor the reluctant groom. The wedding festivities that are featured next are essentially a grotesque spectacle: The wedding canopy over the couple's heads is ripping into shreds as the musicians play their instruments, "righteous men" perform a mitzvah dance, and "Talmudic scholars fill their throats with wine and various delicacies."

A traditional Jewish canopy is made of a tallit and so the shredding of the canopy in "Agunot," as indicated in the introductory Midrash, signifies not only the ruin of the union between the loveless couple featured in the story but also the plan to reestablish Jewish life graced by God in Zion. In a pursuit of a nation committed to "good deeds" young Agnon undermines many established customs involving the duty of matchmaking in traditional Jewish communities, mostly the disheartening belief that a wedding is not a union of love and compassion, but a tribal duty designed for "multiplication

---

modernity and their children's desires.

and replenishment" that will allegedly hasten Jewish redemption.⁴⁵ Dina's fit of rage did not trigger the epic events Agnon presents in "Agunot." They were triggered by the community's misdirected leadership and collective vilification of Ben Uri, a man who dedicated himself to the renewal of Jerusalem as the center of Jewish life while celebrating Ezekiel, who had never wished to be there and was unable to show gratitude for "meriting to ascent to the Holy Land." Far from "the mighty righteous men that were granted the privilege of finding their place in the Holy Land in their lifetime," the narrator reveals, Ezekiel's "feet are planted in the gates of Jerusalem and he stand on her soil [but] his eyes and his heart are pledged to houses of studies and worship abroad . . . Even now as he walks in the hills of Jerusalem, he fancies himself among the scholars of his own town, strolling in the field with them." Joining the endeavor to restore Jewish life in Zion with "a song on his lips all day," Ben Uri actualizes one of the greatest prophecies of redemption: "And the ransomed of the Lord shall return, and come with singing unto Zion, and everlasting joy shall be upon their heads; they shall obtain gladness and joy, and sorrow and sighing shall flee away" (Isaiah 51:11). Conversely, overcome by "sorrow and sighing," Ezekiel in his longing for the diaspora could not be but a destructive force in the attempt to resettle the Land of Israel with a jolly spirit of messianic time. As a result, the celebration of Ezekiel and his famed scholastic virtues are short lived. In no time the entire community comes to recognize that "Rabbi Ezekiel's soul is flawed." Aḥiezer then realizes that his daughter's marriage was a sham and that his grand "repair" plan was in ruins. Humiliated and wholly dejected, he leaves Jerusalem with his daughter.

Aḥiezer's plan to settle the Holy Land failed because, to borrow the title of Ahad Ha'am's essay, "The Wrong Way" to mend Judaism and merit the beginning of a national redemption in the Land of Israel.⁴⁶ It was not the right way because it perpetuated a regressive Jewish way of life based on affluence and religious scholarship that during the long history of diaspora living, in the words of Ahad Ha'am, "weakened and humbled the nation into utter submission" to overbearing communal leaders and esoteric rules inscribed in ancient books for ancient times.

---

45. According to the Talmud the mitzvah of procreation is essential for the messiah to come and so marrying young and multiplying as fast and as much as possible hastens redemption (BT Yevamot 62a).

46. Ahad Ha'am, "The Wrong Way," in *Ten Essays on Zionism and Judaism*, 1–24.

A controversial figure during his lifetime, Ahad Ha'am's writings inspired many of the young men and women who decided to settle the Land of Israel during the Second Aliyah, including authors and essayists, ever since "This is Not the Way" was published in 1889, and he was greatly revered by the literary leadership that young Agnon joined in Jaffa.[47] The influence of Ahad Ha'am on Agnon is palpable not only in his biting criticism of the plutocratic attempt to revive Jewish life in the Land of Israel, but mainly of the religious authority that relied on obsolete rules, customs and traditions to repress all "natural and/or moral foresight" that inspired progressive movements all through the enlightened world and moved nations from the darkness of a repressive past to a bright future of national as well as individual freedom since the middle of the nineteenth century.[48]

It is therefore not surprising that Aḥiezer's renouncement of the Land of Israel and his disgraceful departure from Jerusalem does not bring the story of "Agunot" to its closure. For a Jewish endeavor to merit redemption, and for a revival of Jewish life in the Land of Israel to get on the right path, it is imperative that the rabbi, the community's moral authority and guide, leave Jerusalem at once, return to the diaspora, and dedicate his life to "repairing moored women" (*le-takken agunot*), or "redeem the forsaken in love." Only by this mission, Agnon surely does not refer to saving abandoned women, or even to correcting merciless rulings that forever doom the life of women, as the Hebrew title of the story seems to suggest. In fact, "Agunot" is hardly concerned with the fate of forsaken wives, not even when, in a twist of irony, the rabbi leaves his own wife and vanishes forever in the very end of the story. The main concern expressed all through "Agunot" and is articulated overtly and powerfully in the last chapter of the story is with displaced souls, men and women alike, denied of their God-given impulses and of the home and land their hearts passionately sought to inhabit by rabbinical [mis]reading of Torah's commandments. The decisive voice of condemnation the rabbi hears in his dreams is that of Ben Uri accusing the rabbi of driving him out "from abiding in the inheritance of the lord" (I Samuel 26:19). The obvious allusion to King Saul's ill-conceived attempt to expel David from the land for the sake of holding

---

47. Note that Ahad Ha'am polemic was the impetus for Boris Schatz to establish a progressive art school in the heart of Jerusalem and also for Sh. Ben-Zion, Ahad Ha'am "friend, colleague and disciple" and Agnon's first literary mentor in Jaffa, to move to the Land of Israel and establish the literary periodical "*HaOmer*" where "Agunot" was first published.

48. Ahad Ha'am, "Torah of the Heart."

on to his throne reveals the underlying message Ben Uri's reappearance in "Agunot" upholds: the time has come for a creative spirit like Ben Uri to be included in a Jewish community endeavoring to transform Judaism from a moribund creed into a vibrant national culture of continuation and change that Ahad Ha'am envisioned.[49]

Young Agnon's commitment to revealing the ills of diaspora living and laying the case for a spiritual and cultural amendment of the nation prior to restoring Jewish life in the Land of Israel bind him to the ideology of the Zionist young men and women he joined in 1908.[50] The disparaging portrayal of everything that smacks of a diasporic way of life one hears repeatedly from early Zionist pioneers is front and center in "Agunot" (as well as in other works Agnon published upon his arrival). What struck many readers of "Agunot" from the day it was published, and sets it apart from much of the critical works that were published at the time, is the allegorical veil that allows Agnon to undermine vices of a strictly Jewish way of life in the very literary genre that is known to celebrate its virtues. The achievement of "Agunot" is twofold. Following Ahad Ha'am, Agnon is deeply concerned not only with a soulless nation "enslaved by the Book" but also by Zionist attempts to divorce Judaism from the past. "Agunot" is a novel literary creation in the Land of Israel of the time that in the words of Ahad Ha'am skillfully breathes new life into old Jewish forms, akin to the fictional image of Ben Uri and the ideology that has driven creative artists that gathered around the Bezalel School of Art. The spirit of Jewish creativity was also the main drive of actual young men and women that arrived in the land beginning in 1904 determined to establish a literary center dedicated to Jewish cultural renewal. Agnon's stylistics demonstrate how the "nation of the Book" can turn, in the words of Ahad Ha'am, into a "bookish nation"—a nation that allows for its creative arts and literatures to grow with history and "plant in the farrows of Jewish hearts seeds of new ideas and new desires" without sacrificing its "Jewish image."[51] A deconstructive artist before

---

49. This position is made clear when the soul of the vanished rabbi visits a young, closeted artist in a traditional House of Study in the diaspora late at night when everyone else is asleep. The artist is busy fashioning a *Mizrah* sign, namely his vision of Zion. "Come let's rise and go up to Jerusalem," the artist hears the rabbi saying.

50. The name Agnon which the young author adopted upon the publication of "Agunot" may very well reveal a newly "repaired" Jewish soul emerging from two millennia of hopes, prayers, and dreams, reuniting with its beloved lost land, ready to rewrite the new chapter Zionism has carved for Judaism in the early twentieth century.

51. Ahad Ha'am, "Torah of the Heart."

Agnon's Tales of the Land of Israel

"Deconstruction," Agnon provides in "Agunot" a serious examination of Jewish heritage. He demonstrates how multifaceted Jewish traditions really are and disavows the one-dimensional approach that has come to define Orthodox Judaism. Driven by the love of Zion and inspired by images of redemption, Agnon, much like many of his Zionist peers, asserts that revived Jewish life in the Land of Israel is not possible without a breakaway from communal and religious traditions that were perpetuated in the diaspora. Jerusalem will not be rebuilt through the leadership of the wealthy. It will not be rebuilt by constructing fancy synagogues staffed by rabbinical scholars imported from abroad and "enslaved by the Book." It will not be built by recreating an insular community ruled by halakhic rulings and by refusing to allow spirited, progressive Jews to "abide in the inheritance of the Lord." Redemption in the Land of Israel will come only when passion, compassion, grace, tolerance, and good deeds will be valued over heartless decrees, and Jews of all walks of life will be welcome into a versatile society that allows for every Jew to feel at home in the Promised Land.

Bibliography

Agnon, S.Y. "Vehayah he'akov Lemishor." *Hapoel Hatzair*, January–May, 1912.
———. "Ma'aseh haEz." In *Elu veElu*, 303–5. Tel Aviv: Schocken, 1953.
———. "Agunot." In *Elu veElu*, 329–37. Tel Aviv: Schocken, 1953.
———. "Agunot." In *A Book That Was Lost*. Edited by Alan Mintz and Anne Golumb Hoffman. Translated by Baruch Hochman. Tel Aviv: Schocken, 1996.
———. "Fable of the Goat." In *A Book That Was Lost*, ed. Alan Mintz, and Anne Golumb Hoffman, 199–202. Tel Aviv: Schocken, 1996.
———. *Forevermore & Other Stories*. Edited by Jeffrey Saks. New Milford, CT: Toby, 2017.
———. Prize presentation. NobelPrize.org. Nobel Media AB 2020. Mon. 2 Nov 2020. <https://www.nobelprize.org/prizes/literature/1966/agnon/prize-presentation/>
———. "Rothschild's Luck." In *The Outcast and Other Tales*. Edited by Jeffrey Saks. New Milford, CT: Toby, 2018.
Ahad Ha'am. "Torah of the Heart." *Pardes* II, Odessa, 1894.
———. "The Wrong Way." In *Ten Essays on Zionism and Judaism*. Translated by Leon Simon. London: Routledge, 1922.
Almog, Shmuel. "Ge'ulah in Zionist Rhetoric" [Hebrew]. In *Ha-Nekudah ha-Yehudit: Yehudim be-'Ene 'Atsmam uve-'Ene Aherim*, 65–82. Tel Aviv: Sifriyat Po'alim, 2002.
Almog, Shmuel, Jehuda Reinhartz, and Anita Shapita. *Tzionut vaDat*. Jerusalem: Zalman Shazar, 1994.
Alterman, Nathan. "The People of the Second Aliyah" [Hebrew]. In *The Book of the Singing Box*, 1958.
Bakon, Yitzhak. "On 'Agunot." [Hebrew] *Moznaim* 46/3 (1978) 167–79.
Be'er, Haim. *Gam Ahavatam, Gam Sin'atam: Bialik, Brenner, Agnon, Ma'arkhot-Yehasim*. Tel Aviv: Am Oved, 2002.

Ben-Avi, Itamar. *Hashkafah*, Friday, November 22, 1907, 3.
Ben-Dov, Nitza. "The Raven's Message of Return: S.Y. Agnon and the Zionist Dream." *Studies in Zionism* 14/1 (1993) 95–112.
Biber, Yeho'ash. "Betzalel: Teḥilatah shel 'Amanut Eretz Yisrael." *Sipure Batim*. Tel Aviv: Hotza'at Misrad HaBitahon, 1988.
Brenner, Y. H. "The Eretz Israel Genre and Its Accessories." Personal letter, August, 1910.
———. *From Here and from There*. Warsaw: Sifrut, 1911.
———. "Nerves." *Shalechet*. Lvov: 1910.
———. "MeḤaye Yerushalaim." *HaPo'el HaTza'ir* (Summer 1913).
———. *Breakdown and Bereavement*. New York: Shtiebel, 1920.
Golan, Orna. "The Story 'Agunot' and the Second Aliyah" [Hebrew]. *Moznaim* 32/3 (1971) 215–23.
Govrin, Nurit. *HaOmer: Tnufato shel Ktav 'Et va-Aḥrito*. Jerusalem: Yad Ben-Zvi, 1980.
Gressel, G. "A Priest for the Land." [Hebrew] *Davar*, October 23, 1959.
Halpern, Ben and Jehuda Reinharz, "The Cultural and Social Background of the Second Aliyah." *Middle Eastern Studies* 27/3 (1991) 487–517.
Kaniel, Yehoshua. *Hemshekh uTmurah*. Jerusalem: Yad Ben-Zvi, 1981.
Katznelson, Gidon. "*Agunot shel Agnon: Gilgulav shel Nusah*." *Moznaim* 27/3–4 (1968) 163–73.
Knaani, David. *HaAliyah ha-Shniyah haOvedet veYahasah laDat ve-laMasoret*. Tel Aviv: Sifriyat Po'elim, 1977.
Kushnir, Shimon. *Anshe Nevo: Pirḳe Aliliah shel Anshe ha-Aliyah ha-Sheniyah*. Tel Aviv: Am Oved, 1968.
Morgenstern, Arieh. *Meshiḥiyut yeYishuv Eretz Yisra'el baMaḥatsit haRishonah shel haMe'ah ha19*. Jerusalem: Yad Ben-Zvi, 1985.
Schweid, Eliezer. "The Rejection of the Diaspora in Zionist Thought: Two Approaches." *Studies in Zionism* 5 (1984) 43–70.
Shaked, Gershon. "Midrash and Narrative: Agnon's Agunot." In *The New Tradition*, 244–61. Cincinnati: Hebrew Union College Press, 2006.
Shalev-Khalifa, Nirit. "Yerushalaim haḤadashah: Amanim, Tzionim ve-Sotzyalistim biYerushalaim shel Re'shit haMe'ah ha'Esrim," *Et-mol* 186 (March 2006) 1–5.
Shamir, Ziva. *HaKol biGelal Kotso shel Yod*. Tel Aviv: Hakibbutz Hameuchad, 2014.
Shapira, Anita. "HaMitos shel haYehudi heḤadash." In *Yehudim Ḥadashim, Yehudim Yeshanim*. Tel Aviv: Am Oved, 1997.
Stern, Dina. *Agnon Hamekhuseh min HaAyin*. Jerusalem: Reuven Mas, 2000.
Tsur, Muki. "Anshe haAliyah haSheniyah, Tipuse haOlim veDeyukanam haḤevrati-Tarbuti." in *HaAliyah haSheniyah: Meḥkarim*, 286–93. Jerusalem: Yad Ben-Zvi, 1997.
Tsur, Muki. "heḤalutz, haTipus, haDerekh." www.mukitsur.co.il/הדרך-הטיפוס-החלוץ (September 14, 2014).
Weiss, Hillel. *Agnon—Agunot, Ido veEnam: Mekorot-Mivnim Mashmauyot*. Tel Aviv: Open University, 1979.
Werses, Shmuel. *S.Y. Agnon kiFeshuto*. Jerusalem: Mosad Bialik, 2000.
Yadin, Yigael. *Megilat Milḥemet Bene Or biVene Ḥoshekh*. Jerusalem: Mosad Bialik, 1955.
Zeira, Moti. *Keru'im Anu: Zikatah shel haHityashvut ha'Ovedet biShenot ha'Esrim el haTarbut haYehudit*. Jerusalem: Yad Ben-Zvi, 2002.

3

Agnon's "Tale of the Menorah" Between Buczacz and Modern Israel

STEVEN FINE*

Agnon's "Ma'aseh ha-Menorah," "The Tale of the Menorah," first appeared in *Atidot: Rivon le-Noar*, a cultural anthology produced quarterly for Israeli teens by the Jewish Agency in time for Hanukkah, 1956.¹ It was subsequently integrated into *Ir u-Meloah*, published posthumously in 1973.² The title of our tale plays on Numbers 8:4, "And this is the making (*ma'aseh*) of the lampstand." It is a double entendre. The noun *ma'aseh* refers to a tale or story in both classical and modern Hebrew. In the participle form of Numbers 8, however, it refers to the fabrication of *the* lampstand, *ha-menorah*. Agnon's story (*ma'aseh*) then, is the tale of the ongoing "making"

---

* Many thanks to Jeffrey Saks, Vladimir Levin, Sergey R. Kravtsov, Joshua Karlip and Leah Bierman Fine for their wise counsel and many kindnesses in the preparation of this article. It is dedicated in memory of my friend Ozer Glickman ז״ל, who truly believed in and exemplified "the eternity of Israel"—in all of its (and his) amazing complexity.

1 Agnon, *Atidot: Rivon le-Noar*, 3–11.

2 Agnon, *Ir uMeloah*, 29–37. Owing to its greater availability, I cite this version throughout, and follow the translation of David Stern published in Agnon, *A City in Its Fullness*, eds. Mintz and Saks, 44–56.

"Tale of the Menorah"

Figure 3.1: Hanukkah Menorah, Poland, eighteenth century, North Carolina Museum of Art (photo: Steven Fine).

(*ma'aseh*) of a particular menorah that exemplifies all menorahs. Beyond that, its first publication was as a Hanukkah story, even though the subject was a seven-branched menorah and not a Hanukkah menorah. This publication, then, intimately associates the Temple-like menorah of the tale with the Hanukkah season in a palimpsest that is, in fact intrinsic to the holiday and its ritual vessel. "Ma'aseh ha-Menorah" was first published at the height of a kind of "menorah craze" at mid-century, when belles-lettres, academic studies, archaeological discoveries and visual representations of the biblical lampstand were central to the Jewish public agenda, in no small part owing to the choice of the menorah as a central Jewish icon and then of the Arch of Titus menorah for the "symbol" of the State of Israel (1949).[3] Menorahs were everywhere. From soap and insurance to postage stamps, building facades, the Knesset garden to chocolate Hanukkah candy, scholarship and even comic books, the menorah was a framing element of Israeli visual culture and civil religion. "Ma'aseh ha-Menorah" placed Agnon at the center of the excitement. It expresses what I see as a rather jaundiced—if camouflaged—perspective on the national symbol that was shared by others within his religious Zionist milieu.

Atidot was edited by Shimshon Meltzer and Benzion Benshalom. Meltzer was a prominent Yiddish and Hebrew author and translator born

---

3. See Fine, *The Menorah* and the bibliography there.

in Tluste in Galicia (now Ukraine). Benshalom was associated with the publication of *Atidot* throughout its history. Meltzer positioned himself, like Agnon, as a bridging agent between Eastern European Jewish life and modern Israel. His literary work often steered to themes and subjects dear to Agnon, and the 1967 edition of Meltzer's collection, *Or Zarua: Sefer ha-Shirot ve-ha-Baladot ha-Shalem* was dedicated to Agnon. Within its original frame in *Atidot*, "Ma'aseh ha-Menorah" is accompanied by two black and white woodcuts of rather low quality, though they reflect an approach brought into the Zionist ethos by Jacob Steinhardt and deployed elsewhere by his student, Avigdor Arikha, who illustrated a number of Agnon stories during the 1950s and early 1960s.[4] Each image shows stages in the history of Agnon's menorah against the Chagall-esque background of traditionally garbed Eastern European Jews in a shtetl setting. This nostalgia is far more sugary and wistful than Agnon's often cutting, if loving, construction of prewar Europe and provides an additional overlay to Agnon's social commentary. The Buczacz menorah is part and parcel of the complexities of the modern menorah, its deployment in modern Israeli culture, and, for its first readers, the complexities of the Eastern European Jewish heritage and "Zionist" identity in early Israel.[5]

The ultimate home of our tale in *Ir u-Meloah* is different. The story is placed among a series of vignettes that present the town of Buczacz and its synagogue in microcosm of Eastern European Jewry.[6] It is prefaced with a short tale called "The Other Vessels That Were in the Synagogue," as an exemplar of the vessels made, lost and preserved down to the final destruction by the Nazis—"taken by the evil scum followers of the repulsive scum [Hitler] who killed the entire town and left not one Jew alive." Agnon epitomizes all of the vessels through "Ma'aseh ha-Menorah," explaining that were he to tell all the stories of all the vessels "we would not be able to."[7] In this way, he deploys a story published first as a Hanukkah tale as a larger example of the fate of his town and its sacred vessels. This gloss on the tale allows Agnon to weave "Ma'aseh ha-Menorah" seamlessly into his opus, making explicit his sense the menorah represents all the holy vessels, but is not unique among them. My purpose here is to explore something of the cultures in which this story was created and within which it was received.

4. See Silberman, *Iyyurim le-Sippurei Agnon*, especially unpaginated pages 5, 8–9.
5. Mintz, *Ancestral Tales*, 20–22.
6. Mintz, "I Am Building a City," xvi, xxv; Mintz, *Ancestral Tales*, 1–31.
7. Agnon, *Ir uMeloah*, 29.

THE TALE

"Ma'aseh ha-Menorah" is the tale of a large seven-branched brass menorah in the synagogue of Agnon's hometown of Buczacz in Galicia—today Ukraine. As Agnon tells it, a seven-branched menorah was given to the synagogue by the king of Poland, a gift to a communal leader who served as a court Jew and Jewish communal leader. The gift represented what the king believed was fitting for Judaism and represents for Agnon the space between Jewish self-understanding and the ways that the dominant society understood and influenced Jews. His language resonated with biblical moments as read through Rabbinic interpretation of biblical cases of the dangers for Jews inherent in entering the royal court. These are epitomized in classical rabbinic terms through Esther and Mordecai, Joseph and Pharaoh, and Jacob and Esau—Esau being a cipher for all gentiles, and especially Rome and Christian Rome. Agnon frames the story in a chain that begins with "and it happened in the days of . . . ," *va-yehi bimei* (Esther 1:1), a phrase that the ancient rabbis read as a harbinger of bad things to come.[8] This sense of eternity frames the entire story, which Agnon makes explicit in the conclusion of the tale.

Accepting the gift despite reservations, the Jews of Buczacz felt themselves in a real predicament:

> When they brought the menorah, which was a gift from the king, to the synagogue, the Jews saw it and beheld its seven branches. They said, we cannot place this menorah in the synagogue. If we do, they said to themselves, we will sin against God; on the other hand, if we do not set it in the synagogue, we will insult the king and his gift.
>
> They did not know what counsel to take for themselves. Even Nahman, the counselor to the king, had no solution. He said, this has all befallen us because I frequented the court of the king.
>
> But God saw their distress, and He set the idea in their heads to remove one branch from the menorah and thus make it into an ordinary candelabrum. Then if they placed the menorah in the synagogue, there would be no sin for them in doing so. And if someone mentioned it to the king, they could say, from the day that our Temple was destroyed, we make nothing without marking upon it a sign in remembrance of the destruction.

---

8. See Esther Rabbah 1, proem 11, ed. Tabory, 17–24 and the notes there.

> So they removed the middle branch. Then they brought the menorah into the house of God and placed it on the ark and lit its candles.

In a true balancing act typical of both Jewish legal tradition and a well-tuned political sense (*shtadlanut*) the synagogue leadership removed the central branch, so as not to violate Talmudic strictures—and to maintain their own scruples and agency. Still, the location of the menorah is unusual, as the standard location for a large Hanukkah lamp next to the ark was taken. It was perched on the reading table.

During the infamous Khmelnytskyi uprising (1648–49) when the community was massacred, and the synagogue christened a church "the town's gentiles made the house of God into a church for their gods." The lampstand was buried in the Strypa River by a non-Jewish synagogue attendant whose task had been maintaining the synagogue lamps on Sabbaths and holidays. This is the second apparently benign act of gentile agency in the story, this servant seemingly protecting the bronze lamp as one might an icon, a relic, or a sanctified Church serving vessel. The lampstand was forgotten, only later being recovered from the Strypa after the community was reestablished with the reassertion of Polish rule. Jewish children found it in a kind of ghoulish resurrection of the dead during elaborate late-night penitential prayers (*selihot*) that precede Rosh ha-Shanah:

> That year, on a Saturday night at the close of the Sabbath, on the night that was also the first night for reciting the Selihot, the penitential hymns, the young children were shining candles over the surface of the Strypa. They were doing this in order to make light for the slain martyrs who had drowned in rivers, streams, and lakes. On the first night of Selihot, all the dead whom our enemies have drowned come to pray to the eternal God in the same synagogue in which they prayed during their lifetimes. The other nights of Selihot are dedicated to those martyrs who died by fire, to those who were stabbed to death, to the ones who were strangled, and to those who were murdered. For on account of their numbers, the building could not contain all the slain at once. As a result, they divided up the nights among them, one congregation of martyrs for each night of prayer.
>
> Now while the children were on the banks of the Strypa shining their candles, a great menorah such as they had never seen before suddenly shone forth from beneath the water. They said, that must be the menorah of the dead; for the dead bring with

them their own menorahs when they come to pray. Their hearts quaked in fear, and the children fled.

Some grown-ups heard the story about the menorah that the children had told, and they said, Let us go and see for ourselves! They went and came to the Strypa. Indeed, there was a menorah in the Strypa. The story is true, they said. It is a menorah.

The forgotten and discovered menorah was placed in a prominent location in the new small synagogue. A generation later, not realizing "that their forefathers had already repaired the menorah when they cut off one of its branches to avoid sinning against God or the king" the local Jews installed a large "white" eagle, the Polish national "symbol," in place of the missing central stalk as a sign of Polish patriotism. With the Austrian conquest of Buczacz (1772), the Polish eagle became something of a scandal and was replaced—on order of Austrian army officers—with an Austrian two-headed eagle. This process repeated itself when Poland revolted, and a clearly modernizing Jewish Polish patriot attended the synagogue:

> And so it happened, as he was standing before the Torah, that the man saw the two-headed eagle. He began to scream, This is an abomination! An abomination! Then he grabbed the hammer from around his waist and struck at the two-headed eagle. He paid no attention to the other worshipers, not even when they pleaded with him to stop and not desecrate the Sabbath. He did not listen to them until he had broken the Austrian eagle from off the menorah and cast it to the ground.

Austrian rule was restored and a new double-headed eagle manufactured. Like the Polish eagle before it, the previous eagle was comically melted into Hanukkah dreidels. This detail makes the Hanukkah connection and snidely referencing the frivolity of this repeating process.[9] With World War I and the Russian army approaching the Austrians took all of the metal from the synagogue to be melted for munitions, all except the menorah, which the metalworker buried. Finally, through a miraculous interpretation of Exodus 25, the portion of *Terumah* (which describes tabernacle menorah), a Jewish soldier, maimed in the trenches who had returned to Buczacz, succeeded with the metalworker in digging up the lampstand from beneath the destroyed ruins of the metalworker's own home. It was returned once again to the synagogue but concerned that the Ukrainians might revolt, the Buczacz Jews once again removed the eagle.

9. Many thanks to Jeffrey Saks for his thoughts on Agnon's deployment of dreidels.

To reinforce the widespread futility felt across Europe, especially by Jews, at the end of World War I, the metalworker once again decides to melt the eagle and create dreidels for children:

> He [the soldier] added, Let us also not make a one-headed eagle, like the eagle that is the national insignia of Poland. I have heard that the Ruthenians have revolted against Poland. If they see the eagle of Poland in our synagogue, they will say that we have prepared to go to war against the Ruthenian nation.

The moral of the story, symbolized by the menorah, its broken central stalk, its transitory eagles and multiple dreidels is that "One kingdom comes and another kingdom passes away. But Israel remains forever."[10] Agnon's menorah, in all of its cultural complexity, is a metaphor for the Jewish people itself, and the eternality of Israel being central to Agnon's thought.[11] The story ends at World War I, his *Atidot* readership being all too aware of the recent fate of Buczacz—and of the Jews symbolized by its maimed menorah. The Holocaust connection is made specific in the prologue to our tale in *Ir u-Meloah*.

CONTEXTS

In constructing his "Tale of the Menorah," Agnon—and his audience—were certainly aware that he had placed his Eastern European synagogue lamp, odd as it was, as a Judaized gift of a non-Jewish ruler, in a long tradition of lost and found Jewish artifacts—of Jewish storytelling about gone but always present objects. The origin point for this sense of loss and memory of the Temple. The loss of the Temple vessels in 586 BCE, and their restoration, provided a template for Jewish, and then Christian, thinking about loss and restoration. This is certainly how Jews have read the extended descriptions of the Tabernacle in the Book of Exodus, repeated twice in the "received" Masoretic text of the Hebrew Bible. Comprising large sections of Exodus, Jewish tradition has certainly looked back wistfully to the Tabernacle and its vessels, and the relatively more recent losses of the First and Second Temples. The very invocation of these Divinely ordained vessels in words, in Exodus compulsively, symbolically brings them back, and has sustained

---

10. Cf. Ecclesiastes 1:4 and the rabbinic interpretation cited in Rashi's comment.

11. See "HaSiman," reproduced in *Ir u-Meloah*, 695, where Agnon refers to the year 5689 (1929), the year of the Hebron Massacre, during which his home in Talpiot was marauded, as having the numerical value of *Netzah Yisrael*, the "eternity of Israel."

hope for their physical return throughout Jewish history. They are what biblical historian Peter Ackroyd called a "continuity symbol," which is certainly the leitmotif of Agnon's tale.[12] Nineteenth century Christians, and Jews, piously believed that the menorah was buried in the silt of the Tiber.[13] Agnon's deployment of the Strypa falls within this tradition. Many other myths developed along these lines, leading to the contemporary urban legend that it is hidden in the Vatican.[14] Within nascent Zionist contexts, the modern discovery of menorahs in archaeological sites was exceptionally important for the developing national/cultural ethos. This began with the Zionist "discovery" of the Arch of Titus menorah during the latter nineteenth century, through the uncovering of the Hammath Tiberias menorah by the first Zionist "archaeologist" Nahum Slouschz at Hammat Tiberias in 1921.[15] Presented in academic and popular literatures, this carefully staged discovery was featured in an early Zionist film by Yaakov Ben Dov, produced by Ben Dov's "Menorah" film company.[16] Agnon had a significant predecessor for this story, a Zionist novella produced by Stefan Zweig called *Der begrabene Leuchter*, published in Vienna in 1937 and translated immediately into English as *The Buried Candelabrum* (New York, 1937)[17] and into Hebrew as *Ha-Menorah Ha-Genuzah* in 1946.[18] Agnon had been in contact with Zweig, and his correspondence dating to 1920 is preserved the Zweig Archive in Fredonia, New York.[19] Set in the age of Justinian, Zweig's lampstand underwent travels and travails. Ultimately it was buried in the soil of *Eretz Yisrael* by the road leading to Jerusalem from the coast awaiting by pious Jews awaiting modern "redemption"—presumably by the rising Zionist movement. Scholars of all sorts caught the "menorah bug," most prominently classical historian Yohanan (Hans) Lewy, who imagined that the hidden menorah could be uncovered in the ruins of Justinian's Nea

---

12. Ackroyd, "The Temple Vessels," 166–81.

13. Fine, *The Menorah*, 175–79.

14. Fine, *The Menorah*, 185–207.

15. Fine, *Art and Judaism in the Greco-Roman World*, 23–27.

16. Fine, *Art and Judaism in the Greco-Roman World*, 23–27.

17. Zweig, *Der begrabene Leuchter*; Zweig, *The Buried Candelabrum*, tr. Paul and Paul; Fine, *The Menorah*, 180.

18. Tr. Fishman.

19. This correspondence is preserved in the archives of Reed Library, State University of New York, Fredonia, together with an unpublished Yiddish translation. Many thanks to Kimberly R. Taylor for making these available to me.

Church in Jerusalem.[20] In his late novel *Shira*, Agnon invoked his colleague, the father of Jewish archaeology himself, Eleazar Lippa Sukenik, parodying this intrepid scholar (whom Agnon is known to have respected), his search for Jewish artifacts in the antiquities shops of mandatory Jerusalem, and his discovery of the Dead Sea Scrolls.[21] This sense of discovery and of recovery is essential to the Zionist ethos, with its visions of returning the menorah to modern Jerusalem, and literally marching it under the Arch of Titus in a reverse restoration. This excitement was heightened with the choice of the Arch of Titus menorah as "symbol" of the state of Israel in 1949.[22]

"Ma'aseh ha-Menorah" is more complex. Agnon's seven-branched menorah was not uncovered by archaeologists, nor was it found in the silt of the Tiber or in a Nazi assemblage. Rather, it was planted in the silt and soil of Buczacz—over and over again. It is clearly modeled on large brass synagogue Hanukkah menorahs of the eighteenth and nineteenth centuries, which often have eagles as finials to the central branch—either with one head to denote Poland or two for the Holy Roman/Hapsburg Empire. These were attached to the lampstand with threaded bases for easy installation and removal, depending upon communal preference.[23] These often-huge Hanukkah menorahs were placed to the side of the Torah ark—a position already filled in the Buczacz synagogue.[24]

A silver Hanukkah lamp standing 100 cm. tall from the Dubno great synagogue parallels nicely the complexities of Agnon's menorah, and points to the inspiration for our story. This lamp is described in considerable detail as part of a tour of the Jewish community of Dubno by Rabbi Hayyim Zeev Margaliot in his Hebrew volume *Dubno Rabbati*, issued by the publishing company associated with the *maskilic* Hebrew newspaper *Ha-Tzfirah* in Warsaw in 1910. Margaliot writes that within the synagogue

---

20. Lewy, "A Note on the Fate of the Sacred Vessels of the Second Temple," 123–25, and was collected in his posthumous collection, *Studies in Jewish Hellenism*, 255–58; see Fine, *The Menorah*, 49–52, 54, 74, 180.

21. Agnon, *Shira*, 141–42. On Agnon's acquaintance with Sukenik, see Laor, *S.Y. Agnon*, 341–42.

22. Mishory, *Lo and Behold*, 138–64; Fine, *The Menorah*, 134–62.

23. On standing Hanukkah menorahs, see Narkiss, *The Hanukkah Lamp*, 71–81; Braunstein, *Five Centuries of Hanukkah Lamps from the Jewish Museum*, 12, 18–19, 117–20. On two-headed eagles in Eastern European synagogues, Rodov, "The Eagle, Its Twin Heads and Many Faces," 77–129.

24. On the placement of free standing menorahs in synagogues in this region, Kravtsov, "Synagogue Architecture of Volhynia," 87–88.

a large and heavy Hanukkah menorah, whose candles they light on the eve of every Sabbath and holiday, is made of pure silver. It is made in great beauty (*pe'er*) and glory (*hadar*) with a silver eagle with two heads above. Two small silver tablets are attached to the menorah. On one I see written: "This making of the menorah (*ma'aseh ha-menorah*) was renewed by the Society of the Tavern keepers who added to it much silver, 5576 [1816]." On the second is written: "An eternal sign and offering of remembrance (*minhat azkarah*) of the *gabbai*[s] [sexton(s) of the society] of the tavern keepers and the members of the society. In the year 5597 [1837] the pure menorah that was donated to the synagogue long before (*me'az*) was stolen. It was found damaged, and by the good of their hearts they repaired it again beautifully and finished on Hoshanah Rabba of 5598 [1838]. Forever it will be, until the coming of the Redeemer." They say that this menorah was stolen by a brazen uncircumcised [gentile] whose job it was to extinguish the lamps on Sabbath nights. After he broke it up for sale, he put its parts in a sack and brought them to an acquaintance of his to sell them. A certain man was there and saw this, and the situation was made known by him to members of the [Jewish] community.[25]

Sergey R. Kravtsov and Vladimir Levin note that the Dubno menorah was illustrated by artist Ksawery Pillati in a late nineteenth century drawing topped with a single-headed Polish eagle and not with the double-headed eagle donated in 1816.[26] When the lampstand was photographed in 1910, however, the double-headed eagle had returned! The Dubno Hanukkah menorah was lovingly cared for over generations by a single religious society. Over this period the lampstand saw the addition of a double-headed eagle, theft, reconstruction, and at some point, the replacement of the double-headed eagle finial with a single eagle, and the return of the double-headed exemplar. It was destroyed during World War II, together with the Jewish community of Dubno as a whole—a fact that we know with hindsight (as the readers of *Atidot* and narrator of *Ir u-Meloah* did as well). The repair of the Dubno lamp was associated in a memorial inscription with the biblical "making of the menorah," *ma'aseh ha-menorah*—as, of course, was the lampstand of Agnon's tale. Finally, the pious hope of the inscription, "Forever it will be, until the coming of the Redeemer," rings with messianic tone evident in Agnon's conclusion, "But Israel remains forever."

---

25. Margaliot, *Dubno Rabbati*, 28. See Kravtsov and Levin, *Synagogues in Ukraine, Volhynia*, 233, 236.

26. Kravtsov and Levin, *Synagogues in Ukraine, Volhynia*, 233, 236.

Margaliot's excursus on the menorah is set within the frame of a tour of the synagogues of Dubno and their sacred vessels, as is Agnon's tale in its final literary frame. It is composed in a maskilic Hebrew not unlike Agnon's archaicizing style, replete with biblical and rabbinic references. Agnon almost certainly knew the story of the Dubno menorah, as Margaliot's book is preserved in his personal library.[27] Read in light of Margaliot's tale of the nefarious *Shabbos goy*,[28] Agnon's reference to a gentile servant burying the brass lampstand in the Strypa, to which he ascribes no motive, feels far less benign. Beyond these resonances, Kravtsov and Levin have discovered archival evidence from 1934 for the removal of a gypsum Habsburg double-headed eagle from the facade of a Buczacz synagogue.[29] The eagle was described in an official Polish government document ordering its removal as "this symbol of the times of captivity." The fact that this removal at this late date was a government decision and not that of the local Jews is notable. This change in heraldry was not unique to Jews or Jewish contexts and is documented in Galicia as early as Galician "de facto autonomy" in 1869. Our tale, built on the literary model of *Dubno Rabbati,* is thus rooted in actual political shifts in Agnon's hometown.

A similar symbolic shift took place twice during Agnon's time in the Holy Land, first with the replacement of Ottoman symbols with those of the British Mandate and then symbols of "His Majesty's Government" with the new Israeli national "symbol"—at its center the Arch of Titus menorah. Within its Zionist/early Israeli context, Agnon's menorah asserts the primacy of continuity across the generations, and not a radical "discovery" of an old-new Jewish icon for the "New Maccabees" in the soil of modern Israel. Still, the menorah of our tale began as a seven branched lampstand, and not the traditional eight-plus-one of a Hanukkah lamp. Despite its obvious similarities, it is a new creation distinguished through an essential nuance invisible to its royal Polish donor. Agnon's menorah illuminates the new-old ethos of the religious Zionist community in early Israel, one that hallowed traditional religion in a new and sometimes contradictory idiom—the physical and literary embodiment of the new-old Jew. Large bird-headed Hanukkah menorahs were displayed prominently in the Bezalel National

27. Many thanks to Jeffrey Saks for verifying this in the Agnon House library. Beyond the menorah episode, a broader study of how Agnon's "guide" to Buczacz is indebted to Margaliot's work is a desideratum.

28. Katz, *The "Shabbes Goy."*

29. Kravtsov and Levin, *Synagogues in Ukraine, Volhynia,* 236 n.223, Lviv National Vasyl Stefanyk Library, Ms. UK-31, fol. 431.

Museum (now the Israel Museum) and significantly for our discussion, in the Religious Zionist Wolfson Museum of Jewish Art. This museum was opened in the new Chief Rabbinate building in Jerusalem, Hechal Shlomo, in 1958—two years after our story appeared in print. During the early years of the state, Judaica was streaming into Israel, in no small measure owing to the work of the Jewish Cultural Reconstruction in Europe, Umberto Nahon in Italy, and immigrants/refugees from Islamic lands who brought treasures with them to Israel. Agnon may hint at the Nazi theft of cultural objects in his preface to our story in *Ir u-Meloah*, describing the Nazis who, like, previous persecutors "took" (rather than destroyed) the synagogue vessels—leaving behind only stories.[30] The objects returned, and in Agnon's day were exhibited and interpreted through exhibition—like Agnon's menorah—as both remnants of Jewish "martyrdom"[31] and iconic proof of Jewish "eternality."[32] An exquisite large brass Hanukkah menorah crowned by a two-headed eagle donated more recently to the Israel Museum makes this point implicitly. It was given to the museum by "Arthur Lejwa, a native of Kielce, in memory of the Jewish community of Kielce, annihilated in the gas chambers in 1942."[33] More than a lachrymose history of martyrdom, however, Agnon presents the ingenuity and staying power of Eastern European Jewry, his menorah injecting this theme into the old-new culture of modern Israel at a time after the Holocaust when the Eastern European Jewish experience was often viewed with scorn—or at the very least as a desire for a new beginning.

According to Agnon, the Christian king clearly thought that he was giving the synagogue an object of traditional Jewish piety. Christians had long associated the biblical lampstand with Jews, and the synagogue with the Temple. Jews had as well, applying Temple themes to the synagogue in expanding ways beginning with classical rabbinic sources. Reference to the synagogue as a "small temple," a *mikdash me'at* in rabbinic interpretation of Ezekiel 11:16 that appears in the Babylonian Talmud (Megillah 29a), is the locus of all later conceptions. Throughout our story, Agnon himself fuses this language to refer to the sanctuary of Buczacz.

---

30. Agnon, *Ir u-Meloah*, 29.

31. Grossman, "The Skirball Museum JCR Research Project," 325–26, citing Jewish Museum/New York director Stephen S. Kayser.

32. Herman, "'A Brand Plucked Out of the Fire,'" 29–62, esp. 43–46; Nahon, *Holy Arks and Religious Appurtenances from Italy in Israel*.

33. Benjamin, "A Hanukkah Lamp from Poland," 48–49.

Gifts by Christian rulers to local synagogues were not unheard of in modern Europe. In eighteenth century Germany, for example, one synagogue was

> built in 1789–90 by court architect Friedrich Wilhelm von Erdmannsdorf was a round pavilion in the gardens of the Jews' patron; the synagogue was also known as the Temple of Vesta—which shows the congregation's position before emancipation as the private domain of the Grand Duke of Anhalt-Dessau.[34]

Projecting this line of reasoning into antiquity, British and then German scholars imagined that synagogues with human and mythological reliefs in the Galilee and Golan Heights were gifts by well-meaning Roman authorities, and that Jews abandoned these " pagan" buildings or removed the offensive imagery as soon as they could.[35] There is even a Talmudic precedent, a Roman emperor named Antoninus being said to have donated a *menarta*, a "lamp" of some kind, to a synagogue in late antiquity.[36] The wanted/unwanted gift described by Agnon, then, was not outlandish, and follows historical and literary precedents with which our author was certainly familiar.

Agnon played on the fact that the use of seven branched lampstands by modern Jews was anything but traditional before the latter nineteenth century. While menorah imagery was a common feature of traditional Jewish iconography, seven branched three-dimensional lampstands were unheard of among European Jews before this period owing to a Rabbinic prohibition against reproducing Temple vessels directly. Accepting the gift despite their reservations, the Jews of Buczacz set out to render Jewishly acceptable an object that the king had thought the most Jewish object of all. The removing of the central branch follows rabbinic precedent both for "nullifying" and in creating synagogue lampstands. Thus:

> Our Rabbis taught: No one may make a building in the form of the [temple] shrine [*hekhal*],
> an exedra in place of the entrance hall,
> a courtyard in place of the court,
> a table in place of the table [of the bread of the Presence],
> a menorah in place of the menorah,

---

34. Krinsky, *Synagogues of Europe*, 72.

35. Fine, *Art and Judaism*, 19.

36. PT Megillah 3:2, 74a; Fine, *This Holy Place*, 80; Cohen, "The Conversion of Antoninus," 141–71.

but one may make [a menorah] with five, six or eight [branches]. Nor [may it be made] of other metals.[37]

Seven branched lampstands were known, however, from the latter nineteenth century in Jewish circles associated with Freemasonry, including Bnai Brith lodges, liberalizing synagogues ("temples") and on Zionist regalia of all sorts—especially those associated with the Bezalel School and eventually with Zionist revisionism. Agnon was well aware of the Bezalel School and its early antinomianism, and wrote of this complexity in *T'mol Shilshom* (1945).[38] Seven branched menorahs were even making inroads within Orthodox ritual, the chief rabbinate prescribing, for example, the lighting of such lamps in synagogues on the eve of the first Israel Independence day in 1949.[39]

Agnon's lamp, too, parallels modern custom. Branched menorahs had become so popular in synagogue lighting that even traditional synagogues adopted them, sometimes removing the light from the central branch to comply with the letter of the Talmudic injunction. Agnon, certainly aware of both the complexities of this gift-giving and of the very presence of altered seven branched lamps in modern synagogues, projects the contemporary Jewish solution to this modern problem of synagogue decor back to Buczacz where this "large menorah" was placed on the reading table of the synagogue and not near the ark itself, since that space was already taken (a lamp discussed explicitly in an earlier story in *Ir u-Meloah*[40]), and the local Jews knew that they had to put it somewhere! In a sense, the deletion of a branch from the royal gift is the reciprocal of decisions by eighteenth and nineteenth century synagogue communities—including Agnon's Buczacz, to create free-standing bronze (and in Dubno, silver) Hanukkah menorahs reminiscent of the Tabernacle menorah, the added branches facilitating this innovation. These communities acted on the Talmudic allowance that "one may make [a menorah] with ... eight [branches]."[41]

The foreignness, subsequent "Judaization" and broad acceptance of the Buczacz seven-branched menorah resonates with themes in the then-current negotiation between religious Zionists—for whom Agnon was a

37. BT Menahot 28b (and parallels); Shulḥan Arukh, Yoreh De'ah 141:8.
38. Agnon, *T'mol Shilshom*, 293–94; Werses, *S.Y. Agnon Kifeshuto*, 264–90.
39. Fine, *The Menorah*, 146.
40. 19–20.
41. Maimonides, *Mishneh Torah, Hilkhot Beit HaBekhirah* 7:10 and the sources cited by Narkiss, *The Hanukkah Lamp*, 71–72.

culture hero—and the demands of the broader Israeli civil religion. Rabbi Isaac Halevy Herzog, the first Ashkenazi chief rabbi of the State of Israel and a close friend of Agnon[42] was most ambivalent regarding the state "symbol" and its use of the Arch of Titus menorah on the national emblem.[43] For Herzog, a University of London trained scholar of Semitic languages, the Arch menorah was an imposition upon Jewish memory, and did not reflect an "authentic" Jewish memory itself. He writes:

> In conclusion, our government is not doing well today—when we have merited again the light of Zion, which is symbolized by the menorah, by copying specifically the image of the menorah that is on the Arch of Titus—which was apparently made by foreigners and is not wholly made in the purity of holiness, as is supported by the teachings of our teacher Moses [Maimonides], the genius of geniuses and from other sources derived by the Torah sages. Not only that, but an expert in the past [archaeologist Yigael Yadin[44]] has testified before me that the menorahs represented on caves and in the catacombs in Rome all have three feet [tripods] as do all of the menorahs illustrated on mosaics of synagogue remains in the Land of Israel. My opinion on this is clear and determined.[45]

Adamant as he was, Herzog's campaign was unsuccessful—even among religious Zionists. Within Hechal Shlomo itself, his brother-in-law, British artist David Hillman, created a stained glass window showing the Arch menorah—though as a concession, symbols of the Tribes of Israel do replace the mythological animals in the base of the Arch menorah. Similar to Agnon's conception of the Buczacz menorah, Herzog saw the Arch menorah as a foreign imposition upon Judaism to be managed over time. Unlike Herzog, however, Agnon (with Hillman) shows a way that this religiously unwelcome object might be "Judaized" and integrated into their traditionalizing Jewish memory.

Herzog's approach was closer to the plot of "Ma'aseh ha-Menorah" in dealing with the gift of a large bronze menorah sculpture to the Knesset in 1952. This large lampstand was created by British artist Benno Elkan as the culmination of a project funded by wealthy British Jews. The menorah was

---

42. See Agnon's eulogy for Herzog in *MeAtmzi el Atzmi*, 246–50; and Laor, *S.Y. Agnon*, 306, 400, 406–8, 487, 628.
43. Herzog, "The Shape of the Menorah in the Arch of Titus," 95–98.
44. See Fine, *The Menorah*, 138.
45. Herzog, "The Shape of the Menorah," 98.

donated to the Knesset by the British Parliament. A dedicatory plaque at its base expresses the sentiments behind this gift:

> The Menorah is the work of Benno Elkan. The idea of presenting the Menorah was conceived by members of the Parliament of the United Kingdom and Northern Ireland in appreciation of the establishment of a democratic parliamentary government in the State of Israel. The committee organizing the presentation included members of both Houses of Parliament and representatives of the British people of diverse faiths. Viscount Samuel, President; the Rt. Hon. Clement Davies, chairman; Dr. Alec Lerner, treasurer; Mr. Gilbert McAllister, secretary. The gift was made possible by the generosity of the people of Britain and received strong support from the leading banks of the United Kingdom and large industrial concerns. Many small donations, too numerous to record here, were received from British citizens.

Herzog was asked to judge the halakhic propriety of exhibiting this sculpture within the public sphere. Not only is a free-standing seven-branched menorah a problem in light of the Talmudic prohibition, but Elkan's lampstand is decorated with numerous human figures in three-quarters bas-relief, each scene illustrating a significant moment in Jewish history. Herzog did not suggest alterations to the lampstand, opting for a liberal interpretation of Jewish law. Rather, he ruled that the lampstand be displayed inside the Knesset building and not on the street. He hesitantly endorsed Elkan's menorah realizing "the seriousness of the matter in the event of a negative decision."[46] This "seriousness" related both to the delicate diplomatic relationship between Israel and Britain at the time, but also to the reality that the Israeli government would likely have rejected anything but a positive decision by the Chief Rabbi. The status of Judaism itself within the new state was in jeopardy on many fronts. This was expressed, as in our story, by what others considered the most Jewish of gifts, a seven-branched menorah, Herzog chose to mitigate the tension rather than exasperate it. His stipulation that the lampstand be placed indoors was ignored, and it was placed in a large garden next to the Knesset on King George V Street (and subsequently moved to its current location next to the permanent Knesset building, opened in 1966). He did not object in public this time, as he did with his failed campaign against the state symbol. As in Agnon's story, we find here a menorah, a governmental force that religious

---

46. Herzog, *Letter to Lord Herbert Samuel.*

Jews felt obliged to satisfy, and an artifact that was manifestly "Jewish" yet problematic to Jewish tradition. This case is in many ways more complex, a Jewish government exhibiting an otherwise illicit menorah, made by a Jewish artist and displayed in the public domain. With all of this tension beneath the surface and in full sight, Agnon's tale, both in *Atidot* and in *Ir u-Melo'ah,* asserts the "eternity of Israel"—a real continuity between the complexities of traditional Jewish existence in Eastern Europe and the experience of his Israeli readers.

"Ma'aseh ha-Menorah" is not a simple "tale of the menorah." It is an artifact of the larger menorah craze that affected Jewish life during the twentieth century, particularly at mid-century. It reflects complex and very contemporary realities—projected on and through the idealized yet deliciously complex world of Eastern European Jewry as constructed by Agnon. The changing of eagle heads in Galician synagogues, including in the "real" Buczacz, was an actual reality that Agnon transformed for his Israeli audience. The story quietly engages the lived reality in the new State of Israel, as religiously concerned Jews like Agnon—committed to the state and its institutions negotiated their sense of continuity with received tradition and allegiance to the developing new-old civil religion of modern Israel. Its publication by Meltzer in *Atidot* and its subsequent placement in *Ir u-Melo'ah* makes a still broader claim, quietly asserting continuity between Jewish life in Europe and the new Israeli culture—the menorah of Buczacz representing this continuity. Such continuity was in no way obvious to the revolutionary culture of early Israel. Israeli civil religion was in many aspects a "discovered tradition"[47] (just as Agnon's menorah was itself continually "rediscovered") and was sometimes at odds with traditional Rabbinic approaches—a complexity that Agnon's story, like his friend Rabbi Isaac Herzog in the public sphere, worked diligently to overcome even as each toiled to invoke and hence (re)imagine that very Jewish " past"—and through it the Israeli future.[48] "Ma'aseh ha-Menorah" illustrates the axiom that "One kingdom comes and another kingdom passes away. But Israel remains forever." The eternity of Israel is not a simple one in this "Ma'aseh ha-Menorah"—not for Agnon's archetypical if somewhat comic Jews of Buczacz with their multiple eagle finials and dreidels—and not for Agnon's readership in 1950s and 1970s Israel.[49] Behind Agnon's claim of continuity,

---

47. Lewis, *History: Remembered, Recovered, Invented.*
48. Mintz, *Ancestral Tales,* 13.
49. See Sagiv, "Deep Blue: Notes on the Jewish Snail Fight," 285–313, esp. 295.

of "eternality," lurks a reality of discomforting discontinuity and a hopeful message of synthesis that Agnon wished for in the state called "the first sprouts of our redemption"—but which neither Agnon nor Herzog perceived as a completed messianic project.[50]

Bibliography

Ackroyd, Peter R. "The Temple Vessels: A Continuity Theme." *Vetus Testamentum Supplements* 23 (1972) 166–81.

Agnon, S.Y. "Eulogy for Herzog." [Hebrew] In *MeAtmzi el Atzmi*, 246–50. Tel Aviv: Schocken, 1998.

———. "Ma'aseh haMenorah." *Atidot: Rivon le-Noar* (Winter 1956–57) 3–11.

———. "Ma'ase HaMenorah." In *Ir uMeloah*. Tel Aviv: Schocken, 1973.

———. *T'mol Shilshom*. Tel Aviv: Schocken, 1998.

———. *Shira*. Tel Aviv: Schocken, 1999.

———. "The Tale of the Menorah." Translated by David Stern. In *A City in Its Fullness*, edited by A. Mintz and J. Saks, 44–56. New Milford, CT: Toby, 2016.

Agnon, S.Y., and Stefan Zweig. "Correspondence" (1920). Zweig Archive, State University of New York: Fredonia.

Benjamin, Chaya. "A Hanukkah Lamp from Poland." In *The Arthur and Madeleine Chalette Lejwa Collection in the Israel Museum*, edited by Ruth Apter-Gabriel, Jerusalem: Israel Museum, 2005.

Braunstein, Susan L. *Five Centuries of Hanukkah Lamps from the Jewish Museum: A Catalogue Raisonné*, New York: The Jewish Museum, 2004.

Cohen Grossman, Grace. "The Skirball Museum JCR Research Project: Records and Recollections." In *Neglected Witnesses: The Fate of Jewish Ceremonial Objects during the Second World War and After*. Edited by J.-M. Cohen and F. Heimann-Jelinek. Amsterdam: Joods Historisch Museum, 2011.

Cohen, Shaye J. D. "The Conversion of Antoninus." In *The Talmud Yerushalmi and Graeco-Roman Culture*, vol. 1, edited by Peter Schäfer, 141–71. Tübingen: Mohr/Siebeck, 1998.

Fine, Steven. *Art and Judaism in the Greco-Roman World: Toward a New Jewish Archaeology*. New York: Cambridge University Press, 2010.

———. *This Holy Place: On the Sanctity of the Synagogue during the Second Temple Period*. Notre Dame: Notre Dame University Press, 1997.

———. *The Menorah: From the Bible to Modern Israel*. Cambridge: Harvard University Press.

Herman, Dana. "'A Brand Plucked Out of the Fire': The Distribution of Heirless Jewish Cultural Property by the Jewish Cultural Reconstruction, Inc., 1947–1952." [Hebrew] In *Neglected Witnesses: The Fate of Jewish Ceremonial Objects during the Second World War and After*, edited by J.-M. Cohen and F. Heimann-Jelinek, 29–62. Amsterdam: Joods Historisch Museum, 2011.

Herzog, Isaac. *Letter to Lord Herbert Samuel*, 24 October 1952, Israel State Archives, Office of the Speaker of the 4th Knesset, Public Inquiries, ב/12/592.

---

50. Rappel, *Ha-Tefillah le-Shelom ha-Medinah*.

———. "The Shape of the Menorah in the Arch of Titus." [Hebrew] In *Scritti in memoria di Sally Mayer*, 95–98. Jerusalem: Fondazione Sally Mayer; Milan: Scuola superiore di Studi Ebraici, 1956.

Katz, Jacob. *The "Shabbes Goy": A Study in Halakhic Flexibility*. Translated by Yoel Lerner. Philadelphia: Jewish Publication Society, 1989.

Kravtsov, Sergey R. "Synagogue Architecture of Volhynia." In *Synagogues in Ukraine, Volhynia,* edited by S. R. Kravtsov and V. Levin, 59–138. Jerusalem: Center for Jewish Art, Zalman Shazar Center, 2017.

Kravtsov, Sergey R., and Vladimir Levin. *Synagogues in Ukraine, Volhynia*. Jerusalem: Center for Jewish Art, Zalman Shazar Center, 2017.

Krinsky, C. H. *Synagogues of Europe,* New York: The Architectural History Foundation and MIT Press, 1985.

Laor, Dan. *S.Y. Agnon: A Biography*. [Hebrew] Tel Aviv: Schocken, 1998.

Lewis, Bernard. *History: Remembered, Recovered, Invented*. Princeton: Princeton University Press, 1976.

Lewy, Hans Yoḥanan. "A Note on the Fate of the Sacred Vessels of the Second Temple." [Hebrew], *Kedem: Studies in Jewish Archaeology* 2 (1945) 123–25. Reprinted in *Studies in Jewish Hellenism*, 255–58. Jerusalem: Bialik Institute, 1969.

Margaliot, Hayyim Zeev. *Dubno Rabbati*. Warsaw: HaTzfirah, 1910, 28.

Mintz, Alan. *Ancestral Tales: Reading the Buczacz Stories of S.Y. Agnon*, 1–31. Stanford: Stanford University Press, 2017.

———. "I Am Building a City." In *A City in Its Fullness*, edited by Alan Mintz and Jeffrey Saks, xv–xxxi. New Milford, CT: Toby, 2016.

Mishory, Alec. *Lo and Behold: Zionist Icons and Visual Symbols in Israeli Culture*. [Hebrew] Tel Aviv: Am Oved, 2000.

Nahon, S. U. *Holy Arks and Religious Appurtenances from Italy in Israel*. Tel Aviv: Dvir, 1970.

Narkiss, Mordecai. *The Hanukkah Lamp*. [Hebrew] Jerusalem: Bney Bezalel, 1939.

Rappel, Joel. *Ha-Tefillah le-Shelom ha-Medinah*. Modi'in: Kinneret, Zemorah-Beitan, 2018.

Rodov, Ilya. "The Eagle, Its Twin Heads and Many Faces: Synagogue Chandeliers Surmounted by Double-Headed Eagles." *Jewish Ceremonial Objects in Transcultural Context, Studia Rosenthaliana* 37 (2004) 77–129.

Sagiv, Gadi. "Deep Blue: Notes on the Jewish Snail Fight." *Contemporary Judaism* 35 (2015) 285–313.

Silberman, Orna. *Iyyurim le-Sippurei Agnon* [exhibition catalog]. Tel Aviv: Sifriyyat Sha'ar Tsion, Beit Ariela, 1988.

Tabory, J., and A. Atzmon, eds. *Midrash Esther Rabba*. Jerusalem: Schechter Institute of Jewish Studies, 2014.

Werses, Shmuel. *S.Y. Agnon Kifeshuto*. Jerusalem: Bialik Institute, 2000.

Zweig, Stefan. *Der begrabene Leuchter*. Vienna: Reichner, 1937.

———. *The Buried Candelabrum*. Translated by Eden Paul and Cedar Paul. New York: Viking, 1937.

———. *Ha-Menorah Ha-Genuzah*. Translated by I. Fishman. Tel Aviv: Shreberk, 1946.

4

Reading Agnon's *Only Yesterday* Today[1]

Hillel Halkin

Yakov Malkov was a Ḥabad Ḥasid and a bit of a writer. A day on which an article of his appeared in the newspaper *Havatselet* was a red-letter day for him, since having readers made him feel he was doing some good in the world. Because he had a sensitive throat, he had chosen to live in Jaffa rather than in Hebron or Jerusalem, the sea being a physic for throat conditions—and because a man must provide for his family, and Jaffa was not one of the Land of Israel's holy cities whose faithful received charity from abroad, he had opened a boarding house. In it were three rooms: a dining room, a sleeping room, and a room for his family. In summertime, when vacationers came from Jerusalem to bathe in the sea, he spread a mat in the backyard, moved his family to it, and rented out the third room, too.

∽

---

1. This is a slightly edited version of an essay which first appeared online in *Mosaic Magazine* (December 2018) and subsequently in my *The Lady of Hebrew and Her Lovers of Zion* (Toby Press). Translations of Agnon's *T'mol Shilshom* are my own. Page references are to the Hebrew text published as S.Y. Agnon, *T'mol Shilshom* (Jerusalem: Schocken, 1998); hereafter abbreviated as *TS*. The citations which open this essay appear on 288, 292–98.

At sundown, the boarders returned from their work covered with dust, sand, and plaster and put away their tools. One went to wash his hands and face; a second to wet his throat with a glass of soda; a third to see if there was mail for him on the window sill; a fourth to glance at the day's *Havatselet*. One noticed that the author Yosef Hayyim Brenner was there and hurried to greet him. Brenner shook his hand warmly like a man who would like to give a friend a gift and has only his own warmth to give.

"You should get yourself a glass of tea," he said.

"I will, I will," said Brenner's greeter excitedly, as if made suddenly aware of what he had been missing all along. "I'll go get some tea right away."

But he didn't. Having run into Brenner, it was hard to part with him.

Malkov donned his long, heavy gabardine that came to his feet and put on the special hat that he wore to synagogue and other such occasions. "If you people were in the habit of praying," he said, "we could have a minyan here. Since we're not that fortunate, you'll excuse me for being off to evening prayers."

Glad for the chance to be with Brenner, we told him, "Pray for us, too, Reb Yakov."

Malkov turned to look at us. "You can pray for yourselves," he said.

~

Malkov strode in briskly and called cheerfully, "Good evening, lads! A good evening to you all!" He took off his gabardine, hung it on a peg, doffed his hat, and gave it a loving pat. Seeing his wife standing and talking in the dining room, he scolded, "A person might think you were a rabbi giving a sermon. Back to the kitchen, woman, and tend to your affairs! Yosef Hayyim, you'll have a bite to eat with us."

"I'm afraid not," Brenner said.

"Don't tell me that woman has scared you into thinking there's nothing to eat here," said Malkov. "All the fancy dishes she ate at her parents' made her think no other fare is fit for a Jew. Sit down, brother, have a seat and dig in. Hemdat, here's a piece of fish for you. At the feasts in the World to Come, you'll long for the tail end of its tail. Mapku, you're a regular here: go ask Azulai for a few dozen eggs." (Mapku was Gurishkin, called that by Malkov because he wrote fiction like Avraham Mapu.)

"I'll go, Reb Yakov," said little Yankele.

"You stay here," Malkov said. "You're a *kohen* and I don't send priests on errands, especially if they can't even say kaddish for their own father. Don't you think he's worth at least one kaddish? You'll come to synagogue with me tomorrow and say it. I knew this fellow's father, may he rest in peace," he said to Brenner. "He served God and country. He farmed land in Hadera and caught yellow fever, but he wouldn't leave it even when he was sick. He said, 'It's leaving the Land of Israel that kills a man, not yellow fever.' When he was dying he pointed to outside the window and said, 'Great is our shame, for we have forsaken the land.' Polishkin, put down that *Havatselet*! If you're looking for something to laugh at, try one of Eliezer Ben-Yehudah's rags. Or are you afraid that heathen's clowning will rub off on you? Yosef Hayyim, you're new in this country. You don't know how wise its wise men are. Listen to a penny's worth of their wisdom."

Brenner didn't like to hear talk of Ben-Yehudah, neither for nor against. Out of respect for his host, though, he shut his eyes and listened.

"The year Professor Boris Schatz opened his Bezalel school of arts in Jerusalem," Malkov said, "he decided to throw a Hanukkah party. They made a statue of Matityahu the high priest brandishing the sword with which he stabbed the Greek who sacrificed a pig on the altar, and they ate, drank, and had a bash. The next day Ben-Yehudah published a favorable editorial. His only problem was the statue. Matityahu, he said, was a religious fanatic, not a Jewish nationalist. So long as the Greeks merely overran our country, plundering and killing and laying everything waste, he and his sons in Modi'in didn't lift a finger to stop them. Not until our religion was attacked did they rise up valiantly et cetera et cetera, in honor of which et cetera et cetera we commemorate them for eight days. What do you think would have happened, Ben-Yehudah asked, if that statue had come to life last night? It would have run every last party-goer through with its sword, that's what. The sacrifice on the altar would have been us."

All this while Brenner never opened his eyes, as if better to see what Malkov was describing. When Malkov was done, he opened them and rocked with laughter.

"That's a damned lie, Malkov!" Gurishkin shouted. "A damned lie!"

"That's enough out of you, Mapku," said Malkov, stroking his beard. "You're so used to being an unbeliever that you don't even believe Ben-Yehudah."

Brenner laughed so hard that he had to grip the table to keep from falling to the floor. He stopped to catch his breath, burst out laughing again, and said, "You'll have to forgive me, my friends, for carrying on like this. It's just my vulgarity."

~

It was a lovely night, as most nights are in Jaffa when a hot, dry wind isn't blowing from the desert. The same sea that keeps the desert's parching heat away gave off a sultry redolence in which the flat sand shone. The sand didn't bother the strollers. It was pleasing, as sand is in the dark. And as it was pleasant to walk on, so we were pleased with ourselves. Every one of us knew where his next meal was coming from. Gone were the hard times in which we never went out at night because we were weary or hungry, too poor to afford a crust of bread because all the jobs went to Arabs. Now, the Jewish politicians of Jaffa had been forced to give us the contract for the new school they were building, and even those who claimed we couldn't compete with Arab labor had to admit we knew how to work. . . . Soon the first houses north of Jaffa would be going up and Jewish workers would be the ones to build them. . . . For the time being, only 60 of them were planned. But although 60 houses weren't 60 cities, we who had no grand aspirations thought them grand enough.

~

Brenner was not among the celebrants. What was there to celebrate? Did building 60 houses mean you had caught the messiah's donkey by its tail? Jews built houses. A single money lender in Lodz owned more of them than all the homes due to rise north of Jaffa. Did that make him the Jews' savior? You might say, of course, that building a house in Palestine wasn't like building a house in Poland. But houses were going up in Jerusalem, too, whole neighborhoods of them, and what good did they do apart from adding to the sum total of loafing, good-for-nothing, fawning, quarrelsome hypocrites who lived off the dole sent them by their benefactors in the diaspora, those philanthropists of God's chosen who lived off the fleshpots of Europe and threw their brethren in the Holy Land a bone for their rotting teeth to gnaw on, in payment for which they and their *gesheftn* were prayed for at the Wailing Wall? One thing alone was worth doing: farming the land and living from its bounty. But a plow made no commotion, which was why so few cared to walk behind one. We were simply building a new exile, the exile of Palestine, while thinking we were the deputized redeemers of the Jewish people—a people that had no use for us and didn't know the first thing about us. Only a handful of dimwitted idlers were hypnotized by Zionism's dreams of a glorious past and a future in which everything would be done for them by Arabs so that they could sit at home drinking tea. "Except for the farmers of Reḥovot, my friends, except for the farmers, it's all humbug, humbug, humbug! Yankele, what was it your father said as he lay dying? 'Great is our shame, for we have forsaken our land.' Forsaking the land is the greatest shame of all. Jeremiah knew that. Tell us about your father, Yankele."

Yankele blushed and said nothing. Brenner put a hand on his shoulder and looked at him fondly. Yankele took heart and said, "I never knew my father, because when people began dying of yellow fever in Hadera, the children were sent to Zichron Ya'akov. I'll tell you something I heard about him, though. Once he was asked, 'Well, Reb Yisra'el, are you happy here in the Land of Israel?' My father answered, "I would be if not for one thing. When I walked the streets of my town in Russia with its Jew-hating scoundrels and constables, they spat at my beard and gave me dirty looks and I knew I was in exile. When I prayed, I prayed with a broken heart. Here, we're in our own country. There's no Russian constabulary and no exile. I'm a man without worries, and I'm ashamed to stand before my Maker an unworried man."

Brenner gave Yankele a big hug and began to sing to a tune of Malkov's, "Come, ye children, hearken unto me, I will teach you the fear of the Lord."

∼

The night was a fine one with a fine sea, and Brenner's words were fine words. Once, when we had no work and nothing to eat or do, most of us thought as he did. Now that there were plenty of jobs and you could make a good living, we were like Yankele's father who missed his broken heart. Each of us thought of his own affairs: one of the new clothes he was going to buy, a second of paying for his girlfriend's passage to Palestine, a third of saving up enough to study at a university abroad. Our friend Yitzḥak was thinking of Shifrah.

∼

Midnight came and went. A cool breeze began to blow. The sea changed its tune and foamed with waves that made pockets of water in the sand. Brenner gazed at it as if struggling to grasp its grandeur. He flexed a hand and took Hemdat's as though reaching for a pen while trying to phrase an insufficiently clear thought. "It's time for sleep," he said.

"*Yo,*" said Podolsky. "*M'darf geyn aheym.*"

Podolsky stressed *aheym* and laughed, because none of us had a home to call his own.

"*Kinderlakh,*" Brenner repeated in a singsong, "*m'darf geyn aheym.*"

Once Brenner departed, and a while later Hemdat, all felt how tired they were. Each said goodnight and went his own way, one to his room and another to his bed in a corner of a cheap hotel in Neveh Shalom.

༄

THESE EXCERPTS COME FROM Shmuel Yosef Agnon's long novel *T'mol Shilshom*, published in English as *Only Yesterday.* Set in 1908–1910 in Jaffa and Jerusalem, and appearing in Hebrew in 1945, the novel tells the story of Yitzhak Kummer, a young Second Aliyah (1904–1914) immigrant to Palestine from Austrian Galicia, as was Agnon himself in those years. Unlike the Zionist ideal of the *halutz*, Yitzhak is not a tiller of the soil. Although it was his ambition to be one upon arriving in Palestine several years prior to the scene in Yakov Malkov's boarding house, things turned out differently. Ending up in Jaffa rather than in a pioneer commune like Degania or Kinneret, Yitzhak has become a house painter, a profession he earns well from, especially now that an increase in Jewish immigration at the end of the first decade of the century has led to a construction boom. One of its signs is a plan to build, on the sands north of Jaffa's Jewish neighborhood of Neveh Shalom, the first houses of what will soon be known as Tel Aviv.

Yitzhak does not live in a cheap hotel like Malkov's. He can afford a rented room of his own, as most of his Second Aliyah friends cannot. Nearly all of them are, like him, relatively new arrivals in Palestine from Eastern Europe; most have grown up in religious homes and have put religious observance behind them; most are single and have little prospect of marriage. Few could support a family even if they found a partner, which is difficult because there are more men than women among them. To this, Yitzḥak is an exception. While shy with women, he has had a romantic relationship with a fellow immigrant his age named Sonya Tsvayring, and he is, at the time of the evening at Malkov's, in love with Shifrah, the only child of Reb Feysh, a religious zealot in the ultra-Orthodox Jerusalem neighborhood of Meah She'arim.

Although Yitzḥak dreams of marrying Shifrah, a match between him and a daughter of the Old Yishuv, as the anti-Zionist, ultra-Orthodox community of Palestine is called, is hardly imaginable. Only unlikely circumstances could have led to their even meeting. Knocking on a door one day to ask for a glass of water after he has moved from Jaffa to Jerusalem, Yitzḥak finds it opened by an elderly couple he recognizes from the ship that brought him to Palestine. These are Shifrah's grandparents, who are staying with their daughter Rivkah, Reb Feysh's wife. Invited in by them, Yitzḥak chats and returns a second time, when he is served refreshment by their granddaughter. At once he is as smitten by her as "Adam was when God set Eve before him."

None of this would have happened had Reb Feysh been at home, since while he might have tolerated Yitzḥak's presence there once, he surely would not have welcomed him a second time. Soon afterward, however, Feysh is felled by a sudden stroke that leaves him speechless and semi-comatose, thus enabling Yitzḥak to keep visiting by offering his assistance to the now providerless women. The neighbors gossip. Rivkah, though grateful to Yitzḥak for his help and less extreme in her views than her husband, is uncomfortable with the situation. So is Shifrah. Still in her teens, she cannot conceive, even while feeling an attraction to Yitzḥak, of anything developing between them. When once they meet by chance out-of-doors and Yitzḥak, seeing they are alone, seeks to hold her hand as no young man from Meah She'arim would dare do, she runs away in a fright. Yet not only is he determined to marry her, he decides to pave the way for it by returning to Jaffa and asking Sonya to release him from whatever obligations he might have incurred to her. Amused that he should think he has any (their brief romance has meant less to her than to him), she assures him that he is free—and it is at this point that we encounter him at Malkov's.

In all this there is an irony that no one is aware of, namely, that Yitzḥak himself has been the cause of Reb Feysh's condition. This is because, approached by a stray dog while standing in the street at the end of a day's work, he playfully painted the Hebrew words *kelev m'shuga*, "Mad Dog," on the animal's side. Spreading through the city, news of a rabid dog on the loose creates panic. It is talked about everywhere; the newspapers are full of it; new sightings keep being reported. One is by the headmaster of a French-speaking school, who, ignorantly reading the Hebrew consonants of *kelev* from left to right instead of the other way, takes the dog's name to be Balak. This is the name of the Moabite king who in the biblical book of Numbers hires the sorcerer Balaam to put a curse on Israel, and it is Balak, as henceforth the dog is known, suddenly appearing in front of Reb Feysh in Meah She'arim, who gives him such a fright that he ruptures a blood vessel in his brain.

∼

Yitzḥak is nineteen or twenty when, his family's oldest child, he leaves their Galician shtetl for Palestine, about which he is as naïve as he is idealistic. Since childhood he has avidly read Hebrew and Zionist literature and accounts of First Aliyah farming colonies, which have imbued him with a romantic view of the Land of Israel. *Only Yesterday*'s opening paragraph is a medley of the clichés they have cluttered his mind with:

> Like our other comrades of the Second Aliyah, Yitzḥak Kummer left his native town and country for the liberation of his people, setting out for the Land of Israel to rebuild it from its ruins and be rebuilt by it. As far back as he could remember, there wasn't a day he hadn't thought of it. He had pictured it as a blissful place whose inhabitants were graced by God. Its villages nestled amid vineyards and olive groves; its fields were laden with grain; its fruit-festooned valleys teemed with flowers and were ringed by forests that rose to a cloudless blue sky; joy reigned in every home. By day, all plowed and sowed and planted and reaped, harvesting their grapes and olives, threshing their wheat, and treading out their wine in their presses; when evening came, they sat beneath their vines and fig trees, each man surrounded by his wife, sons, and daughters. Gladdened by their labors and grateful to be where they were, they thought of their days outside the Land as one thinks of sorrowful times in happy ones and felt doubly blessed. Yitzḥak was an imaginative type and his imagination was guided by his heart.[2]

---

2. Agnon, *T'mol Shilshom*, 5.

Although Yitzḥak is disabused of his illusions only gradually, the process begins immediately with his arrival in Palestine.[3] Rowed ashore from his ship in Jaffa port by bawling Arab longshoremen who overcharge him, he next has his luggage snatched up by a Jew who commands him to follow.

> The man led him through marketplaces, side streets, alleyways, and back yards.... The sun blazed down from above and the sand steamed up from below. Yitzḥak's skin was on fire; his every fiber was aflame. Although a barrel of sweat, his lips were dry, his throat was parched, and his tongue felt like toast.... His escort brought him to a yard and a dark house crammed with gunnysacks, baskets, boxes, crates, bundles, and ropes and said, "I'll have a table set and call you when your meal is ready." Yitzḥak reached into his jacket pocket for the letters of recommendation he had brought to let his host know he was a worthy guest.[4]

It is a comic moment. Inappropriately dressed in a jacket and tie and stunned by the savage Middle East heat that no one has warned him about, Yitzḥak, who has traveled with letters of recommendation from Zionist politicians in Galicia in the belief that they will make an impression in Palestine, thinks he is being invited to a fellow Jew's home in a brotherly gesture of welcome. In fact,

> while his host had not misjudged Yitzḥak's worth, Yitzḥak had misjudged his host. The man was an innkeeper and cared only for exacting what he could for food and lodging.... Yitzḥak bore it cheerfully. "Tomorrow," he thought, "I'll have a job working in the fields and won't need any of my money." What difference did it make how much he was made to pay now?[5]

This, too, is an illusion that quickly bursts. The next day Yitzḥak sets out for nearby Petaḥ Tikvah, the country's largest Jewish farming colony, and goes from door to door looking for work. None is to be had. The farmers hire mostly Arabs, and if there are jobs for Jews, they have been taken long ago. Yet now, too, he puts the best possible face on things. Told by a farmer's wife to try the next-door neighbor and discovering that the latter's house has been abandoned, he fails to see that he has been cynically treated. Rather, he wonders, "How strange: a house whose neighbors don't even know no one lives in it!"

3. Agnon, *MiKan u-miKan*.
4. Agnon, *T'mol Shilshom*, 31.
5. Agnon, *T'mol Shilshom*, 31–32.

His trusting nature, however, also works to his benefit. He is drowsing on a park bench one day in the German Templar neighborhood of Sarona, his money all but gone, when a Templar, mistaking him for a worker who has fallen asleep while taking a break, hands him a paint can and a brush and orders him to get to work on a nearby fence. Instead of replying "Go paint it yourself," Yitzḥak obeys without questions, is paid for his labors at the day's end, and is told to return the next day. It is the start of a profession that gives him security and status in a world of semi- or unemployed young immigrants. Although at first a mere "smearer," as he is called by a fellow painter, he eventually masters his new trade and becomes skilled at it.

It is the combination of innocence and a steady job that piques Sonya's interest in him. Sexually experienced, as he is not, she finds him a challenge—a virginal young man who must be made a conquest by creative means but who is also well-mannered and well-dressed, can afford to take her out for coffee or ice cream, and can be counted on not to disappear on the next ship to leave Jaffa, as her previous boyfriend Yedidyah Rabinovitz has just done. Yitzḥak is Rabinovitz's friend, too, and it is in Jaffa's port, to which the two have come to see him off, that he and Sonya have their first conversation. The description of their meeting is a fine example of what the Israeli critic Nitza Ben-Dov has called Agnon's "art of indirection," his masterly ability to convey subtleties of character and situation in passing and without comment, leaving the reader to notice them or not.[6] Yitzḥak and Sonya have just returned to shore after parting from Rabinovitz aboard ship.

> A chill cloaked the autumnal silence of a diminished world. The smell of the sea mingled with the smell of rotting oranges. Yitzḥak and Sonya walked wordlessly until they left the sandy shore for a city street. Sonya plucked a sprig of jasmine from a bush and sniffed its flowers, tossing some over her shoulder. "I think I'll have my shoes shined," she said. Hiking up her dress, she placed her foot on the box of an Arab shoeshine boy. He straightened her leg, buffed her shoe, spat on his brush, dipped it in polish, and set to work until the shoe gleamed like a mirror. Yitzḥak thought of how she had stood on the tips of Rabinovitz's shoes to kiss him on the forehead. He rubbed his forehead and stared at his hand. Placing her other foot on the box, Sonya told the Arab to make sure to do a good job, as if valuing the second shoe more than the first. And then what had happened? Yitzḥak tried to remember. Then

---

6. Ben-Dov, *Agnon's Art of Indirection*.

Rabinovitz had dusted his shoes with a silk handkerchief. "*Finis*," Sonya said. She paid the Arab and turned to go. Yitzḥak walked beside her, sometimes closer and sometimes further away.

In silence, they reached the boulevard. It was lined by consulates, offices, and shops, in one of which Rabinovitz had worked. Since it was closed for the Sabbath, it didn't know yet that he had left it to go abroad. Above it was a balcony over which hung the white, blue-lettered sign of the municipal information and employment bureau. Yitzḥak had been there many times with friends as down-and-out as himself. A melancholy muteness brushed his lips.

Sonya glanced at the shut store's sign and said, "Rabinovitz won't be back anytime soon. He's like Yarkoni. They come like a house on fire and leave like thieves in the night. Now Gurishkin will think he's the center of the world. Do you know Ya'el Ḥayyut? Gurishkin is running after her friend P'ninah. You don't? That's no great loss. Have you seen Gurishkin's mustache lately? It droops over his mouth like two bananas." She brought the jasmine to her nose and sniffed it.

Yitzḥak walked unobtrusively by her side. He couldn't think of a single clever thing to say. All he could answer to her questions was "Yes" or "No." Not that he cared about her. Or if he cared, it was only because she was his friend's girlfriend. Being unused to female company, he stepped as carefully as if she were a countess or a duchess. This amused her more than it annoyed her. Or perhaps it annoyed her more than it amused her. She glanced at him and asked, "Is this how you behave with a woman in Galicia?"

Yitzḥak blushed and looked down at the ground. "The only women I've ever talked with," he said, "are my mother and my sisters."

Sonya had encountered Yitzḥak before and wondered what Rabinovitz saw in such a provincial. She threw him another look and shut her eyes. Then she straightened the tips of her collar and laid a hand on her heart. When they reached Neveh Shalom, she pointed to a side street with the sprig of jasmine and said, "That's where I live." For a moment, she seemed about to say more. She thought better of it, shook Yitzḥak's hand, and turned into the street. Yitzḥak headed home.[7]

In an incisive study of *Only Yesterday*, Amos Oz points to some of the seemingly minor details in this passage that reveal more than they may

---

7. Agnon, *T'mol Shilshom*, 73–75.

appear to at first glance.[8] The dust Rabinovitz wipes from his shoes, for instance, tells us all we need to know about the shallowness of his feelings for Sonya. What man who genuinely cares for a woman would rush to wipe away, even from his feet, her last traces? And is not Sonya herself, in deciding on a whim to polish her own shoes, making a parallel statement? (Perhaps, having noticed what Rabinovitz has done, she is even paying him back tit for tat. Her needless bossiness toward the shoeshine boy shows her need to be in command.) And while she may or may not be fully conscious of the symbolism of her act, she is surely aware of the opportunity it gives her to show off her legs to Yitzḥak. Her disdainful conviction, expressed as though to a confidant, that Rabinovitz will not return, and her disparagement of Gurishkin, are signals, too, that she is already available for a new partner and considers Yitzḥak an eligible candidate.

Does Yitzḥak understand her signals? If he does, it is only subliminally. His hand travels to his forehead to ascertain what a woman's kiss there might feel like and is then stared at as if the kiss might have rubbed off on it; yet in first denying to himself that he is drawn to Sonya and then admitting that he is but only because of their shared friendship with Rabinovitz, he is struggling to suppress the sexual feelings she arouses. She, for her part, scarcely able to believe his naïveté, is uncertain how to proceed. Should she reassure him that she is a proper young lady who needn't be feared? She primly straightens the tips of her collar. Should she let him know she is an emotional being who will respond to any overtures on his part? She lays a hand on her heart. And what can it be that she refrains from saying at the last moment? Is it "Drop by some time" and does she change her mind because she realizes this might scare him off?

Like Rabinovitz, Sonya's friends, some of whom we have met at Yakov Malkov's, are Yitzḥak's as well. Although most come from Russia and think of Galicia as a backwater, their stories are similar to his. They, too, came to Palestine dreaming of being pioneers, of " plowing and planting and sowing and reaping," and they, too, whether because the opportunity has not presented itself, or because they lacked the courage to face the hardship that seizing it would have entailed, have failed to live up to their dream. Construction work in Jaffa, though it, too, is physical labor, leaves them feeling that they have not given themselves fully to the land as they have been told they must do by idolized figures like Brenner and the Zionist thinker A.D.

---

8 Oz, *Shtikat haShamayim*, chapter 4; translated by Harshav as: *The Silence of Heaven: Agnon's Fear of God*.

Gordon (who also makes a cameo appearance in the novel). And Yitzḥak, if anything, feels this even more keenly, since as a house painter, it seems to him that he is simply coloring what others have made.

Yet life in Jewish Jaffa, when there is work, is not unpleasant. There is the sea. There are miles of empty beach. There is a small-town atmosphere in which everyone knows everyone, an informal, easy-going code of manners, and the carefree camaraderie of young people unburdened by adult responsibilities. Yitzḥak and Sonya's friends rarely talk seriously; they prefer to banter and joke, for though having taken their place in Zionism's vanguard by coming to Palestine, they are uneasy with the role, as if its weight were too much for them. Many have left for greener pastures, like Rabinovitz, who plans to make money abroad, and many who have remained have doubts whether they should have. They belong to a small minority of Jews in an Arab country and Zionism's progress is too slow for them to have confidence in its success or to derive from it the sense of purpose that might replace the religious faith they have lost.

In regard to religion, Yitzḥak is no different:

> He behaved like the rest of us. He didn't go to synagogue or put on *t'filin* or observe the Sabbath or the holidays. At first he tried making a distinction between not doing what he should have done, such as praying regularly, and doing what he shouldn't have done, such as eating non-kosher food, but he didn't persist in this. In the end, he did what was forbidden without qualms.
>
> None of this involved thinking very hard about such things. It was a matter of being surrounded by people who had come to believe that religion was of no importance, and that having no need for it, they had none for its commandments. On the contrary: because they sought to live honestly, it would have been hypocritical to perform rituals they were far removed from. If Yitzḥak thought about it at all, he was vaguely guided by the notion that the Jews of Palestine were divided into an Old Yishuv and a New Yishuv, each with its customs. Since he belonged to the new one, why keep those of the old one? Even when he changed his opinion of other things, he didn't change it of this.
>
> And yet if his opinions didn't change, he still missed the home, the Sabbaths, and the holidays that he no longer had. Although he never entered a synagogue at such times, he often sat silently communing or humming a ḥasidic tune until he forgot his workaday woes. He was not the only one. Jaffa was full of ex-yeshiva students. Sometimes, when getting together, they waxed nostalgic

over ḥasidic tales and melodies or imitations of rabbinic sermons. The generation before theirs had sung songs of Zion. Their generation had had enough of these. When their souls overflowed with longing, they looked for what was lost where they had lost it.[9]

If Yitzḥak, a descendant of the renowned pietist Yudl Ḥasid, the fictional protagonist of Agnon's novel *The Bridal Canopy* who settles in the Land of Israel in old age, is unlike his friends in such matters, it is because he occasionally muses about returning to Jewish practice. Even when toying with this idea, however, "he threw himself the sop of doing only what demanded the least effort, such as saying his bedtime prayers—and then, too, he said them less as a matter of duty than as a nostrum to help him fall asleep."

There is an emptiness in the lives of the young Second Aliyah immigrants in Jaffa that they try to ignore. So long as Yitzḥak is involved with Sonya, he, too, is hardly aware of it. Having never had such a relationship before, he has no way of knowing that the excitement he mistakes for love is simple sexual pride and a newfound sense of manliness. Fooled into thinking that Sonya is in love, too, he contemplates marriage, only to be rudely awakened when, her conquest of him accomplished, she loses interest in him and lets him know that their affair is over. Once again, he is painfully slow to read her behavior, taking as long to understand her wanting to be done with him as he did her wanting to take up with him. This only forces her to be more cruel:

> Once he ran into Sonya and insisted on accompanying her on her way. The talk came around to Jerusalem.
> "I've never been there," Yitzḥak said.
> "Anyone with blood instead of paint in his veins," Sonya said, "goes to see it."
> She added:
> "I've seen everything in Jerusalem there is to see. What didn't I see there! I saw Bezalel and Professor Schatz, and Ben-Yehudah's workroom, and the desk he wrote his big dictionary on. . . . All that time, I never slept a wink. Every day I went to see the ancient sights and every night I walked the Old City's walls with the art students and danced with them in the moonlight."
> A pale flush spread over her face as on the night she gave Yitzḥak his first kiss. His heart trembled like the golden gossamers playing over her lips and he reached out to stroke her hair. She

---

9. Agnon, *T'mol Shilshom*, 63–64.

turned her head away and said, "Let's go." When they reached her street, she shook his hand and said goodbye. Before he could say it too, she was gone.[10]

Dancing in the moonlight, Sonya makes clear to Yitzḥak, is not for dullards like him. In the end, half comprehending that he is no longer wanted and half still hoping to please her, he takes her advice and leaves Jaffa for Jerusalem.

∼

Jaffa and Jerusalem, pre-World War I Palestine's two major cities, are opposite poles between which *Only Yesterday* moves back and forth. Apart from a brief account of Yitzḥak's travels to Palestine with which the novel begins, its four parts are divided equally between them, with Parts I and III (in which the scene in Malkov's boarding house takes place) set in Jaffa and Parts II and IV in Jerusalem. Jaffa is coastal, flat, sandy, and humid; Jerusalem, land-bound, mountainous, rocky, and dry. Jerusalem is central to Jewish history and sacred in Jewish tradition; Jaffa, never a hub of Jewish life, is marginal to both. In the one city live Jews, some with roots in it going back generations, who are predominantly religious, anti-Zionist, and Yiddish-speaking; in the other, secular Zionist newcomers who do their best to speak Hebrew.

There were exceptions, of course. There were Jews in Jaffa like the religious Zionist Yakov Malkov—an actual historical figure like Brenner and Gordon—and militant secularists in Jerusalem such as the students and teachers at the Bezalel School of Arts, or the circle around Eliezer Ben-Yehudah, the great Hebrew lexicographer who edited the daily *Ha-Tsvi* and the weekly *Hashkafah,* both rivals of the pro-Orthodox *Ḥavatselet*. But though geographically the two cities were only several hours apart by train, the journey between them was one between two worlds.

Only Yesterday's description of Yitzḥak's arrival in Jerusalem has a lyricism, not often found in Agnon's prose, that makes it very different from that of his arrival in Jaffa. At the train station he finds a wagoner to take him to a hotel.

> A breeze stirred, brushing the rocks and sifting the dusty earth. The air had changed. Its brittle silence could have been the quiet weeping of the mountains. Yitzḥak was overcome by a hushed

10. Agnon, *T'mol Shilshom*, 139–40

> sadness, as if tidings were on the way that might be either good or bad. Good being the stronger force, he hoped for it while faint-heartedly fearing the worst. The old wagoner steered his horses at an easy pace while humming the melody of a prayer under his breath.
>
> Yitzhak peered ahead. His heart began to pound like a man's nearing a long-awaited destination. Soothed by the strains of the wagoner's prayer, he felt his fears melt away. Before him, laced with gold and veined with red fire, were the walls of Jerusalem, washed by a drift of gray and blue cloud that etched in them tones of fine silver, of burnished bronze, of lustrous pewter, of rare electrum. Yitzhak leaned forward, wanting to say something. His tongue mutely sang a soundless song. He sat back again, dancing in his seat.[11]

Yitzhak feels he has come home as he never did in Jaffa. He quickly finds living quarters and a job, and since most of his neighbors and fellow workers are observant Jews, he gradually reverts to the Orthodoxy that he has merely fantasized returning to until now. Now, too, his religious behavior is more a matter of social conformism than of considered conviction, but the way of life it conforms to is that of the shtetl he grew up in. Often, he goes to the Western Wall on Friday nights to participate in Sabbath eve prayers, which he once knew by heart and has partially forgotten.

> Yitzhak would stand praying, in part from memory and in part from his prayer book. Sometimes he felt more drawn to the simple, heartfelt chanting of the Misnagdim and sometimes to the tuneful crooning of the Hasidim; sometimes to melodies ecstatic with the awe of God and sometimes to ones that caught fire from their own rapture. And amid them all, his heart sang its own song, his native town singing in it. Transported, he felt purged of all guilt, once again a blameless child, as unstained by sin as he had been, a boy among boys, in those faraway days.[12]

The guilt he feels purged of is multiple. It is for having abandoned his family in Galicia; for having failed to live like a *halutz* in the Land of Israel; for having betrayed his friend Rabinovitz with Sonya and compromised, so he thinks, her good name; for having forsaken religion. His Zionism is no longer what it was. One day as he is at work with two other painters who know nothing about his past, he starts to sing.

11. Agnon, *T'mol Shilshom*, 145–46.
12. Agnon, *T'mol Shilshom*, 201.

Yitzḥak's companions turned to look at him wonderingly. They had never heard anyone sing while at work.

"Are you a cantor's assistant?" one asked.

"No," Yitzḥak said. "Why?"

"On account of your singing."

"I just like to sing," Yitzḥak said.

"Are you a Zionist?"

"What makes you ask?"

"I've heard the Zionists sing a song called Hatikvah."

"What else have you heard about them, my friend?"

"I've heard that they want to hasten the Redemption by committing all kinds of sins."

"Why would they want to sin?"

"Because it's written that the messiah will come in a generation that's all righteous or all sinful. Since it's easier to be sinful, that's what they've chosen to be."

Yitzḥak did not respond. Gone were the days in which he had sought to make converts to Zionism. Nowadays, he was happy if no one sought to make an anti-Zionist of him. Yet whether for good or for bad—who was to say?—such things had their effect. If outwardly he was beginning to resemble a Jerusalemite, he was becoming more like one inwardly, too. When his fellow workers took a break for the afternoon prayer, he prayed with them; when they shared their meager lunch, he joined them in the grace after meals. If not for Bloykop the artist, his Jerusalemization would have been complete.[13]

Bloykop is one of two people Yitzḥak gets to know in Jerusalem who fit no conventional mold. A former Bezalel student and fellow Galician, he is, though not an observant Jew, an artist with a Jewish sensibility. "There's not a moment in Jerusalem," he tells Yitzḥak,

> that isn't eternal. Not everyone can see that, though. Jerusalem only reveals herself to her lovers. We should hug ourselves, Yitzḥak, for having the good fortune to live here. At first, when I kept comparing Jerusalem to other cities, I saw all its faults. In the end, my eyes were opened and I saw *it*. I saw it, brother, I saw it! What can I tell you, my friend? Words can't describe a fraction of a fraction of it. Pray for me, brother, that God give me a long enough life to show you with my brush all that I see and feel. I don't know if I believe in

---

13. Agnon, *T'mol Shilshom*, 170.

God, but I know that He believes enough in me to let me glimpse what most people never do. If I'm given the time, I'll paint it.[14]

Bloykop, who is dying of tuberculosis, is not given the time, and his death, which leaves behind a grieving wife, is a blow to Yitzḥak. Although painting houses and painting pictures may have little in common, Yitzḥak has not previously thought of paint as a medium for anything but covering things. That it can serve also to uncover them is a revelation. Dimly, he conceives of himself and Bloykop as standing on the same ladder, he on the lowest rung and Bloykop on one of the highest. While he is only to rise one rung more, which happens when Bloykop teaches him to be an expert sign painter, thereby increasing his earning power and professional standing, his being taken into Bloykop's confidence and shown his art gives him, too, a glimpse of what "most people never see."

The second such person is Arzef—a taxidermist and an even more eccentric figure than Bloykop. Born into Jerusalem's Old Yishuv, he left the yeshiva studies he excelled in to go his own way.

> What had made him choose the odd profession of stuffing the skins of walking, flying, and crawling creatures? No one knew. Like Adam in the Garden of Eden, he lived by himself without a wife, children, worries, or complications, surrounded by mammals, birds, reptiles, spiders, and scorpions with whom he got along in perfect harmony. None had the slightest cause for complaint, not even when he took its life, since this only led to its acquisition by one of the great museums of Europe. Professors and scientists beat a path to his door with offers of money and honors. Arzef was no more impressed by the honors than he gave a fig for the money... It was enough for him to regard his handiwork and know that no animal in the world was the worse off for it. On the contrary: more than one Palestinian bird considered extinct had been rescued by him for posterity. All he cared about was the fauna of the Land of Israel mentioned in the Bible and in the Jerusalem and Babylonian Talmuds. He hunted it, discarded its flesh, and stuffed it to give it lasting existence. This was on the first six days of God's week. On the seventh he rested like everyone, rolling out a mat beside his front door and reading a book on it.[15]

As opposed to the visionary Bloykop, Arzef does not seek to see through or past the surface of things. He is fascinated by the surface itself, and his

---

14. Agnon, *T'mol Shilshom*, 164.
15. Agnon, *T'mol Shilshom*, 179.

only desire is to capture Nature, quite literally, as no artist or sculptor can do, and make it live forever. He kills to immortalize, and the immortality granted by him evokes the Garden of Eden before Death entered the world. He is a restorer working in God's atelier, and like God he labors six days a week and takes the Sabbath off.

Each in his own way, Bloykop and Arzef are religious personalities with a firm compass in life that is not oriented either to Jewish observance or to pioneering Zionism. They remind both Yitzhak and the reader that there are other possibilities of personal and Jewish fulfillment in Palestine than those offered by the New and Old Yishuv. Precisely because they are such autonomous beings, however, they are not models for imitation. Yitzhak can admire both but he cannot hope to become like either. They make him feel that for him the choice *is* between the new and the old, Jaffa and Jerusalem—and the longer he lives in Jerusalem, the farther from Jaffa he drifts even before meeting Shifrah and painting "Mad Dog" on Balak.

∾

Although Balak is only the second most famous animal in Hebrew literature, his name links him to the first. This is Balaam's donkey, which, struck by its master for balking beneath him on a narrow path, complains, "What have I done unto thee, that thou hast smitten me these three times?" *What have I done?* is Balak's complaint, too, but, unlike the donkey, he never gets an answer.

From the moment Yitzhak plays his prank on him, Balak, until then just another stray dog living in Jerusalem's Jewish neighborhoods, undergoes a drastic change of life. He has not been averse to being painted. It is a hot day and the cool, wet stroke of Yitzhak's brush on his fur is pleasant, so much so that he begs for more and is driven away with a kick. This causes him to take off on the run and soon reach the streets of Meah She'arim, where, to his astonishment, pandemonium breaks out. Whoever sees him, flees; screaming mothers grab their children and dash home; merchants, before bolting from their stores, pelt him with their weights, scales, and measures. Being a Jewish dog, he puts a Jewish construction on things.

> He knew enough to realize that a rabbinical court must have been sent to check the merchants' weights and scales. "Arf, arf," he barked, which meant: "Are you foolish enough to think I can swallow all your false weights and keep the court from impounding

them?" And in fact, had the weights weighed what they should have, they would have killed him; it was God's mercy that they didn't. "Heavens above!" he cried. "Jews have sinned and I'm to blame?" Before he could get out the words, every last man, woman, and child had sped home and locked their doors. Meah She'arim was emptied of all but a single dog.[16]

Only when such scenes recur wherever he appears does it dawn on Balak that something about him must be the cause of them. His adventures, which occupy long parts of *Only Yesterday,* tell of his increasingly frantic attempts to discover what this is. At first, he takes refuge in Jerusalem's Christian and Muslim quarters, where nobody can read the Hebrew writing on him and he lives and eats well, playing with the local dogs and nipping and being nipped by them.

> But he found no solace there for his soul. The food he crunched with his jaws could not replace the ground snatched from under his paws. The whole world wasn't worth the small corner of it from which he had been exiled. By now he had lived so long among the Gentiles, swayed by their heathenish ways and filled with their heathenish swill, that his addled brain no longer knew a shofar from a church bell. Yet even now he disdained the revenge of apostasy and still woke to howl at midnight, it being written in the tractate of Berakhot that dogs howl in the night's middle watch.[17]

Longing for Jewish cooking and company, Balak returns to Meah She'arim and is again driven from pillar to post. A glimpse of his reflection in a store window causes him to connect the marks he sees on himself with the sign painter, and his suspicion that these are related to his adversity is heightened when the French headmaster bends over him to read them. But what do they signify?

> Balak wagged his tail and said to himself, "It's just as I thought. This whole kettle of fish is someone's fault. It's all because of that scoundrel of a painter who made a sign of me. Do I deserve to be hounded just because some good-for-nothing scribbled on my fur?"
> It is in the nature of Truth's seekers to seek it in its entirety. Balak was no exception. Having set his heart on the truth, nothing but the whole truth would do. "Ahr, ahr," he barked, crouched at

---

16. Agnon, *T'mol Shilshom,* 212–13.
17. Agnon, *T'mol Shilshom,* 227–28.

the headmaster's feet. "Are you going to tell me what it says? Tell me everything!"

Just then the school janitor [whose Hebrew is better than the headmaster's] came along, saw the dog and the writing, and took to his heels. "He knows the truth! He knows the truth!" Balak thought. "Only what am I to do now that he's run off with it?"

Indeed, Balak was still far from the truth. Nevertheless, his pursuit of it helped him to live with his predicament. As the divine poet has said,

Blessed art thou, Science, which doth console
When the waves of misfortune o'er me roll.¹⁸

Although Balak may not know that the author of these Hebrew lines is the 18th-century kabbalist and philosopher Moshe Ḥayyim Luzzato, he is something of a poet himself. One night as he is lolling peacefully while Meah She'arim is asleep and unable to harm him, letting the angry frustration that has been building up in him drain away, a poem comes to him. He is composing its final stanza,

Upon the earth
Walks no one now.
All is silent.
Bow wow wow,

when Shifrah's father Reb Feysh emerges from the darkness. What is Feysh doing out-of-doors in the dead of night? He is posting writs of excommunication on the walls of Meah She'arim that he is afraid to put up by day, lest the neighbors he is excommunicating for being less pious than himself tear them down before they can be read. Balak, who "took no interest in politics or religious disputes and didn't know the difference between one faction of Jews and another," thinks Feysh is out to enjoy the quiet night and greets him with a friendly bark. Alarmed, Feysh drops his lantern and glue pot while his posters are borne away by the wind.

> Reb Feysh's soul was borne away with them. "What is it, Feysh?" soothed the mission he was on with a reassuring hug. "Never fear!" His soul cajoled into returning, he ran after the posters. They, however, reasoning quite logically, "If a mere agent of the law is trying so hard to retrieve us, surely we who are the law should be trying even harder to be retrieved," swerved in midair and flew straight at him, their anathemas flapping in his face. As white as

18. Agnon, T'mol Shilshom, 223.

shrouds, they were uncritically presumed by him to be the ghosts of the ancestors of the excommunicated men.

Feysh shrieked, turned, and ran the other way, chased by the posters, and tripped over the dog. It let out a yelp. Terrified, he went sprawling. No agent of the law should have to go through what he did.

Balak saw Feysh lying on the ground and was nonplussed. What was he to make of it? One minute a man was running on two feet and the next he was lying on all fours. "I'd better smell him," Balak thought. "Either he's not really a man or else he is one and needs help." Reb Feysh came to just in time to find a dog sniffing at him and took off for dear life. Balak remained where he was, thoroughly mortified. No helping hand should have to feel what he felt.[19]

Reb Feysh staggers away and collapses again in the street. Found by the neighbors in the morning, he is carried home and put to bed, never to rise from it again.

∼

In Princeton University Press's published version of *Only Yesterday,* translated by Barbara Harshav, the passage I've translated above begins:

> And Reb Fayesh's soul also flew away. That Commandment began clinging to him and said to him, What's wrong with you, don't be afraid. And it tempted him until his soul returned. He started running and gathering up the posters. Those scraps of paper made their own inference. If Reb Fayesh, an emissary of the Commandment, is running, we who are the Commandment itself should run even faster. They immediately began rolling away and striking him in the face. And every single note cackles with those words Reb Fayesh wrote on it. In his innocence, Reb Fayesh thought that the forefathers of the excommunicated rose up from their graves and came to take vengeance on him, for the notes were white as shrouds of the dead.[20]

There are, it would seem, different ways of translating Agnon. However, I quote from Harshav's *Only Yesterday* not so much to illustrate this point as to explain why Agnon's Hebrew confronts a translator with unique and in part insoluble problems.

---

19. Agnon, *T'mol Shilshom,* 237–8.
20. Agnon, *Only Yesterday,* translated by Harshav, 325.

What happens in this passage? Reb Feysh, shocked by the appearance of a dog he believes to be rabid, drops what he is holding and his posters blow away. As he struggles to master his fear and collect them, the wind shifts and bombards him with them, causing him to panic again and run the other way. Stumbling over Balak, he falls, passes out, regains consciousness, sees Balak smelling him, leaps to his feet, and vanishes in the darkness, leaving the dog to feel once again that it has done something wrong without knowing what.

All of this borders on slapstick, and Agnon makes the most of it by relating it from Feysh's and Balak's perspectives. Lacking all self-awareness, Feysh projects his fear, his attempt to overcome it, and his unconscious self-recrimination for excommunicating blameless Jews onto the soul that deserts him, the task he has set out to perform, and the personified posters that physically attack him after he first thinks they are trying to help. (Not that he doesn't know that posters can't reason talmudically, but in true primitive fashion, he thinks of himself as the cause of all that happens to him.) Balak's mental processes are equally crude. Since human beings, in his experience, do not lie down in streets, seeing Feysh sprawled in one makes him wonder, in a parody of syllogistic thinking, whether Feysh is truly human.

Harshav's translation is more literal than mine. Her "commandment" is closer to Agnon's *mitzvah* than is my "mission" or "law," and her "clinging to him" is closer to Agnon's *m'gafefto* than my "soothed [him] with a reassuring hug." But literalism brings one no closer to Agnon's meaning if its literary associations are ignored. Whereas in modern colloquial Hebrew the verb *l'gafef*, rendered by Harshav as "to cling to," has the sense of to paw clumsily or intrusively, in the Hebrew of the rabbis that Agnon is evoking it means to embrace lovingly. Feysh's sense of duty is, so to speak, putting a comforting arm around him, not desperately clutching at him.

The association Agnon has in mind is actually more specific. In Shir ha-Shirim Rabbah, an ancient collection of midrashim related to the Song of Songs, we read:

> When God declared [on Mount Sinai], "I am the Lord thy God," [Israel's] souls were immediately borne away [by fear]. Seeing that they [the Israelites] had died, the angels began to embrace and kiss them [*hithilu ha-malakhim m'gafefin u-m'nashkin otam*] and said, "What is it? Never fear!" . . And He [God] cajoled them [*hayah m'fateh otan*] until their souls returned.[21]

---

21. Shir ha-Shirim Rabbah 6:3.

Clearly, Agnon wrote his account with this midrash in mind. Although he could not have expected most of his readers to be familiar with it, Feysh certainly would have been.

Rabbinic language, however, pervades Agnon's prose even when his characters are not learned Jews. Take Yitzḥak and Sonya's conversation about Jerusalem. The following elocutions in its opening lines are characteristic of rabbinic as opposed to modern Hebrew:

> *Once he ran into Sonya.* "Ran into [her]" is *m'tsa'*[set aleph]*ah lah*, a talmudic idiom not used in the revived Hebrew spoken in Jaffa in the early 20th century.
>
> *The talk came around.* The verb for "came around," *nitgalgel*, is in the passive *nitpa'el* construction rather than the active *hitpa'el*, another throwback to rabbinic diction.
>
> *"I've never been there,"* Yitzḥak said. Translated literally, this reads, "Said Yitzḥak, 'I've never been there.'" Whereas, in modern Hebrew as in English, identifying phrases like "he said" appear at the end or in the middle of a quotation, quotations in rabbinic literature begin with speaker identification, the verb always coming first.
>
> *"Anyone with blood instead of paint in his veins,"* Sonya said, *"goes to see it."* This sentence, too, begins with "Said Sonya," and her word for "paint" is not the modern Hebrew *tseva* but the Mishnaic *mey tsva'im*, literally, "colored water." Although one might argue that this is her way of sharpening her insult, the expression is not one she would have known or thought of inventing.

There is scarcely a paragraph in Agnon's work that does not contain such archaisms. They are an integral part of his style, and an untranslatable one, since English, having never passed through a rabbinic period, has no equivalents of rabbinic language. To hope to create them by parallel archaisms like "Once he chauncéd upon Sonya," or "Quoth Yitzḥak, 'I've never been there,'" would be patently absurd. Chaucer and Sir Thomas Malory do not evoke the rabbis. Nothing in English does.

One must distinguish between the archaic element in Agnon and the same element in 19th-century Hebrew novelists like Avraham Mapu, Peretz Smolenskin, and Micha Yosef Berdichevsky, who were struggling, each in his way, to forge a language usable for fictional purposes. Mapu, in adopting biblical diction in *The Love of Zion*, was not being deliberately anachronistic. In the absence of a spoken language to serve as an arbiter of what was contemporary and what was not, he chose a stylistic option offered by literary Hebrew, none of whose different stages of historical development had effaced any of its predecessors. He could hardly have written archaically even had he wanted to, there being practically nothing in the Hebrew of his day, from the biblical period on, too superannuated to be used. Although Hebrew underwent a steady process of modernization in the course of the 19th century, from which the spoken Hebrew of the early 20th evolved, the doors to the past remained open.

This was no longer true when Agnon started writing Hebrew fiction in Jaffa in 1908. There was now a spoken language in Palestine to whose speakers some things sounded natural and some did not, some belonged to the present and some to the past alone—and that Agnon's Hebrew was suffused with the past was recognizable at once. It had in it more of "the dust of the study house" than of "the soil of a homeland," wrote Brenner, though he thought Agnon a writer of great promise.[22] Its archaizing, which was to remain a permanent feature of Agnon's prose, was intentional.

This is not to say that Agnon wrote in the rabbinic Hebrew of any specific time or place, or that he eschewed all new developments in the language. When Sonya says, "I've seen everything in Jerusalem there is to see. What didn't I see there! I saw Bezalel and Professor Schatz, and Ben-Yehudah's workroom, and the desk he wrote his big dictionary on," she is speaking, though her phrasing might not have startled Rabbi Akiva, the Hebrew of her day, and it is not until the conclusion of her remarks, where the moon by whose light she danced is the Mishnaic *l'vanah* instead of the modern (and biblical) *yare'aḥ*, that she is given an archaism again. Her Hebrew is in a dialect all its own, and so in general is Agnon's—an integration of 20th-century and rabbinic language, from the Mishnah's to the ḥasidic homily's, so seamless and modulated according to its needs that its components seem never to clash.

The Israeli intellectual historian Eli Schweid has said of this Hebrew that it stands

> halfway between the revolution of modern Hebrew literature and the conservatism of the Hebrew literature that preceded it. Uniquely among modern Hebrew authors, Agnon reverted to an eclectic rabbinic style because such Hebrew, with all its limitations, facilitated a total engagement with Jewish culture throughout the ages rather than with that of his own age alone. He did not recycle it. He developed it in two directions, first by layering it with

22. *Kol Kitvei Y.Ḥ. Brenner*, 2, 320.

contemporary spoken Hebrew, and second, by finding an artistic way of harmonizing its aesthetic lapses and dissonances [owing to its different periods].[23]

This is well put. Yet it misses, I think, an important point—namely, that in setting itself an alternative course from the one taken by twentieth-century Hebrew, Agnon's prose was also a protest against the latter.

Spoken Hebrew's revival in Palestine, and its rapid ascendance to a position of dominance in everyday and cultural life there, was a remarkable and historically unprecedented success, without which Zionism could never have achieved its goal of recasting Jewish identity in a new, national mold. It was a success, however, that was adulterated from the start. The Hebrew that was revived was heavily influenced by Yiddish, the native tongue of most of its adoptive speakers. Its grammar departed in many ways from that of biblical, rabbinic, and 19th-century secular Hebrew alike. It was peppered with loan words and calque idioms—from Yiddish, from Russian, from German, from Ladino, from Arabic, from English, and from Turkish. Its vocabulary and expressive capacities, though they grew greatly in the course of the century, remained limited compared with those of European languages, in part because the establishment of spoken standards consigned to instant obsolescence whole strata of Hebrew's past that could previously have been mined by every Hebrew writer.

At the same time, therefore, that it was rapidly expanding to meet the demands of modern life, Hebrew also shrank drastically, shedding layers overnight that normal languages took centuries to outgrow. Nor could this shrinkage be compensated for by the kind of rich folk language, inherited from parents and ancestors, that is spoken by native populations everywhere. Ordinary Jews had spoken this way, too, in Yiddish, Ladino, and Judeo-Arabic, but the Hebrew they learned to speak in Palestine was an immigrant tongue, acquired from fellow immigrants who had had no native population to learn from. At its most demotic, it was semi-creolized, consisting of a Hebrew base on which were imposed numerous non-Hebraic elements. At its most educated, it had a bloodless cultivation.

Palestinian Hebrew literature, of course, was not stunted in this fashion. Writers like Brenner were the products of intensive Jewish educations in Eastern Europe. The Hebrew they wrote was cultivated. They knew their sources and made use of them. But they no longer could make use of them

---

[23] Schweid, "*HaDisonans haSignoni b'Sippurei Agnon*,"; anthologized in Barshai, *Shai Agnon ba'Bikoret haIvrit*, 282–83.

as freely. Much of the language of these sources was now strange or comical to Hebrew readers who were also Hebrew speakers, especially if they were secular Zionists like Yitzḥak Kummer's friends in Jaffa. Much was hopelessly *passé*. What had never before been archaic in Hebrew now became so.

Agnon's Hebrew is a refusal to acquiesce in this. It poses and attempts to answer the question: what might modern Hebrew have been like had it not undergone so sudden and brutal a rupture with the past? How could it have kept in touch with its rabbinic heritage and exploited it better? How much of what has ostensibly been lost to it can be restored by a skillful enough author?

There can be no such refusal, however, that is not also a critique of the secular Zionism that gave birth to such a Hebrew. And nowhere is this critique of secular Zionism more in evidence in Agnon's work than in *Only Yesterday*.

∽

Balak does not remain in Meah She'arim for long. Impelled to keep wandering by his search for the truth no less than by the way he is treated, his fame spreads beyond Jerusalem. Scholars come from afar to investigate his case. An anthropologist publishes an article about an ancient custom among Jerusalem's Jews of casting out a dog to expiate their sins—a possible result, he speculates, of Islamic influence, dogs being regarded by Muslims as unclean. This leads to international protests by animal lovers and even to anti-Semitic broadsides against Jewish cruelty.

Throughout the second half of *Only Yesterday*, in which Balak plays a prominent role, Agnon has great fun with him. He has him break into the rhymed prose of Hebrew and Arabic medieval narrative. ("The dog set out with a strut in its gait, preening itself as though of high estate, and with each step that it stepped and each leap that it leapt a recital of its future reward and the wicked's requital ran through its brain with this refrain: *Out, damned fleas and cursèd mites! Afflicted be all parasites / for their itches and their bites!*"[24]) He uses Balak's wandering to satirize different elements of Jerusalem's Jewish and non-Jewish population. He comments by means of Balak on human credulity, on the genesis of folk beliefs, on the Hebrew spoken in Palestine. (Since a mad dog in rabbinic language is *kelev shoteh*, not *kelev m'shuga*, Balak, we are told, cannot be mad in any traditional sense.) He parodies anthropomorphic religious thought with a cosmogonic

---

24. Agnon, *T'mol Shilshom*, 220–1.

myth of Balak's own making, according to which the earth and sky were created by a primeval dog and eagle born from the stomach of a camel. When the sky, frightened by the eagle's screeches, weeps endless tears, filling the seas and flooding the land, the great ancestor dog, perched on the eagle's wings, bites it in retribution, and the rents he makes in it become the moon and stars.

Biting is increasingly on Balak's mind. As his plight worsens, so does his physical condition. He doesn't feel well. His head hurts. He is thirsty all the time, drinkable water being hard to find since the country is suffering from a drought. He drags his tail between his legs and drools. His timidity gives way to pent-up aggression.

> "Ay!" cried Balak in his torment. "Why am I persecuted everywhere? Why is everyone out to kill me? Whom have I harmed? Have I bitten anyone? Why can't I have some peace?" Arf, arf, he barked, appealing to the heavens. "Are you going to give me a place to rest? Are you going to give me justice?"
>
> The more he barked, the more he was assailed with sticks and stones. Balak bit the sticks and the stones and went on barking. "Why bite us?" they asked. "Do we have any choice? Bad people grab us and do what they want with us. If you're looking for revenge, go bite them."
>
> "What am I, a mad dog, that I should go bite people?" Balak asked.
>
> "Then go complain to them," said the sticks and stones.
>
> "Do you think they care about my complaints?" Balak asked. "They themselves say, 'Might makes right.'"
>
> "In that case," said the sticks and stones, "you had better show them your might."[25]

Balak is also closing in on the culprit responsible for his sufferings. As he roams the city one night, his senses tell him to start digging and he finds one of Yitzḥak's discarded paint brushes.

> He sniffed its bristles and his hide tingled as it had on that day when the painter dripped something wet on it. This time, though, it didn't tingle with pleasure. It tingled with fear. His eyes filled

---

25. Agnon, *T'mol Shilshom*, 363.

with blood and he let out a sound. It wasn't a yelp or a yowl or a moan, but something new. It was the sound of vengeance.[26]

Meanwhile, Yitzḥak returns to Jerusalem. Having achieved the closure he sought with Sonya, he now feels free to ask for Shifrah's hand. The scene in which he does this—quite literally, yet without an explicit word—is a marvel of delicacy. Arriving in Jerusalem as evening is falling, he finds a hotel in which he leaves his belongings and hurries to Reb Feysh's. The small apartment is lit by a lantern.

> Shifrah was standing by a basin of water, washing her father's undershirt. She tugged at her sleeves and raised her eyes to Yitzḥak. They were not the golden, dreaming eyes he remembered. Or if they were, their gold was dulled and their dream had no interpreter. But though not the same Shifrah, she was even more beautiful.
>
> Rivkah sat knitting in a corner. At Yitzḥak's appearance, she threw him a wondering glance. "I'm coming from Jaffa," he said, looking at Shifrah.
>
> Rivkah nodded. "I heard you were there," she said.
>
> "I've just arrived," Yitzḥak said, "and here I am. How is Reb Feysh?"
>
> Rivkah shone the lantern on her husband and sighed.
>
> Reb Feysh lay in bed. The fleshy sacks beneath his sunken eyes twitched. Rivkah looked at her husband and said, "All our enemies should be as well as he is."
>
> "So nothing has changed," Yitzḥak said.
>
> "Thank God for that," Rivkah said. "No change could have been for the better."
>
> Reb Feysh stirred and seemed to stare at Yitzḥak. Rivkah moved the lantern away. "Why don't you sit down?" she asked. "Sit, Yitzḥak. So you're back in Jerusalem. Let me get you some tea."
>
> "That's kind of you," Yitzḥak said. "Jaffa is growing by leaps and bounds. A new neighborhood is going up with 60 houses. There's work for everyone—for me, too."
>
> "Will you be going back there?" Rivkah asked.
>
> "If you'd like me to," Yitzḥak said, "I will."
>
> Shifrah blushed and stared at the floor. He rested pleading eyes on her and blushed too.
>
> A dog barked outside. "Go be with your father," Rivkah told Shifrah. "Whenever Feysh hears a dog bark," she said to Yitzḥak, "he's frightened."

---

26. Agnon, *T'mol Shilshom*, 365.

> The door opened, a neighbor entered, saw Yitzḥak, and turned to leave. Holding a lump of sugar, Yitzḥak said, "Good woman, there's no need to run from me."
> He took a last sip of tea, set the sugar on the table, stroked his beard, said "It's time I was off," and got to his feet. "Good night," he said to Rivkah with a nod. He went to Shifrah, took her hand, and said good night to her, too. Rivkah looked on in wonder. "Is this the young man?" the neighbor asked. Yitzḥak smiled at her. "It is, it is," he said, giving Shifrah's hand a squeeze.
> Shifrah withdrew her hand. "Good night," she said. Yitzḥak stroked his beard and departed. Rivkah took the lantern and went to the doorway to light his way. Shifrah stood and listened to his footsteps. When he was gone, Rivkah returned and hung the lantern on its peg.[27]

With which of the understated details in this passage does one begin? With Shifrah's instinctively obeying the code of modesty she has grown up with by automatically lowering the sleeves she has raised to do the wash even before knowing who the unexpected visitor is? (If it is a woman, there is no need to do this.) With her leaving the conversation entirely to Rivkah, guided by the same code and her trust in her mother? With her eyes that tell us, as they perhaps tell Yitzḥak, that she has been suffering from his absence without acknowledging to herself that this has been the cause of her unhappiness? With Yitzḥak's finding her "even more beautiful" because a woman one loves, no matter how wan, is always beautiful? With Rivkah's first moving the lantern toward Feysh and then away from him because, while she wants Yitzḥak to see him, she is worried that, even in his unconscious state, he might see Yitzḥak? With Yitzḥak's self-confidence, which he has never exhibited before and now has because he has matured and because, for the first time since coming to Palestine, he feels sure he is doing the right thing? With Rivkah's warmth toward him despite her fears of social disapproval? (She is under no obligation to be so friendly, much less to offer him the tea that she serves, East European-style, with a lump of sugar to sip it through.) With his twice stroking his beard in a gesture typical of the observant Jew he has become—a conscious or unconscious signal that, consciously or unconsciously, must register on Rivkah and Shifrah? (We have seen Yakov Malkov make this same gesture in his boarding house.)

---

27. Agnon, *T'mol Shilshom*, 377–9.

With the narrator's leaving us to guess what Rivkah hopes or fears to hear when she asks Yitzḥak if he plans to return to Jaffa?

Yitzḥak's answer to this question is in effect a proposal of marriage, and Shifrah's blush conveys that she understands this well. He does not get a response because the bark of a dog (is it Balak?) mercifully spares Rivkah the need to give him one. Yet he has reason to feel encouraged. When he boldly takes Shifrah's hand before her astonished mother and neighbor with every awareness of what he is doing (neither he nor she has forgotten the time this caused her to flee from him), she does not pull it away at once but only when he squeezes it—and then, too, she returns his "Good night," watches as her mother goes out of her way to light the dark street for him, and gets up from her seat to listen to him walk off.

Only Yesterday makes Yitzḥak and Shifrah clear a few more hurdles before they are wed, but the outcome is no longer in doubt. Abetting it are Rivkah's discovery that Yitzḥak is a descendant of the pietist Yudl Ḥasid (ancestry counts for much in Meah She'arim) and the unexpected support of the wise neighbor, who, having discerned the young couple's feelings for each other, urges Rivkah to promote the match. Even then, Meah She'arim is about to boycott the wedding when an eminent rabbi decides to officiate at it in tribute to an old friendship with Rivkah's father. This changes everything, and at the last minute, we are told, "so many neighbors, men, women, and children, came to celebrate with the bride and groom that there wasn't a place left to stand in."

Yitzḥak and Shifrah are blissful. One evening after finishing his work,

> Yitzḥak was preparing to return home to his wife. His need to be with her was still like a bridegroom's. Shifrah sat alone with her thoughts, marveling how, since the wedding, they had been only of Yitzḥak. She looked around as if to detect whether anyone had noticed the change in her. What she saw in the mirror on the wall made her marvel even more. Apart from the married woman's kerchief on her head, nothing about her looked different. And yet she felt like another person . . . Standing beneath the wedding canopy with Yitzḥak, she had been sure there would never again be such a moment in her life. Now, every moment was its equal. She went to

the stove to check the dinner she had cooked and wondered why, though it was ready, Yitzḥak was still not home.[28]

Yitzḥak has been delayed. On his way home he has encountered a crowd gathered on a corner to listen to a street preacher inveigh against the sins of the age, for which the drought is God's punishment. Suddenly, Balak appears. The crowd scatters in all directions. Yitzḥak, who has been in Jaffa and not known of the mad-dog hysteria in Jerusalem, calmly stands his ground and explains when told to flee that there is nothing to be afraid of because—so he shamefacedly confesses—it was he who painted *kelev m'shuga* on Balak's side. Incredulity is followed by a wave of relief.

> No one feared the dog any more. And since no one did, no one understood why anyone ever had. In their newfound courage, all mocked the cowards who had run from it. The cowards, in turn, resolutely blamed the newspapers, which had stirred up panic. That was the press for you. It had nothing better to write about and so it wrote about that. One day it scared you with dogs and the next with mosquitoes.
>
> The dog frightened no one, least of all Yitzḥak, who had forgotten it the moment he painted it. But the dog had not forgotten him. It understood only too well that it owed all its troubles to the sign painter. It had looked for him everywhere, barking when it saw him and barking when it only imagined that it had.... Make sense of it if you can: so long as Balak was in his right mind, he was feared to be mad; now that he wondered if he wasn't going mad, all fear of him was gone.[29]

Balak has indeed gone mad. He has rabies, contracted, it would seem, while playing with the dogs in Jerusalem's Gentile neighborhoods. Face-to-face with Yitzḥak as the crowd begins to disperse,

> [he] fixed weary eyes on the sign painter's feet and saw they hadn't moved. "Whoever knows the truth," he thought with a sigh, "is afraid of nothing. But the truth is heavy and few can bear its weight—I could help him to bear it."
>
> Yitzḥak stood there crestfallen, like a man awaiting sentence. He noticed the dog, snapped his fingers at it, and said, "Did you hear what they said about you? They said you were mad." He hadn't meant to offend Balak; he just needed someone to talk to and was too ashamed to talk to anyone else. Balak, though, thought

---

28. Agnon, *T'mol Shilshom*, 455.
29. Agnon, *T'mol Shilshom*, 452.

> otherwise. He glanced up at Yitzḥak in alarm, the whites of his eyes vanishing and their pupils turning black. His mouth foamed and his teeth shook in their sockets. Then he shook all over. He wanted to jump on Yitzḥak. In the end, he looked back down and nuzzled the ground.[30]

Yitzḥak turns to go home.

> Balak wagged his head and thought, "He has somewhere to go—and I'm an outcast with nowhere, despised and downtrodden." His tongue hung from his mouth as if about to fall out. He tried putting it back in place and couldn't. Something sweet trickled between his teeth. His other senses in abeyance, a craving bubbled up there like a spring. Every tooth stood on edge. His body stiffened. Before Yitzḥak could walk off, the dog leaped on him and sank its teeth into him. Having bitten him, it took to its legs and ran off.[31]

Yitzḥak returns home, falls ill, and dies after several weeks of frightful torment. "And we, dear friends," laments the narrator, "are left dumbfounded when we regard all that befell Yitzḥak. Why was this man, who was no worse than any other, punished in such a fashion?"

But there is a silver lining in the clouds that form on the day of Yitzḥak's funeral. Soon they begin to pour. The drought is over. It rains and rains. When the rain finally stops,

> every bush and blade of grass gave off a good smell, most of all the orange trees. The entire country was a blessed garden of God's and blessed were all its inhabitants. And you, our stalwart brothers in Kinneret and Merḥavia, in En-Ganim and Um-Guni, as Degania once was called, went to work in your fields and gardens, doing what our friend Yitzḥak was not privileged to do. Our friend Yitzḥak never got to plow, sow, and farm. And yet like his ancestor Reb Yudl and other pious Jews, he was granted a grave in the Holy Land. Let the mourners mourn this suffering soul who died badly. We prefer to tell of our brothers and sisters, the sons and daughters of God's people, who tilled the earth of Israel to their everlasting glory. Yitzḥak's adventures are done. The annals of our other comrades will be told in the book of *The Field that Was*.[32]

Such a book was never written.

---

30. Agnon, *T'mol Shilshom*, 453.
31. Agnon, *T'mol Shilshom*, 455–6.
32. Agnon, *T'mol Shilshom*, 464–65.

Although not all have chosen to read it in such a manner, *Only Yesterday*'s ending, with its sentimental description of a life of happy toil on "the earth of Israel," is pure parody. It matches that of the novel's beginning, the two framing the story between them like twin bookends. This may seem an odd thing for Agnon to have done with what is not, despite all its humor, a comedy. But Agnon was a writer who liked to toy with his readers and never shrank from the risk—indeed, he enjoyed courting it—of being misunderstood by them. One might say, almost tongue-in-cheek, that *Only Yesterday* was written to fool the bookstore browser who weighs a purchase on the basis of its first and last paragraphs.

There is a fundamental difference between these paragraphs, however. *Only Yesterday*'s opening lines ridicule Yitzḥak Kummer's rosy picture of conditions in Palestine at the time he sets out for it. Ultimately disappointed by a life in Jaffa that is not like the one he imagined, Yitzḥak moves to Jerusalem, reverts to religion, and ends up in anti-Zionist Meah She'arim, where he perishes, as it were, by his own hands, having set in motion the events that lead to his death. One can analyze his character and motives from many angles, and Agnon's critics have done so at length, but this remains the novel's bare synopsis.

Only Yesterday's last lines, on the other hand, come after Yitzḥak's death and do not reflect his point of view. They express that of the nameless narrator, a shadowy presence who regularly refers to "our friend Yitzḥak." What about him, or the collective "we" of the Second Aliyah in whose name he speaks, is Agnon burlesquing?

It certainly isn't the Second Aliyah's *ḥalutzim*, for whom Agnon had great respect. Rather, it seems an inescapable conclusion, the parody of *Only Yesterday*'s ending is aimed at the Labor Zionist ideology that romanticized and mythologized the figure of the *ḥalutz,* making it a yardstick by which all other forms of Zionism were judged lacking.

"Many a critic," writes Amos Oz, "has found ample grounds in *Only Yesterday* for generalizations about the Second Aliyah, ... which seemingly broke with religion, family, and Tradition only to break in the end [in individuals like Yitzḥak] with its own pioneering ideals"—"seemingly" because Oz's understanding of Yitzḥak is of someone who never really broke with his past at all. The values Yitzḥak grew up with, Oz writes, remain *his* yardstick, so that "from the shtetl proceed all his fantasies of the shade-giving vines and fig trees of Palestine, and to the shtetl they return." He and his friends in Jaffa "will never be reborn or shake off the dust of exile. On the contrary: they will carry it with them wherever they go."³³

Unlike the pioneers of Kinneret and Degania, in other words, Yitzḥak is unwilling or unable to remake himself radically and is thus sucked back into the world of religion in its most regressive form. He has tried to live by a "naïve synthesis," as Oz puts it, of Jewish tradition with the revolutionary ideals of the Second Aliyah, and when this synthesis breaks down, as it must because of its internal contradictions, he reverts to where he has come from and then some.

Such would indeed appear to be the narrator's judgment of Yitzḥak at the conclusion of *Only Yesterday*. Oz's seconding of it, however, is surprising given the astute reader that he is, because it is a judgment that is meant, as I have said, to be laughed at. The novel's closing clichés are as mawkish as its opening ones. Substitute the communes of the Second Aliyah for the First Aliyah colonies that Yitzḥak Kummer has read about and the two passages are highly similar.

Oz accepts at face value the narrator's insistence in *Only Yesterday* that Yitzḥak's fateful mistake was not having become the pioneer that he dreamed of being. In this, the narrator is faithful to the Labor Zionist narrative, never more widely accepted than it was in the 1940s when *Only Yesterday* was written, of the *ḥalutz* as an unequaled paradigm of Zionist self-fulfillment in whom the trapped religious energies of Judaism were freed and rechanneled into Zionist fervor and construction.

But while this may be the narrator's opinion in *Only Yesterday*, it is not, the novel's ending makes clear, Agnon's. The whole issue of Yitzḥak's failure to become a *ḥalutz*, I would submit, is a red herring that is repeatedly dragged through the novel in order to throw us off the trail. Becoming a housepainter in Jaffa rather than a field hand in Degania was hardly, after all, a negation of Zionism. The Yishuv needed house painters, too, and could no more have succeeded without Jewish workers in Palestine's cities than without Jewish farmers in its countryside; in fact, a very small percentage of Zionist immigrants to Palestine in the years in which *Only Yesterday* takes place ended up living in agricultural settlements. Yitzḥak's feelings of guilt at not being one of them are real, but they tell us only about his failed expectations of himself, not about his failure as a Zionist. In denying him his Zionist credentials and classing him with his ancestor Yudl Ḥasid, who came to Palestine in order to die and be buried there, the narrator

---

33. Oz, *Shtikat ha-Shamayim*, 73–74.

simplemindedly echoes Brenner's declaration of "Except for the farmers, my friends, except for the farmers, it's all humbug, humbug, humbug!"[34]

In truth, if Yitzhak makes a mistake, it is, like the narrator, to buy into this belief, which is mocked by *Only Yesterday*'s ending just as he himself is mocked by its beginning. Challenging us at the last moment to see through a narrator whose good sense we have trusted until then is the sort of game Agnon delighted in playing. There are other examples of this in his work, the most germane being the conclusion of his 1951 novel *To This Day*, set during World War I in Berlin. Its story, too, is told by a sophisticated observer who, keenly aware of the foibles of others, ends his account with an unwitting exposure of his own foolishness that forces the perceptive reader to rethink what he has read.

The statement made by the ending of Only Yesterday is in fact the opposite of the one Oz attributes to him. Yitzhak's regression to Meah She'arim does not come from his inability to "shake off the dust of exile." It comes from shaking off too much of it by throwing religion and its values overboard in a Jaffa in which his friends do not even say kaddish for their fathers. This undermines his Jewish and human equilibrium, and in an attempt to regain it, he lurches too far in the other direction.

Although Yitzhak's story is unique, he himself is portrayed in the novel as anything but that. "He made," the narrator tells us,

> no special impression on anyone. There were many young men like Yitzhak, none of whom drew the slightest attention. There was nothing unusual about his appearance or conversation. Talking with him left you with no great desire to do it again, and it was possible to encounter him in a public place and not recognize him. Unless you happened to be fond of him, you didn't notice he was there.[35]

Yitzhak is a Zionist Everyman, even if what happens to him does not happen to every Zionist. His life is his own; his fate, if we are to regard it as more than just a curiosity that would hardly justify a 600-page novel, must suggest something greater.

But what? Agnon wrote *Only Yesterday* in Jerusalem during the years of World War II, when the Old Yishuv was a much smaller part of the city's population than it had been in 1910. By then, it had long lost its battle with the New Yishuv. In Palestine as elsewhere, religion was assumed to be on

---

34. Agnon, *T'mol Shilshom*, 297.
35. Agnon, *T'mol Shilshom*, 170–71.

the wane before the wave of a secular future. Non-observant Jews turning or returning to a life of Jewish observance were extremely rare. Although the irony of a young Zionist coming to Palestine in the early 20th century only to swallowed up by an ultra-Orthodox quarter of Jerusalem would not have been lost on Agnon's Palestinian readers, it would not have symbolized anything significant in the world they knew.

Indeed, Agnon's readers in 1945 could only have been puzzled and disappointed by the apparent absence in *Only Yesterday* of the great and terrible concerns of the day: the cataclysmic world war that had just been fought, its murder of European Jewry, the desperate struggle for a Jewish state that lay ahead, in which victory was far from assured. How could the greatest living Hebrew author, as Agnon was already regarded at the time, have spent the years in which this was happening writing as lengthy a work of fiction about a life as peripheral as Yitzhak Kummer's?

Perhaps the answer lies with Balak.

Balak has puzzled readers of *Only Yesterday* even more than Yitzhak has. What is he doing in the novel? Agnon, who had written a rudimentary version of Balak's story in the early 1930s before greatly expanding it in *Only Yesterday*, was well aware that this question would be asked. In a chapter that he wrote and decided to delete, he addressed it and the reader directly:

> I know you're displeased with me for mixing one thing with another and confusing animals with human beings. In your opinion, dear reader, I should have kept Yitzhak and the dog apart and made of them two separate stories. Moreover, you're annoyed at me for letting a dog talk and giving him language in which to think about things that no bird or beast has the slightest need to think about, ... [especially since] a shrewd critic has already established that horses do not speak like people.[36]

The identity of this critic would have to be searched for, but the horse alluded to is clearly that of Mendele Mokher Sforim's novella *The Mare*, first written in Yiddish in 1873 and later rewritten in Hebrew, in which the animal of the title is a personification of the Jewish people. Most critics of Agnon have rejected such a view of Balak and offered other interpretations of him. He is Yitzhak's alter ego; he is Yitzhak's repressed erotic and aggressive self; he is a demonic force let loose on a helpless world; he is the eternal

---

36. Published from the Agnon Archives by Hagar, *Shai Agnon: Meḥkarim uTeudot* (Jerusalem: Mossad Bialik, 1978), 164–65.

victim of inscrutable Fate; he is all these of things and still more; he is none of them, being only a dog. And a marvelous dog he is, sniffing, scratching, squatting, rolling in the dirt, barking, growling, yelping and yowling, cocking his ears and dragging his tail as dogs do.

Still, he is, as has been observed, a very Jewish dog, and nothing is more Jewish about him than the way the world fears him, reviles him, drives him into exile, hounds him from place to place, and seeks to kill him without any reason that he can discern. Can it be a coincidence that Agnon wrote about him during World War II? Is it conceivable that he could have done so without having had Europe's Jews in mind?

I think not. *Only Yesterday* is a book written in the shadow of the Holocaust.

Falsely thought by his persecutors to be mad, Balak becomes mad. The Jewish people, though it had every reason during and after the Holocaust to go mad, too, remained remarkably sane. But madness, like rabies, incubates before it appears. If the first great fear expressed in *Only Yesterday* is that a Zionism that is too secular will one day swing like a pendulum to its opposite extreme, the second is that sooner or later, today or tomorrow, a madness contracted from Jewish history will claim the Jewish people as its victims, as Yitzḥak is Balak's victim and Balak is Yitzḥak's. Not even love (for who can doubt Yitzḥak and Shifrah's?) will save them then.

Agnon, the wiliest of all Hebrew authors, believed in the synthesis that Amos Oz calls naïve and was apprehensive for a Zionism that rejected or failed to achieve it, just as he was apprehensive for a Hebrew language detached from its roots. In terms of the great debate between the great Zionist thinkers Ahad Ha'am and Micha Yosef Berdichevsky that continues to rage, in one form or another, in Israel to this day, Agnon was an Ahad Ha'amian like Bialik as opposed to a Berdichevskyan like Brenner. Yet unlike Ahad Ha'am and Bialik, he was an observant Jew, though one who had lapsed during his years in Jaffa.

When he returned to religion, however, he did not do so like Yitzḥak. The Orthodoxy he practiced until his death in Jerusalem in 1970 was a measured one. Indeed, the more one reads him, the more impossible it becomes to determine whether his Judaism was a matter of faith, ancestral loyalty, cultural conviction, inborn conservatism, a deliberately chosen bulwark against disorder, or some combination of these things. He had no more qualms about turning his accomplished sense of irony against this Judaism than about turning it against anything else.

Reading Agnon's Only Yesterday Today

Irony, present in all of his work, was a balancing act for Agnon, keeping him equidistant from everything he wrote about, and a careful sense of balance characterized everything he wrote, from his language and sentence structure to his delineations of character and fictional plots. *Only Yesterday* is a novel about the loss of balance in one young man and its possible loss in an entire people. It may strike its readers today as being more timely than it did in 1945.

Bibliography

Agnon, S.Y. *Only Yesterday*. Translated by Barbara Harshav. Princeton: Princeton University Press, 2000.

———. *T'mol Shilshom* [Hebrew] Tel Aviv: Schocken, 1945.

Agnon, S.Y., and Gershon Shaked. "Ḥelkat haSadeh haNatushah." *Moznayim* 32/3 (February 1971) 212–15.

Agnon, S.Y., and Sarah Hagar. *Shai Agnon: Meḥkarim uTeudot*. Edited by G. Shaked and R. Weiser. Jerusalem: Mossad Bialik, 1978.

Ben-Dov, Nitza. *Agnon's Art of Indirection: Uncovering Latent Content in the Fiction of S.Y. Agnon*. New York: Brill, 1993.

Brenner, Y.H. *Kol Kitvei Y.Ḥ. Brenner*. Tel Aviv: Dvir & HaKibbutz Hameuchad, 1960, 2, 320.

———. *MiKan u-miKan*. Warsaw: Sifrut, 1911.

Hagar. *Shai Agnon: Meḥkarim uTeudot*. Jerusalem: Mossad Bialik, 1978.

Halkin, Hillel. "Reading Agnon's *Only Yesterday* Today." *Mosaic Magazine*, December 2018.

Mokher Sforim, Mendele. *Die Kliatshe*. Translated by Joachim Neugroschel as "The Mare" in *The Great Works of Jewish Fantasy and Occult*. Woodstock, NY: Overlook, 1986.

Oz, Amos. *Shtikat haShamayim: Agnon Mishtomem al Elohim*. Jerusalem: Keter, 1993.

———. *The Silence of Heaven: Agnon's Fear of God*. Translated by Barbara Harshav. Princeton: Princeton University Press, 2012.

Schweid, Eli. "HaDisonans haSignoni b'Sippurei Agnon." *Gazit* 17:7–12 (1960); anthologized in A. Barshai, ed., *Shai Agnon ba'Bikoret haIvrit*. Vol. 1. Tel Aviv: Schocken, 1991.

5

The Art of Agnon Annotation

Discussing Professor Avraham Holtz's Monumental Edition of Agnon's *T'mol Shilshom*

AVRAHAM HOLTZ AND JEFFREY SAKS IN CONVERSATION

Avraham Holtz, professor emeritus of Hebrew Literature at the Jewish Theological Seminary in New York, is the author of a large body of important scholarship concerning Hebrew Literature in general, and Agnon specifically, and most notably, the fully annotated and illustrated edition of Agnon's *Hakhnasat Kallah, The Bridal* Canopy.[1] Since that significant contribution, Holtz has been at work on a parallel edition, fully annotating Agnon's *T'mol Shilshom, Only Yesterday*.

Professor Holtz was ordained as a rabbi and received his doctorate from the Jewish Theological Seminary of America, where he taught and served as Chair of its Department of Hebrew Literature and as Dean of Academic Development. He is an Honorary Member of Israel's Academy of the Hebrew Language and has published several articles about aspects of the Hebrew language in the Academy's various publications, in addition to

---

1. Agnon, *Hakhnasat Kallah*.

THE ART OF AGNON ANNOTATION

scholarly articles in the field of Hebrew literature, many of which are related to various aspects of Agnon's works.

In the context of Yeshiva University's conference on *Agnon's Stories of the Land of Israel*, Holtz spoke about his work in annotating Agnon, in general, and specifically his focus on *T'mol Shilshom*, which is perhaps Hebrew literature's most significant novel of *Eretz Yisrael*. He discussed these topics in conversation with Jeffrey Saks. What follows is an edited transcript.

Jeffrey Saks: Your work on Agnon's *Hakhnasat Kallah* is truly unparalleled in Hebrew literature, although of course there are examples in other cultures. How did that first great annotation project inform what you have been doing for these past two-plus decades in working on *T'mol Shilshom*. What was the background to these two colossal undertakings?

Avraham Holtz: I suppose it all has something to do with the fact that I never forget that Agnon was a Galitzianer, as am I on both of my parents' sides. (*Audience applause*)

JS: There aren't too many other audiences where that line would get applause! (*Audience laughter*)

AH: I grew up with one Galitzianer grandfather and we spoke Galitzianer Yiddish. And my grandfather, Shulim Nadel *z"l*, taught me how to read Hebrew. So I read in his native Galitzianer accent, and I thought that that was the only way to read. But when I went to Hebrew School, they just decided that that's not the way to pronounce words. My teachers there insisted that I read according to the Litvish Ashkenazic pronunciation and accents. A few years later, I went to Herzliya Hebrew High School, where they did not teach Agnon, and then I went to Herzliya Teachers Seminary, where they also did not teach Agnon. I guess he wasn't part of the corpus, or part of the Zionist idea, I don't exactly know. In 1952 I went to Israel. Before I left, my Hebrew grammar teacher, the late Daniel Persky, approached me and cautioned me in thick Ashkenozis: *Avrohom, hizoher shelo yikalkalu es ho-Ivris shelcho,* "Take care that they not ruin your Hebrew!" Despite his warning I came back from Israel speaking and reading in the more "modern" and more Israeli Sefaradit accent. The first Friday night after my return, when he heard me recite Kiddush in Sefaradit, my grandfather said: *Yetzt farshtei Ich goornisht,* or "Now I don't understand a thing!" Agnon had the same problem—and the recordings of him speaking, reading, or being interviewed which are available online all bear this out; listen and you'll hear his struggle to overcome his native Galitzianer accented Hebrew. I mention all of this because I think it's essential to understand where Agnon's writing emerges from. If one reads the title of the book as *Hakhnasat Kallah* and doesn't at least hear in his mind the Yiddish "*Hachnosses Kalle*," he's missing something. Professor Dov Sadan insisted that I indicate in my book that the protagonist's name is Reb Yeedl and his famed wagon-driver's name should be read or pronounced as Nussin Nutte (not Natan Neta).

JS: There's an amusing passage at the beginning of *T'mol Shilshom* when Yitzḥak goes out on his first day looking for work as a laborer, in which Agnon renders his not-yet Sefardi accent by visually representing all the letter *tavs* as *samekhs*, so the reader knows Yitzḥak is speaking in Ashkenozis.

AH: Correct, so the reader will hear in his mind the name of the city as *Paisach Tikva*, for example. The reader knows Yitzḥak is a Galitizianer and speaks the Hebrew he brought with him on the ship from home—and he's made fun of because of it. And of course, Agnon wanted to replicate that pronunciation in order that we follow Yitzḥak Kummer as his language becomes acclimated or acculturated, or whatever it is that he has to do. In truth, I don't think that he actually does speak much Hebrew at any point in the book. Presumably most of the dialogue would have been spoken in Yiddish, and Agnon renders it into Hebrew for us. (There is even mention that Regel-HaMetukah speaks to his dogs in Yiddish; that everyone spoke in Yiddish amongst themselves unless Ben-Yehudah was around to catch them!) At one point there's a woman from his hometown who reminds Yitzḥak that he's forgetting his Buczaczer Yiddish, and he's beginning to pronounce words in some other way, and Heaven help us, he's introducing all kinds of Arabic words and other phrases that we never heard about in Buczacz. What's he doing? But at any rate, back to the beginning. Agnon had his own way of getting even with that young man who made fun of Yitzḥak. There's a passage in the Prologue, when Yitzḥak is on the train, that relates that when one of the hasidim wanted to curse the Zionists, fearful lest God Himself wouldn't understand Hebrew, translated his invective to Yiddish!—*Di epikorsim vus zaanen in inzere tsaatn* ("The heretics of our times!")—but he pronounces it in a Galitzianer Yiddish, slightly different than Buczaczer Yiddish. This is how I came up with the idea that, I hope, in the new book on *T'mol Shilshom* we'll include a CD with voice recordings, so the readers can get a true sense of how it all sounded.

JS: When you started the work on *Hakhnasat Kallah* did you have a model in mind? How did it originate and evolve?

The Art of Agnon Annotation

AH: The origin of the work on *Hakhnasat Kallah* began with my monograph, *Ma'aseh Reb Yudil Hasid* (Jewish Theological Seminary, 1986). In that work I dealt with the "archeology" behind the novel, identifying the principle source in hasidic literature on which Agnon drew, the Yiddish work *Nisim veNiflooes*, a kind of hagiography of Reb Avraham Yehoshua Heschel, the Apter Rav. That's where I got the idea that the other sources might be "excavated" as well. I understand now that if *T'mol Shilshom* (in its hardcover edition) contains 607 pages with 31 lines to a page, each and every page requires another type of expertise, different kinds throughout the book. Through the literary allusions, the linguistic problems, the biblical and rabbinical sources, references to liturgy and realia, foreign phrases—you name it and it's in there as questions that arise from the text. It was also very important to me to situate all of the stories within the actual geography of eastern Galicia, and that's how we came to produce the detailed map which was researched and drawn by my wife Toby. We were able to chart out the actual route that Reb Yudel travels throughout the book. Once I got into the work of "excavation" I realized how much I, and presumably other readers, didn't understand, how much required study and research, and that's what guided me. I knew I needed to develop an apparatus to organize all the information, and I found a model in Gifford and Seidman's annotated edition of Joyce's *Ulysses*.[2]

JS: Why was it obvious that this edition of Ulysses should be the model? You have drawn our attention in the past to other scholarly work, meta-scholarship, on the work of annotation. Why was this model preferred over a different model?

AH: With Ulysses you have an annotator wrestling with a book that has two different editions, two different layers of the text. So, too, with *Hakhnasat Kallah*, which Agnon rewrote four times. Curiously, the first edition was published in America. Then, quite typically, Agnon came back to it, revising and expanding it each time. In my preliminary monograph I examined the kernel story of the Apter Rav guiding an impoverished man to go out seeking a dowry for his daughters. That story is what stands at the core of *Hakhnasat Kallah*—quite literally the money needed to bring the bride under the marriage canopy. Agnon's achievement in expanding the story was also, in the process, creating a Hebrew language to tell it in! We, the Hebrew readers in the twentieth century know that it's not really Hebrew, because these people didn't really speak Hebrew. Maybe they prayed

---

2. Gifford and Seidman, *Ulysses Annotated*.

in Hebrew, but they didn't actually speak Hebrew. And he created his own Hebrew. So, part of my job for this book was to recreate the Yiddish which is hidden "between the lines," because Agnon crafted all the dialogue in the novel. In the *Nisim veNiflooes* it's almost entirely a plot recitation with no character dialogue. I very much wanted the reader to understand and experience that.

JS: Was the original plan to first prepare a critical edition of the text and then to pursue all of the other annotations?

AH: When Racheli Edelman, Schocken's granddaughter and the current publisher, first asked me about the work I had begun she wanted to know what I was aiming at in the proposed work. I began to spell out for her the scope of what needed to be involved in the annotations and explained that what I want to do is to guide the reader through the book. She correctly observed that "Jews don't read that way. Jews read everything on the same page." She took down a copy of Schoken's *Mikraot Gedolot* from the shelf and said, "That's how we'll publish it." Curiously, that Hebrew Bible was published in Berlin in 1937, already after Hitler had come to power.

JS: Interesting. It was Mrs. Edelman's idea. The irony, of course, is that one of the critiques of the book, from a very specific sector, was that it had trampled on the holy, by graphically modeling an Agnon book after a page of Talmud!

AH: Yes, they said, "How dare you take the Gemara page and apply it to Agnon and his *ma'ases*! It's desecrating the *Daf*!" You can understand the whole attack by the fact that I came from Jewish Theological Seminary. Only somebody coming from the Seminary would do such a sinful thing. (*Laughter*) And curiously enough, just last week somebody called me up. He's writing a book about all these kinds of things among the Haredi community. So he said: Do I have permission to quote? I said: "Please!" So, I sent him the review which had appeared in the *Yated HaShavuah*.[3]

JS: So let me turn our attention to the next topic which you already foreshadowed. In an essay, a couple of years back on the website of *Tablet Magazine*, the literary critic Adam Kirsch shared his thoughts on first reading *T'mol Shilshom* in translation.[4] It has relevance for your work, but maybe even more so for our work at the Toby Press in now trying to render Agnon in English translations with annotations. Kirsch writes:

---

3. *Yated HaShavuah*, 15.
4. Kirsch, "Pilgrim's Progress."

THE ART OF AGNON ANNOTATION

> The biblical diction of [Agnon's writing] is a key to *Only Yesterday*. [Translator] Barbara Harshav works hard to render the echoes of biblical and rabbinical Hebrew in the modern Hebrew of Agnon's novel. But this can't really be done in English, which is one reason why the novel's texture ends up feeling thin: The plot and characterization are forced to bear much of the weight that, in Hebrew, must be borne by the language itself. Still, enough of these antique resonances come across to show how the language of *Only Yesterday* embodies its theme, which is the vertigo that results when a 20th-century Jew returns to the land his ancestors left 2,000 years earlier.

Now here he is referring to having read the novel and experiencing the novel in translation, but if I'm understanding you correctly that's part of what you're trying to do for the contemporary Hebrew reader as well, so could you say a word about what the contemporary Hebrew reader encounters in Agnon, and how your editions aim to accomplish that for the contemporary Hebrew audience.

AH: For example, it became clear to me, while working on this book, that to enter the world of Second Aliyah Jaffa and Jerusalem today's readers need maps, pictures, and perhaps especially music. Agnon's works are full of music, and all kinds of sounds. I have a file called "*Kolot T'mol Shilshom*" [Sounds of *Only Yesterday*], and I could have done the same thing for Hakhnasat Kallah but the technology wasn't as advanced back when I worked on that book. Remember, *T'mol Shilshom* takes place from 1908 through 1911, when Tel Aviv is just beginning to be built. Our maps will have to leave out most of Tel Aviv (which consisted of only a few houses, just being built), and center on Yaffo, although only certain streets in Yaffo. Yerushalayim is not the contemporary city we know; only certain streets and neighborhoods existed, and we have to map them to understand the dog Balak's journeys around town.

JS: So by way of example, and we planned this out in advance, there is a central passage at the beginning of the third book of *T'mol Shilshom* when Yitzḥak is returning by wagon from Jaffa back to Jerusalem. I'll read it, or adapt it from the English translation, and you can comment, or "orally annotate," as we go along [*Only Yesterday*, 378–79]:

> One of the passengers said to the carter, Perhaps, Reb Zundl, you can sing something by Bezalel Hazzan . . .

AH: One mistake: His name should be pronounced *Zindl!* I won't keep interrupting, but it's important to appreciate the language, or the tension in

Agnon between modern Hebrew and the Hebrew that he wanted to evoke. *T'mol Shilshom* is set in the early twentieth century—it's a different country (and a different language) than the State of Israel today. It's a different place. Agnon was part of that. He came in 1908. I almost think I know the ship in which he came, and I am looking for a picture of that ship because if it wasn't that ship it was a similar ship. How did he get there? How does one travel through Galicia to Trieste and the Mediterranean Sea? . . .

JS: You can see why the project has been going on for 25 years! (*Laughter*) That's the note on having read only half a sentence! So one of the passengers said: "Perhaps you can sing something by Bezalel Hazzan?"

AH: I'm going to interrupt you again because I wanted to question one thing that occupies me many times over. Was this person an historical figure? Did he live? Is this his name? Do we have pictures? Because if we have a picture, I think the picture ought to appear in my volume. But right now, we have this strange wagon-driver, called in the awkward English translation a "carter"—but he's a *Balagole*—I should say *Balagoole*, but OK. At this point more than halfway into the novel Yitzḥak is finally coming around to Sefaradit. The wagon has already entered the outskirts of Jerusalem. Who are the primary settlers there? The original ones were Sefaradim and Litvaks! And if you were a Galitzianer you were an outsider. And nothing helped you unless you changed your Hebrew and Yiddish pronunciation. You have to be Litvish. Agnon always felt like an outsider because of his accent.

JS: Moving on:

One of the passengers said to the carter, Perhaps, Reb *Zindl* you can sing something by Bezalel Hazzan, like, *Then all shall come to serve You* [*Veye'esoyu kol lovdecho*].[5] The carter laughed and said, I knew you would call me Zindl, but Zindl isn't my name, my name is Avreml. The man said to him, Didn't I hear them calling you Zindl? Said he, They call me Zindl because my younger brother was named Abraham after me.

I'll skip to the end:

And now you want me to sing you Bezalel Hazzan's *Then all shall come to serve You* [*Veye'esoyu kol lovdecho*]. That, my friend, is impossible, for once I was traveling on the road and I started singing *Then all shall come to serve You*, and the horses started quaking and shaking and jumping and leaping until their yoke came undone to serve the Holy One Himself. You

---

5. A piyyut (liturgical poem) of great antiquity, recited as part of Rosh Ha'Shanah Musaf.

think I'm telling you made-up things. The God's honest truth I'm telling you, just as my name is Avreml and not Zindl.[6]

AH: And now I can tell you that this is a real person and a real tune. I propose that this hazzan was one Bezalel Shulsinger—and that's a great name for a *hazzan*, or perhaps, of course, that's how he got his family name. He was born in Uman, lived 1779–1873, was also known as Bezalel Odesser as he served as the *hazzan* in Odessa for many years before moving to Jerusalem. His tunes gained great popularity and were widely disseminated by his students and followers. We even have a photograph of him. Now my next chore is to discover exactly which tune to this piyut *Then all shall come to serve You* [*Veye'esoyu kol lovdecho*], which is a centerpiece of the service on *Yamim Noraim*, was composed by Bezalel. There is one tune which is fairly well known and still widely sung which I suspect is the very version of Bezalel Hazzan that Agnon is referencing. It is recorded in different versions but I recommend a recording by Vizhnitzer hasidim which we uploaded to YouTube.[7] The description of the tune as causing the horses to start "quaking and shaking and jumping and leaping until their yoke came undone to serve the Holy One Himself" is perfectly imaginable when you listen to the *niggun*. You sing along and the horses gallop right off the page!

JS: Before we turn our attention back to another piece of what certain academics call the realia—a major agenda, a major aspect of the annotation is to uncover or to reveal, or to simply cite the very many sources in *Tanakh*, in the Talmud and rabbinic literature, in a variety of works from every layer of Jewish literature and every corner of the Jewish bookshelf, that Agnon is directly or indirectly referencing, or working in echoes of, or is subverting in the text. And just the simple act of footnoting every Gemara and every Midrash and every line from the prayerbook is a major effort and part of the work. And presumably between the original work starting back in the 1980s to the current work at hand that's changed slightly. We know that you're a little, how shall we say it, Luddite, technophobic, but nevertheless all this has been made easier with the advent of the many digital resources, searchable databases, etc. But here we get to a very interesting question about the work of annotation as interpretation. Because these are not mere footnote references to specific chapter and verse; the very act of annotating is also an act of interpreting, because Agnon is doing different things when he's citing a variety of sources.

6. Agnon, *Only Yesterday*, 378–79.
7. Available at https://youtu.be/EGTONe-SIYw.

AH: Correct

JS: Sometimes he's merely borrowing, and we've all encountered this in different aspects of Agnon scholarship. Someone will identify a particular source that Agnon is clearly echoing or riffing off of. In some cases, people will identify a reference to something and will try to build a whole mountain of interpretation based upon their "find." But the reader or another scholar may think they're making a mountain out of a molehill. And sometimes a reference is just a reference, as Sigmund told us; sometimes Agnon's just borrowing a turn of phrase for its rhythm, its cadence. He's not trying to do the kind of intertextual bridge building, although often he is doing precisely that. When he does, sometimes he's doing it to draw your attention to a passage in *Tanakh*, so that the reader will consider the Jerusalem of *Tehillah* relative to Jeremiah's Jerusalem. In other cases, he'll build in a reference which serves as an intertextual key to unlocking the entire story or as an axis for interpretation. For example, the reference between the lines to a Rashi in Ta'anit 8a, which references a folktale of the "weasel and the well." Identifying that reference, one can then begin to unlock something underneath it and between the rabbinic and Agnonian text. On other occasions Agnon is quoting a source subversively, ironically. And it's not always clear to the reader, and readers of good conscience can debate what he's doing in any one place. How do you see the act of annotating the source work, not the realia, not knowing how much this kopek was worth, or the distance between this shtetl and that village, but the source work annotation? How do you view that as an act of interpretation for the reader?

AH: A perfect example of this is the presence of rabies in *T'mol Shilshom*. Of course, we all remember the character of the dog Balak, a very controversial figure, but a very obviously central figure in the novel. For some scholars and critics, he's perhaps more important than Yitzḥak Kummer himself, the human protagonist. Throughout the book Agnon never uses the word *kalevet*, the modern word for rabies. This has led some people to false conclusions about what is going on in the plot. Rather, Agnon assumes that every Hebrew reader would know that a *kelev shoteh* is a rabid dog. What he does is to reference a passage in Yoma (83b) of what a rabid dog, a *kelev shoteh* in the Mishnah's language, looks like:

Our Rabbis taught: Five things were mentioned in connection with a mad dog [*kelev shoteh*]. Its mouth is open, its saliva dripping, its ears flap, its tail is hanging between its thighs, it walks on the edge of the road. Some say: Also it barks without its voice being heard.

Agnon doesn't have to tell us that the dog is affected by *kalevet*, we know it from his borrowing of the Talmudic symptoms:

> Balak enters Meah Shearim walking on the sides of the roads and his mouth gapes open and his saliva drools and his ears droop and his tail is between his legs and his eyes are bloodshot and he barks and his voice isn't heard. He stood still and cleansed his body of the forbidden food in it. He folded two of his legs beneath him and sat on them in the style of an Ishmaelite and put out his tongue and breathed like a blacksmith's bellows and looked all around and didn't see a living soul, for Meah Shearim was gathered inside to hear Rabbi Grunam.[8]

So, in this case, the unmentioned Talmudic text gives us the key to understanding the description. But here I will expand on this a little bit. Earlier in the book, there are various descriptions of Balak smelling and sniffing things, as dogs do. Professor Alexandra Horowitz, a researcher of animal cognition at Barnard College, has just published *Being a Dog: Following the Dog into a World of Smell*,[9] a follow-up to an earlier book called *Inside of a Dog: What Dogs See, Smell, and Know* (2009). The description of Balak's journeys, led by his nose, from the tip of his sniffing nose to his wagging tail, are described scientifically in Horowitz's books. Agnon got the description down perfectly. Horowitz describes it as "There is no such thing as 'fresh air' to a dog. Air is rich: an olfactory tangle that the dog's nose will diligently unknot."

At any rate, as we know Yitzḥak Kummer becomes a painter and he has this nudnik dog sniffing around, the dog that keeps getting in his way. So he chases the dog off but Balak keeps returning to him. Then, in the pivotal moment in the novel, Yitzḥak does something with the paint, it's not exactly what he does with the paint but the paint, on its own somehow, drips and writes on the back of the dog: *Kelev meshuga!* Now that's not a Hebrew phrase exactly, but Yiddish: *A meshiginne hint*, a mad dog. Agnon is making a comment about the Jews in Meah Shearim who are Torah scholars, but Yiddish-speaking ones. Had Yitzḥak written "kelev shoteh" they would have understood it as *A kelev shoyteh*, a "foolish dog." Agnon did not want them to miss the point that this is a rabid dog, so he writes *kelev meshuga*, which all Yiddish speakers understand as a rabid dog.

---

8. Agnon, *Only Yesterday*, 618.
9. Horowitz, *Being a Dog*, 29.

JS: Or they react to Balak as if he's a rabid dog, which he is not actually yet at this point in the story. Perhaps he becomes rabid through the "incantation" now inscribed on his skin.

AH: That's right. But without the Yiddish echo they wouldn't understand what's the big deal with a "silly dog." But once the dog is marked by what they would have understood as a rabid dog, they run away from it. Everyone that is except for Yitzḥak, who ultimately gets bitten by Balak once he really has become rabid, with the tragic consequences at the end of the novel.

At any rate, one of my editors at Schocken serves another purpose as the "common reader." She keeps an eye out to let me know what we can assume the average Hebrew reader, the common, regular reader in Israel, will or will not understand about the text, and this was one of the examples.

JS: What contemporary readers don't know is, unfortunately, often quite shocking.

AH: Absolutely. But to go back a moment to the comparison of the description of a rabid dog with the passage in Yoma, Agnon sneaks in a symptom which does not appear in the Talmud. He writes that Balak's *einav tosesot dam*, his eyes are bloody ("bloodshot" in the English edition). That does not appear in the Talmudic description. That made its way in from another source. Agnon's daughter, Emunah Yaron mentions in her memoirs, *Perakim MeḤayyai*, that when Agnon wrote about any animal, he consulted a book by Alfred Brehm for specific information, and Agnon consulted veterinary manuals that describe rabies and accounts of cases of rabies epidemics in Palestine.[10] Some of these materials are still in his library at the Agnon House. Emunah Yaron's reference to Brehm led me to the popular German encyclopedic twelve-volume *Tierleben* (published in English as *Life of Animals*). Parenthetically, both the German and the English version of Brehm's work are available online in their entirety. Brehm concludes the detailed section on the dog with a description of rabies, in which he states that in the advanced stages of the disease "the eyes [of rabid dogs] become red and inflamed."[11] This, I suggest is the source for Balak's bloody or bloodshot eyes. Here, Agnon drew upon other sources, and seamlessly wove this detail into the Talmudic description of a rabid dog.

---

10. Yaron, *Perakim MeḤayyai*, 62.
11. Volume 2, page 108 in the original German; volume 2, page 213 in the English.

JS: Before we conclude I want to ask just one last question. Part of my own first encounter with *Hakhnasat Kallah* was through using, and being aided by, your work. On my maiden voyage through the novel as a novel, I relied on your book. I didn't read the novel with your annotations in hand but used it as a reference on the side. As a reader, once one starts to go down the annotation rabbit hole it becomes hard to enjoy the novel, to let the words of the prose enter you without constantly stopping and starting. But part of that encounter with *Hakhnasat Kallah,* through your work, was that it's a time machine. It helps us bridge the chasm that really does exist between us in the twenty-first century and the world Agnon describes of the nineteenth century. We stand at a great remove from the events described. And part of the achievement of your work, and part of the benefit of encountering Agnon through the works of Avraham Holtz is the wormhole that we're allowed to get back to that world, and now hopefully soon the world of the Seond Aliyah in *T'mol Shilshom.* Since we're talking today about *Sippurei Eretz Yisrael*, give us one insight, one small little nugget, briefly, of something that you have uncovered that opened up a window to what it meant to be a young man coming to Yaffo or to Yerushalayim in 1908.

AH: It's useful to follow Yitzḥak Kummer's journey from Galicia to Yaffo. Yitzḥak is certainly not an autobiographical projection of Agnon (in the way that the character Hemdat is), but there are places and dates that align between the fictitious character and the autobiography of his creator (or at least the partially fictionalized autobiography Agnon put forth). Let's assume that he arrived in Yaffo on Lag B'Omer 1908. He meets a person who fools him initially, the owner of some type of inn in Yaffo. There's an extremely significant Hebrew volume by Gur Alroey called *Immigrantim* (Jerusalem: Yad Ben Zvi, 2004). Every chapter presents a historical study of an aspect of what it meant to be an immigrant to *Eretz Yisrael*—what each wave of immigrants encountered, the people and places. Often the immigrants were taken advantage of by those already established locals who were out to swindle them of their money. It's a real portrait of some very unpleasant people and unpleasant times, fraught with problems. So, what Yitzḥak Kummer encounters in that world, first of all, is the sense of being an immigrant, a new-comer in the Land of Israel. When he's on the ship at sea, before arriving, Yitzḥak has the naiveté to mention that, although he has no family in *Eretz Yisrael*, it's all right because *Kol Yisrael haverim*, the whole Jewish people is like one extended family. Well, the response to that from an older and wiser person is: yes, yes, that's wonderful, but that's what you say on *Shabbes Mevorchim (laughter)*, as an aspirational prayer, but he better brace himself for the realities of the here and now. Yitzḥak remembers this and it echoes again later when he encounters just such harsh realities. Little did he know at the time of the ship voyage that the older man is the grandfather of the woman he will ultimately marry. At any rate, that's part of the beauty of the story. The insight of the immigrant experience as depicted by Agnon, something of course with which he had personal experience, can really be heightened through some knowledge of the historical reality depicted. Among the charms of Alroey's book is that he prefaces each chapter with a quote from, what else, Agnon's *T'mol Shilshom*, and cites Agnon frequently in the book.[12]

JS: We have to end. We could stay here talking all day, but that would prevent you from writing another ten annotations and completing the task before you—and we can't afford that delay!

Bibliography

Agnon, S.Y. *Hakhnasat Kallah*. Tel Aviv: Schocken, 1995.

———. *Only Yesterday*. Translated by B. Harshav. Princeton: Princeton University Press, 2000.

Alroey, Gur. *Immigrantim*. Jerusalem: Yad Ben Zvi, 2004.

———. *An Unpromising Land: Jewish Migration to Palestine in the Early Twentieth Century*. Stanford: Stanford University Press, 2014.

Brehm, Alfred Edmund, Oskar Boettger, Wilhelm Haacke, Eduard Pechuël-Loesche, W. Marshall, Eduard Oskar Schmidt, and Ernst Ludwig Taschenberg. *Brehms Tierleben. Allgemeine Kunde des Tierreichs*. 3rd ed. Leipzig: Bibliographisches Institut, 1890–1893.

Brehm, Alfred Edmund. *Brehm's Life of Animals: A Complete Natural History for Popular Home Instruction and for the Use of Schools*. Translated by Wilhelm Haacke and Eduard Pechuël-Loesche. Chicago: Marquis, 1895. Vol. II, 213.

Gifford, Don, and Robert J. Seidman. *Ulysses Annotated: Notes for James Joyce's Ulysses*. Berkeley: University of California Press, 1988; 2nd exp. ed., 2008.

Holtz, Abraham, and S.Y. Agnon. *Ma'aseh Reb Yudil Hasid*. New York: Jewish Theological Seminary, 1986.

Interview with Abraham Holtz. *Yated HaShavuah*, 18 Tammuz 5756 / July 5, 1996, 15.

Horowitz, Alexandra. *Being a Dog: Following the Dog into a World of Smell*. New York: Scribner, 2016.

12. An expanded, English edition of Alroey's book was published as *An Unpromising Land: Jewish Migration to Palestine in the Early Twentieth Century*.

———. *Inside of a Dog: What Dogs See, Smell, and Know.* New York: Scribner, 2009.
Kirsch, Adam. "Pilgrim's Progress." *Tablet Magazine,* September 27, 2011.
Mikraot Gedolot. Berlin: Schocken, 1937.
Yaron, Emunah. *Perakim MeḤayyai.* Tel Aviv: Schocken, 2005.

6

Hometown and Homeland

The Dialectic between *Eretz Yisrael* and Buczacz in Agnon's Late Works

Alan Mintz*

It is wonderful to be here at Yeshiva University, and it is fitting to have an Agnon conference here. We in America have a long history with Agnon, and a lot of the important Agnon scholarship has been done here on these shores by the likes of Arnold Band, Avraham Holtz, the late Shmuel Leiter and others. There are many ways in which, I think, in the future, Agnon readers will be Americans. In part, because for us Agnon's work serves as

---

* Alan Mintz ז״ל, professor at the Jewish Theological Seminary, was one of the preeminent scholars of Hebrew literature in general, and Agnon specifically. His final scholarly products before his untimely death in May 2017 were a critical edition in English of Agnon's *A City in Its Fullness* (co-edited with Jeffrey Saks) and his monumental study, *Ancestral Tales: Reading the Buczacz Stories of S.Y. Agnon* (Stanford: Stanford University Press), which was published just days before Professor Mintz's passing. The present essay draws on elements of *Ancestral Tales* and was delivered as a conference paper at Yeshiva University in November 2016. We have intentionally retained the feel of the oral presentation in this written essay, which was prepared from the transcript of that talk by Alan's former doctoral student, Dr. Beverly Bailis, who currently teaches Hebrew and Modern Jewish Literature at Brooklyn College as a Visiting Scholar.

a living bridge between the world of tradition and the world of modernity. These are issues that are very much alive for us here.

In Israel, unfortunately, a lot of the resonance of religious life for secular Jews has been kind of poisoned by the *Rabbanut*, the chief rabbinate, and official religion, and the fact that you have to read Agnon for the *Bagrut*, Israel's high school matriculation examination, just the way in which you have to read Shakespeare. So, if you speak to an average Israeli, a literate, young Israeli today, and you ask about Agnon, he or she might respond, "Oh, we had to read that story *Tehilla*," or something like that. The act of reading Agnon carries with it a kind of burden that we do not suffer from here. Again, I think that in the future, whether in Hebrew or in the gathering body of Agnon's work in English translation, American Jews will be uniquely positioned to understand Agnon and to help Agnon continue in the world of Jewish letters.

My goal today is to reflect on the relationship between *Eretz Yisrael* and the world of Eastern European Jewry. I came to this because I have been working for many years on the body of stories that Agnon turned himself toward in the last fifteen years of his life. In the mid-1950s through the '60s, until his death in 1970, he began to write stories about his Galician hometown, Buczacz. Many of the stories were published in *Haaretz*, but also in many other publications. About half of them were published during his lifetime, and then the rest after his death. The second of the posthumous volumes, entitled *'Ir uMelo'ah, A City in Its Fullness*, was published in 1973 with the editorial guidelines given to his daughter, Emunah Yaron.

We have something that is interesting here, namely, why does Agnon, beginning in the mid-'50s, turn his attention to the enterprise of writing about Eastern Europe? He does not depict Buczacz during the years of his childhood or even within the personal memories of his family. Rather, he writes about the eighteenth century. He begins in the seventeenth century, in the generation after the Khmelnitski pogroms, and goes to the mid-nineteenth century, around the time when the Jews of Galicia received the vote, together with other minorities within the Austrian Empire. We are speaking about early modern times, which encompassed the beginnings of the Haskalah, but came before the upsurge in various ideologies, including socialism, Zionism, and the rise of assimilation. Agnon chose in the last period of his life to write about what we might call the classical period of Polish Jewry, and to center it on one town, his Buczacz. He had treated

Buczacz in many other ways before, and I will get to that in a moment. The question then arises, what does this body of work mean?

First, I want to begin with an earlier period, with Agnon's major novel, *A Guest for the Night*, which was first published serially in 1938–39 in *Haaretz*, right on the eve of World War II. The novel is based on the kernel of an actual "homecoming" visit Agnon made for a number of days in the summer of 1930. The narrating "Guest," a figure very much like Agnon, named Shmuel Yosef, returns to his hometown and spends almost a year there, for various motives we will discuss in a moment. He calls the town Shibush rather than Buczacz. Shibush means error or mistake and it is a play on words, obviously, of Buczacz. It is the last of Agnon's major dealings with Buczacz before the war.

Prior to *A Guest for the Night*, many other works were also set in Buczacz, such as *A Simple Story*, set prior to World War I. Likewise, while Buczacz is not a focus in *The Bridal Canopy*, it takes place in the milieu of Galicia around the time of the Napoleonic Wars. There is also the novella "In the Heart of the Seas," which is about an *Aliyah* from Buczacz to *Eretz Yisrael* on the part of a group of hasidim in the nineteenth century.

I suppose that *Guest for the Night*, though, is really the swan song. It is a reckoning with the world of Buczacz, in which a middle-aged Hebrew writer from *Eretz Yisrael* comes to spend time in his hometown, and his motives are two-fold. Initially, he is hoping to reignite some kind of spiritual life in this town. The town has been the victim of what he calls the *hurban rishon*, or "first destruction," that designates World War I, which for Galicia was truly a decimation. Every character in the novel is injured and maimed and broken in some way, while the *beit midrash*, the study house, stands abandoned.

The novel's protagonist arrives with a little money. He heats the *beit midrash*, gets a fire going there, and during the winter, he succeeds in getting people to come back to it. He gives *shiurim*, lectures on the traditional texts, and so forth, but this endeavor fails. He cannot reignite the metaphorical fire or the warmth of the *beit midrash*, and must acknowledge over the time of his stay in Buczacz that he was there for his own purposes. He was there in order to understand his own childhood, in order to bring back into his own life the world of Buczacz from which he had departed a long time ago. He left when he was twenty years old, and he essentially never came back. He made two very brief visits, but that was all. He was in *Eretz Yisrael*, and then in Germany for twelve years, and then he returned to

Jerusalem. It is a reckoning for him, and he has to recognize also that he cannot return Buczacz to himself.

There is therefore a great sense of failure: the world of East European Jewry represented by Buczacz is slipping away; it is depicted as something irretrievable. Yet, in the last pages of the book, there is a palpable connection between Buczacz and *Eretz Yisrael* that becomes manifest through the symbol of the key to the *beit midrash*.[2]

The protagonist, Shmuel Yosef, has the key. It is the key to the *beit midrash*, and he loses it. However, when he gets back to Jerusalem, his wife finds it in a crack of one of his valises. He puts it in a box and takes the key to the box and hangs it around his neck. He then evokes the statement in Megillah 29a: "In the future, the synagogues and the study halls in Babylonia will be transported and reestablished in *Eretz Yisrael*."[3]

The synagogues and the study houses of the diaspora will eventually be transported, fixed, or replanted in *Eretz Yisrael*, and this is the consolation that forms a kind of coda for this epic novel.

In many ways, though, the novel suggests a leave-taking. It is a leave-taking on the eve of the Holocaust from the world of Buczacz, which has already been decimated through World War I, and that is where it rests. In this sense, we have to put that valedictory parting from Eastern Europe, from Buczacz, next to the revived wave of creativity involved in the Buczacz stories that Agnon is writing in the mid-1950s, and that consists of about 140 stories, some very long, some very short. The volume *A City in Its Fullness* is 737 pages in Hebrew, so this is a work which is quite formidable. Yet, it was something that even close readers of Agnon did not quite fathom while it was happening, because the stories were published here and there, and there were other things that he was writing and projects he was

---

2. Yael Feldman has written very eloquently about the image of the key in her essay, "How Does a Convention Mean? A Semiotic Reading of Agnon's Bilingual Key-Irony in *A Guest for the Night*," 253–69.

3. The larger passage from which this line is taken reads: "Rabbi Elazar HaKappar says: In the future, the synagogues and the study halls in Babylonia will be transported and reestablished in *Eretz Yisrael*, as it is stated: 'Surely, like Tabor among the mountains, and like Carmel by the sea, so shall He come' (Jeremiah 46:18). There is a tradition that these mountains came to Sinai at the giving of the Torah and demanded that the Torah should be given upon them. And are these matters not inferred through an a fortiori argument: Just as Tabor and Carmel, which came only momentarily to study Torah, were relocated and established in *Eretz Yisrael* in reward for their actions, all the more so should the synagogues and study halls in Babylonia, in which the Torah is read and disseminated, be relocated to *Eretz Yisrael*."

bringing to completion. It was not possible until later to truly appreciate how much of his attention was turned in this direction.

Even when the stories were being published, there was very little attention given to them, because in the midst of the 1950s and '60s, a period that was preoccupied with state building, the ingathering of the exiles, national security issues and so forth, to be reading about the *alter heim* was just not of interest to most Israelis. He had to give material to the Schocken family for *Haaretz*, and I am sure this is not the material they wanted. They wanted stories about *Eretz Yisrael*, about the holidays and so forth. Even when these stories were gathered and published in 1973, the book was largely overlooked (especially as it had the bad fortune of appearing on the eve of the Yom Kippur War).

Even within the Agnon oeuvre, the first publication of the posthumous volumes was the novel *Shira*, which totally captured the imagination of the reading public. They were waiting for it because it contained a lot of great gossip about Hebrew University professors and German emigres. People's appetite had been whetted and he was waiting to publish it because it was a roman à clef. Conversely, when *A City in Its Fullness* came out shortly afterwards, it just lay there, in part because many of the wonderful stories are set amidst a lot of seemingly ethnographic material about rituals and customs of various sorts. So even for people who are dedicated Agnon readers, this is somewhat of an unknown continent, requiring a shift of our interest to Eastern Europe to hold our attention.

When turning to this body of work, I would like to present the notion that Agnon's producing this corpus of stories about Eastern Europe constitutes a very weighty assessment or critique of Ben-Gurion's political Zionism. It is not about the enterprise of *Eretz Yisrael* as a metaphysical entity, but it is a statement that essentially says that the institution that is being built through political Zionism is deficient in significant ways. It is presented as cut off from the roots of Eastern Europe Jewry because the state has constituted itself as a radical discontinuity, rather than a perpetuation of a grand or golden tradition, which is not just about religious observance, but something much larger. It has to do with the life of Eastern Europe. It has to do with the two pillars that Agnon reimagines Buczacz around, which are based on the key concepts of "Torah study and synagogue worship," or in the traditional formulation: *'al haTorah ve'al haAvodah*. The degree of animosity of the state toward those enterprises were pushing them into the corner of some kind of institutionalized status quo, resulting in an inherent limitation to the fullness of the state, if it cannot connect to these sources. Likewise, as we will see, there is a critique of Buczacz, as well.

I want to read a few texts with you. The first is the foundational text, a myth of origins, about Buczacz. It is the first story that appears, after the epigraph or motto, in *A City in Its Fullness*. This story is very different from the rest of the collection. The rest of the stories move from depictions of life under the Polish nobles, before the partition, to the many differences after 1772, when Galicia is created as an entity, as a province of the Austrian Empire.

This story, however, is written in a kind of biblical haze, as a foundation myth, which is on almost every point totally historically mistaken, but all the more interesting because of its aspirations. What I am interested in here is the fact that the founding of Buczacz is conceived of as a failed *Aliyah*, an arrested ascent to *Eretz Yisrael*, and the very spot on which it is arrested is precisely where the city is built and where Buczacz will be established. It is founded upon an aspiration which fails because of its naiveté. Agnon devotes this book to Buczacz, but this gigantic enterprise rests upon a foundation which is, for lack of a better word, aspirational, but with failure embedded in it as well. So, let me just read a little bit here at the beginning:

> When was our city founded, and who was its founder? Long have all the chroniclers labored to find this out in vain. But some few facts have been revealed to us, and I am herewith setting down a faithful record of all I know.[4]

In this passage, the origins of the town are lost in the haze of myth. The historians, he maintains, really do not know what happened. The narrator claims to know a little bit and he will tell you the little bit of truthful information that he knows. Here is the nub of it:

> There once was a band of Jews who were moved by their own pure hearts to go up to the Land of Israel, together with their wives and their sons and daughters. They sold their fields, their vineyards, their male and female servants, their houses, and all their property that could not be transported. They obtained permission from the authorities to leave their city. They purchased provisions and set forth on the road.[5]

---

4. Agnon, "Buczacz" in *A City in Its Fullness*, 31.
5. Agnon, "Buczacz" in *A City in Its Fullness*, 31.

In the beginning there was an aspiration. This caravan of Jews decided that they wanted to go to *Eretz Yisrael* and they proceed to do just this. They sold all their belongings and all their appurtenances, and they just set out for the road. The problem arrives in the next sentence:

> They did not know the road to the Land of Israel, nor did anyone they met along the way know where the Land of Israel was. They only knew that it was in the East . . .

They know that *Eretz Yisrael* is in the east, and they just set east. The assumption here is they are setting forth from the ancient Jewish communities of the Rhineland Valley. (For the storytelling purposes it does not concern Agnon that this seems to have been historically untrue: The first Jewish residents of Buczacz were immigrants from Poland.) In his construal of the story these are Jews from the great Ashkenaz, and they set out east. The story then relates how they began their journey, and how they keep asking people where *Eretz Yisrael* is. The peasants they come across, if they had ever heard of *Eretz Yisrael*, assume it is in heaven, and not a territorial location. They keep going and they keep going. They set out right after Passover when the roads are open, and they continue until it gets to be cold and they cannot go any further and they have to set up camp.

They camp out in a place which is full of wonderful forests and beautiful ponds, and they happen to meet a party of Polish nobles who are out hunting. This place is, according to this story, uninhabited. There are no indigenous residents. We know that, of course, the Ruthenian Ukrainians were there, but in the story this region is depicted more like how Palestine was imagined as a "land without a people." The nobles invite them to come back to their estates and spend the winter with them, which they do, on a provisional basis. They plan to stay just for this one season, because it is too cold to travel. They had not really considered what it would take to get through the winter. They should have gone south to Trieste and taken a boat, but the lack of any kind of worldliness or practicality is what makes their *Aliyah* impossible.

They reside with the Polish lords and they bring a great deal of prosperity. When their temporary residence turns more permanent, they decide they need to create a sense of community, so on Mondays and Thursdays they all gather to read the Torah. Then, when the holidays come, they have an encampment for the Days of Awe, and then it becomes hard to depart after Sukkot, at the end of the High Holiday period when autumn turns once again to winter.

Finally, they build a synagogue, and around it the town. It is the Jews who build it, and then the nobles give them a charter, since it is in the nobles' interests that they remain, and that becomes the city of Buczacz. Yet, there remains a sense of regret:

> It would have been better if they had not *given in* to the noblemen and had gone their way right after the snow had cleared and were now settled before the Lord in Jerusalem; but having *yielded* and not made the pilgrimage, they now had to take active steps to enable themselves to perform all the rites of God that we are commanded to perform.[6]

The keyword here, which appears twice in the Hebrew original, *nitpatu* (translated here as "given in," and then as "yielded") carries with it the sense of "being seduced." In other words, they allowed themselves to be drawn into the comfort of being able to stay out the winter, the comfort of having their needs provided for, of being of use as administrators, farmers, and shopkeepers to the Polish nobles. Rather than remaining steadfast in their resolve to go to *Eretz Yisrael*, they settled there. And, *since* they settled there, they had to build the institutions of a community and Jewish life grew up around that.

But my focus here is on the motif of *nitpatu*, that they had "compromised" with themselves, or "given in." They had allowed themselves to be persuaded. There was a failure of nerve, and it is upon that compromise with their needs and with reality, and the practical things that are pointed to in the story, such as the vulnerability of pregnant women and older people, that constitutes the reason for not going to *Eretz Yisrael*. Instead, they built a Jewish community, and the stories that follow, and the book as a whole, is a tribute to a fully functioning Jewish community, with a self-governing city-state, based on the norms of study and worship. The stories depict many deviations from those norms, and life with an uncomfortable relationship to various governing authorities, but nonetheless an organic Jewish community is formed, and it fulfills its vocation of serving the Lord, studying His texts and living a good life. That is the story of Buczacz.

The question that arises here is, namely, why do you need a Jewish state in the modern world if we once had places like Buczacz? To what degree was Buczacz insufficient as an example of a Jewish polity? I use the word polity here because I think even in this historical situation, each of these different towns around Eastern Europe, was, in a sense, a kind

---

6. Agnon, "Buczacz" in *A City in Its Fullness*, 35, italics added.

of independent polis. Around them were many villages which took their directions from the rabbinic authority of that town, a kind of regional rabbinic authority. What we have here, then, are Jews living an autonomous Jewish life. Before the partition of Poland, the Polish nobles gave a great deal of autonomy to the *Kahal,* the governing council of a town or city. Most problems were resolved internally through Jewish courts. If this is the case, then, what is wrong with this picture? Why is this not the ideal?

In order to address these questions, I will turn to another story, a 90-page novella, entitled "In Search of a Rabbi, or The Governor's Whim." *A City in Its Fullness* is organized into different books, and this novella appears at the beginning of the second book, which introduces the question of rabbinic leadership. In this novella, Buczacz, which views itself as a very important Jewish metropolis, is in fact presented as a third-rate Jewish community. It is full of Torah, but it does not have enough money to attract the kinds of rabbis that it deserves. The chronicle details how it once had a great rabbi, lost the rabbi to another town, and how other rabbis keep getting stolen by up-and-coming nouveau riche cities like Stanislaw and other places. While Buczacz produces great rabbis, only to have them "kidnapped" by other communities, they are so proud that they will not appoint a rabbi if they cannot find somebody who is equal to their own (perhaps inflated) self-image so they suffer long periods without a rabbi.

This novella begins with an historical prologue, in which Agnon references the Council of the Four Lands. In the Lithuanian-Polish commonwealth, the communities were essentially independent city-states, but there was a larger structure that would meet twice a year at the great commercial fairs to deal with more global issues and policy. This included mostly Rabbinic sages, but also educated laymen. It was disbanded by the Polish state a few years before the conquest of Poland and its division in 1772. Agnon's depiction of the Council reads as a kind of encomium or elegy for this time:

> Shortly after the passing of our Rabbi, the glory was exiled from the Jewish people and Polish Jewry's mighty scepter was shattered with the disbanding of the Council of Four Lands which would meet twice a year at the fairs. These fairs drew myriad, noble merchants from throughout the land, and the rabbis and lay-leaders would gather to consider the affairs of the community, seeking counsel on Jewish affairs, and establishing decrees and ordinances according to the needs of the time and place, so that all should

walk in the good path, and perform righteousness and justice in the eyes of God and fellow man.[7]

The passage goes on to explain that, as opposed to other nations that have sovereign structures and power, the only power which the Jews possess is *koah haTorah*, "the power of Torah," and, nevertheless, they are able to "formulate and promulgate decrees and ordinances" because they are "accepted by the entire people like the edicts of kings." In contrast, with an earthly king, while he makes edicts, nevertheless people disregard them and rebel against them. Yet, in the case of Israel, they accepted the validity and the power of the legislation of the Council as if it were the Sanhedrin in the Temple. Ultimately, though, came the end of the existence of the Polish commonwealth. The ruler saw fit to cancel the Councils, and look what happened:

> Stanislav August [1732–1798; last king of Poland] arose and disbanded the Council of Four Lands which had existed for two hundred years. But the land itself was torn from Poland. Poland disbanded the Council, and God Himself sent three other cruel nations [Russia, Prussia and Austria] and disbanded the Polish kingdom.[8]

I want to conclude by putting this in the framework of the problem we have raised. On the one hand, as mentioned above, writing in the 1950s and 1960s, Agnon is in dialogue with the nativist Zionism of Ben-Gurion and those of his generation who saw the establishment of Israel as a "victory over the Exile, which was conceived of as a gentile-ridden and shame inducing aberration that made Jews dependent for survival upon the obfuscations of religion."[9] Against this view, Agnon presents Buczacz, and other independent, autonomous Jewish city-states, as a highly evolved corporate organism that "deployed a politics appropriate to the challenges that faced it and, in the best of times, maintained a balance between this-worldliness and religious culture."[10] Yet, if Buczacz in some way is exemplary or represents such kinds of autonomous Jewish communities, then why is it not ideal, and why does one still need a state? The problem, as depicted in the

---

7. *Ir uMeloah*, 316.
8. *Ir uMeloah*, 316.
9. Mintz, *Ancestral Tales*, 158.
10. Mintz, *Ancestral Tales*, 158. For more on Agnon's "embroiled dialogue with Zionist historiography," see the continuation of this discussion in *Ancestral Tales*, 158–59.

passage above, is that it did not have ultimate Jewish power. Such communities were capable of self-regulation once there was not a forced measure from above to disturb it. Once there was, things began to change. After the Polish partition in 1772, once the communities of Galicia came under Austrian rule, the sway of rabbinic law was greatly diminished.

To conclude, I titled my talk "The Dialectic between *Eretz Yisrael* and Buczacz" because I think that is what Agnon has in mind. This massive imaginative project of creating Buczacz was, in a sense, a critique of the insufficiency of political Zionism. During the years that Agnon was writing these stories, he corresponded with his great reader and critic, Baruch Kurzweil, who asked Agnon, "What are you working on these days?" and he responded by saying, "I am building a city."

If you consider this sentiment in relationship to Ben Gurion building a state, the State of Israel, which Agnon, as a religious Zionist certainly supported, then during this time, there was a kind of counterweight, where Agnon was building an imaginative world. He used the word *boneh*, "to build," and this use of language suggests not reconstruction or re-imagining, but rather, a type of creative work. It is primary work. In other words, the way that he recouped post-Holocaust Buczacz was to build it according to his likes. He employed the whole toolbox of modernism that he had brought to the process of writing to reimagine Polish Jewry through the lens of his world, and that creative endeavor was his contribution to a fuller dialectic between *Eretz Yisrael* and Buczacz.

Bibliography

Agnon, S.Y. *A City in Its Fullness*. Edited by Alan Mintz and Jeffrey Saks. New Milford, CT: Toby, 2016.
———. "A Guest for the Night." Tel Aviv: *Haaretz* 1938–39.
———. *Hakhnasat Kallah*. Tel Aviv: Schocken, 1931.
———. "In the Heart of the Seas." In *Two Scholars Who Were in Our Town and Other Novellas*. Edited by Jeffrey Saks. New Milford, CT: Toby, 2014.
———. *Ir uMeloah*. Tel Aviv: Schocken, 1973.
———. *Sipur Pashut*. Tel Aviv: Schocken, 1935.
Feldman, Yael. "How Does a Convention Mean? A Semiotic Reading of Agnon's Bilingual Key-Irony in *A Guest for the Night*." *Hebrew Union College Annual* 56 (1985) 253–69.
Mintz, Alan. *Ancestral Tales: Reading the Buczacz Stories of S.Y. Agnon*. Stanford: Stanford University Press, 2017.

7

"Always I Regarded Myself as One Who Was Born in Jerusalem"

Agnon's Nobel Speech in Light of Psalm 137

JEFFREY SAKS

IN 1966, THE NOBEL Prize for literature was awarded to S.Y. Agnon. This was a major event for the Jewish world at large and for Israel in particular. He was the first Israeli to win a Nobel in any field, and he is the only Hebrew-language author ever to have received the Nobel Prize in literature. In Israel, Agnon's award was viewed as a major diplomatic coup, and a ripe opportunity for the young state to gain attention as a cultural force on the world stage. Let us recall that the year 1966 is but a moment in historical memory from the Holocaust. As such, the prize was perceived as recognition not only of the Jewish people's physical survival of the smokestacks of Auschwitz but of its self-reconstitution as a sovereign nation—such an entity bests its enemies but no less develops a meaningful culture.

For Agnon, too, the Nobel Prize was an affirmation: of what Hebrew as a language of Jewish life, learning and literature had reached. Agnon had been a young "combatant" in the great Hebrew wars, joining the likes of Bialik and others often against Eliezer Ben-Yehuda. The battle concerned the existential state of the Hebrew language: was it to be revived, as the latter firmly held, or only reconstituted, as Agnon believed? In Agnon's view, Hebrew could not have been revived, because in order for something to be revived it first had to be dead, which as a language of prayer and scholarship it never was. It was precisely those sources of learning, and especially rabbinic Hebrew, that Agnon sought to distill and recast as modern literature.

Agnon's sense of self-worth has been well documented, as has his biting mock modesty. Upon notification of his award he declared, "To be able to write a single sentence properly in Hebrew is worth all the prizes in the world"—it may be safely said that he was happy to receive the Nobel Prize, an award which had been sought for decades. Significantly, at nearly eighty, Agnon was much older than the typical Nobel laureate in literature. The world expects at least one final piece of work from the recipient of a Nobel. Not so in Agnon's case. Although he was toying with *Shira* and with the stories that would become *A City in Its Fullness* and a few other unfinished pieces of business, his career was essentially over. And here he was in 1966, in his white tie and tails, Agnon and his wife and the king of Sweden.

It might be said with some certainty that the Swedish Academy had never met a laureate quite like Agnon. Upon hearing his or her name announced, the Nobel laureate is expected to walk to the podium, accept the prize, and shake hands with the king. That is the extent of the expected interaction: the recipient is then meant to return to his or her seat. Agnon, however, took the opportunity to engage in an extended discussion with King Gustav.[1] The king was a tall, lean man and Agnon rather short and stout; the king, being hard of hearing, leaned over to listen as Agnon chattered on and on. Later, during his speech, Agnon famously recited the blessing one recites in the presence of a king of flesh and blood. The significance and theatrics of the occasion were not lost on the Hebrew author.

Agnon shared the Nobel Prize with Nelly Sachs, a German Jewish poet who wrote lyrical poems about the Holocaust. The highly acclaimed author was not happy about the idea of sharing the prize with Sachs, whose work has not received a great deal of diffusion and who until today remains relatively unknown (the force of her verse not being well conveyed in translation). While there was precedent for the literature prize being divided, it is not common to do so, and in fact this was the last time it was done. The constitution of the Nobel Committee makes it clear that a shared prize does not indicate that the recipients are somehow "half worthy." Each recipient

1. Video footage at www.nobelprize.org.

of a shared Nobel Prize must be worthy of having received it on his or her own. Not infrequently, scientific research is conducted in collaboration with others, in which case a shared prize is well understood. In the field of literature, this sort of collaboration is markedly less frequent.

Unusual as it was, on the Stockholm stage, Ingvar Andersson of the Swedish Academy faced the two authors, Agnon and Sachs, and informed them, "This year's literary Prize goes to you both with equal honour for a literary production which records Israel's vicissitudes in our time and passes on its message to the peoples of the world." Turning to Agnon, he continued, "In your writing we meet once again the ancient unity between literature and science, as antiquity knew it. In one of your stories you say that some will no doubt read it as they read fairy tales, others will read it for edification.[2] Your great chronicle of the Jewish people's spirit and life has therefore a manifold message. For the historian it is a precious source, for the philosopher an inspiration, for those who cannot live without literature it is a mine of never-failing riches. We honour in you a combination of tradition and prophecy, of saga and wisdom." And he went on to say, "We honour you both this evening as the laurel-crowned heroes of intellectual creation and express our conviction that, in the words of Alfred Nobel, you have conferred the greatest benefit on mankind, and that you have given it clear-sightedness, wisdom, uplift, and beauty. A famous speech at a Nobel banquet—that of William Faulkner, held in this same hall sixteen years ago—contained an idea which he developed with great intensity. It is suitable as a concluding quotation which points to the future: 'I do not believe in the end of man.'"

Faulkner, the great author of the American South, created through words a wholly realized world, Yoknapatawpha County in Mississippi. This literary world recalls a southern Buczacz. In Agnon we meet a young man from Buczacz who leaves his hometown, almost never to return. But our protagonist never really leaves Buczacz at all—when he dies, an old man, he is still there in Buczacz, it is part of him. In like manner, Hannibal is part of Mark Twain, and Newark remains in Philip Roth. Faulkner uttered these lines when the ashes were still settling on Auschwitz. He was conveying the power of literature as a vivifying force—somehow culture can be nearly destroyed, and yet in the spring the buds will again emerge. In Agnon's writing this was the message broadcast in the shadow of the Holocaust in

---

2. The story which could be read as fairy tale or for edification is "In the Heart of the Seas" in S.Y. Agnon, *Two Scholars Who Were in Our Town and Other Novellas*, see at 156.

nowhere less than in the State of Israel and in no delivery system less significant than the ancient Hebrew language, which was now reawakening.

At this point, we, too, return—to Agnon in the Stockholm limelight: we see him rise to deliver his speech—a speech that is written in Hebrew. Indeed, such a speech would have been unimaginable in any other tongue, and for two reasons. First, Hebrew, Yiddish and German were the only languages Agnon could speak; second, it was inconceivable that the Israeli Hebrew laureate would deliver his thanks to the Swedish Academy in anything other than the Holy Language in which he toiled. Abba Eban, then foreign minister of Israel, thought that he ought to have a hand in crafting Agnon's speech: after all, from a diplomatic standpoint, the Nobel Prize ceremony was an unprecedented opportunity to advance Israel's diplomatic goals. Agnon, however, took a different view of the matter. It is said that he retorted, "Tell Abba Eban that when he receives the Nobel Prize, he can write his own acceptance speech."

Thus, Agnon would write his own speech, and he would deliver it in Hebrew. A small glitch remained: not a soul in the room save the laureate, his wife, and a small handful of guests could understand the language. Agnon's solution was to deliver the opening section in Hebrew, after which the full text would be read on his behalf in English. As a piece of rhetoric, Agnon's text is decidedly bizarre. Of the slightly more than two thousand English words in the speech, a solid half was biographical in nature.[3] By way of introduction, the prize-winning author told his audience the Talmudic tale of men of distinction of Jerusalem, who would only dine with those they knew personally (Sanhedrin 23a). One can imagine that at this point, the king of Sweden might have glanced at the old Jewish author with the big black skullcap and mused: What is this rabbi yammering on about? Perhaps answering that unspoken question, at this moment Agnon tells the audience, "I must tell you something about myself, then." And so Agnon does.

Significantly, Agnon's biography was amongst his greatest artistic creations. Everything about him, from his date of birth to the date of his *aliyah* to his very name was part of the myth, part of the fable the author had crafted about his own identity. It is a matter of historical record that he was born in the summer of 1887. Agnon claimed that he was born on Tisha B'Av 1888, which fell out on August 8th that year (the numerically lyrical 8th of the 8th month, '88). As it happens, Tisha B'Av did not fall out

---

3. The speech in its English translation is available in *Forevermore & Other Stories*, 264–69.

"As One Who Was Born in Jerusalem"

on August 8th that year, nor did Tisha B'Av fall out on Agnon's birthday the year before. Agnon was born around Tisha B'Av in 1887. This birth year obfuscation was likely related to draft-dodging efforts. Yet, we might suggest a further signification: for a writer possessed by the notion of the relationship of diaspora and redemption, the symbolism of being born on Tisha B'Av would have been of chief importance.

Indeed, Agnon anchors his name in such ideas, deriving his pseudonym from the Hebrew term *agunot*; not the *agunot* of estranged husband and wife, but the *igun* of the Jewish people being both chained to its Father in heaven and being distanced from Him. If one begins from the Midrashic notion of God and the Jewish people in the bonds of matrimony, these marital partners are clearly in need counseling. God has not divorced the Jews, but perhaps we might say that they are separated over these many years since their banishment from Jerusalem. The Jewish people itself is an *aguna*. God has apparently abandoned us; we are akin to the proverbial abandoned wife: such themes echo time and again in the Agnon oeuvre. In Stockholm, Agnon's biography may well have struck the uninitiated as rather odd from a rhetorical point of view, especially compared to other Nobel laureate speeches. Yet, what Agnon offered was not biography *qua* biography; rather, it was biography *qua* midrash. In effect, what Agnon provided for the Swedish Academy and the world was a myth of himself that melds into the myth of the Jewish people.

At this point, we might note Agnon's rendering of the line that until recently emblazoned a the fifty Shekel bill in the State of Israel: "As a result of the historic catastrophe in which Titus of Rome destroyed Jerusalem and Israel was exiled from its land, I was born in one of the cities of the Exile. But always I regarded myself as one who was born in Jerusalem." Agnon went on to say, "In a dream, in a vision of the night, I saw myself standing with my brother-Levites in the Holy Temple,[4] singing with them the songs of David, King of Israel, melodies such as no ear has heard since the day our city was destroyed and its people went into exile. I suspect that the angels in charge of the Shrine of Music, fearful lest I sing in wakefulness what I had sung in dream, made me forget by day what I had sung at night; for if my brethren, the sons of my people, were to hear, they would be unable to bear their grief over the happiness they have lost. To console me for having

---

4. Agnon was, in fact, a Levite, descendent of the tribe of Temple choristers.

prevented me from singing with my mouth, they enable me to compose songs in writing."[5]

This particular autobiographical claim, like so many made by Agnon, is quite outlandish. Yet much can be gleaned from the story he chose to tell about how his work unfolded. By all rights, as Agnon tells the tale, he ought to have gotten up every day, gone to the Temple in Jerusalem, and there sang the psalms of King David, thus performing the job of a Levite. As that position has been closed on account of the destruction of and exile from Jerusalem, he instead wrote stories. Those twenty-three tomes of modern Hebrew literature are a compensation for such holy work having been denied him. Agnon, according to Agnon, was compensated to compose in prose what was formally sung in praise. Making a radical statement, the author likens his work to nothing less than Temple worship.

Setting aside for the moment the grandiloquence of Agnon's move, we might consider just how this work serves as a consolation for the trials and tribulations of Jewish history. Agnon alludes to this notion recurrently, both in his works of fiction as well as in occasional essays or talks:[6] these passages are beautiful portrayals of the purity of religious experience as it is depicted in the author's stories, through eyes of the child: the child in his grandfather's house, the child with the Bible or prayer book, the child receiving his first pair of *tefillin*, the young boy going off with his father and grandfather, his first memories of going to *shul* on Yom Kippur, the splendor of Yom Kippur. Such transmission does indeed communicate the mystery, the grandeur of the religious experience.

Here Agnon presents a major leitmotif of his production: "I was five years old when I wrote my first song. It was out of longing for my father that I wrote it. It happened that my father of blessed memory went away on business and I was overcome with longing for him and I made a song." Agnon, we recall, had learned in *heder* and had a very close relationship with his father, who was a Torah scholar, having penned a volume on Maimonides' monumental code of Jewish Law. In the Nobel speech as well as in a variety of other places in his writing—both in the guise of autobiography as well as outright fiction—Agnon recounted that his very first composition came to him almost prophetically as a statement of poetic longing and

---

5. Agnon uses the terms *shir* and *shirah* interchangeably to mean both literal poetry as well as prose, or literature or art in general.

6. See passages in autobiographical comments at prize speeches, e.g., in *MeAtzmi el Atzmi*, 26, 55–56; in works of fiction such as "The Sense of Smell" in *A Book That Was Lost*, 149–56.

"As One Who Was Born in Jerusalem"

lamentation for his beloved father, traveling on business to the regional fair, absent from the happy home in Buczacz in which young Shmuel Yosef Czaczkes (Agnon's birth name) was raised. This motif, namely, writing, storytelling, and creativity itself as a balm for pain, runs like connective tissue through Agnon's work. One need not be adept at unpacking literary symbolism to suggest that a little boy's longing for his father might also be read on the national plane of Israel's pining for its Father in heaven. Such polytextured writing lies at the core of Agnon's genius, and accounts for why a writer who was apparently so steeped in the "old world" of eastern European Judaism was honored in Sweden as one of the greatest of modern authors.

Agnon, recognized early on as a prodigy, enjoyed a happy childhood with his parents and four younger siblings. His father worked in the fur trade and would leave several times a year to attend the regional fairs. The little boy is sick for the absence of his father, he comes home and places his head on the "handles of the lock"—a powerful symbol of longing for a lost love and, allegorically, for the Divine (Song of Songs 5:5), words of immense longing, of unfulfilled desire. He knows that on the other side of the door his Abba won't be there. So what happens? A wail emerges from my heart and he cries out, "Where are you father, father? Where can you be found?" Right away another cry comes forth, "I love you with a love so profound" (the spontaneous cries of the boy come out as a rhymed Hebrew couplet). Agnon is not composing a poem; rather, these words are flowing from him. When we sing or pray, we must generate words; in prophecy, the words come to us from somewhere else.

Agnon is not claiming prophetic vision. Yet we have here a description of the artist as a young man, and the initiation of the artist to his craft, that of the art of writing. The art of composing is one that comes through some kind of nearly divine inspiration but is depicted as the immediate reaction to pain and loss. That, at least, is the art of writing for Agnon; a response to suffering, a response to longing. It is about standing with one's hand on the handle of the lock, fully present to the uncertainty of the fulfillment of his desires. Gershon Shaked observed that Agnon, like Kafka, portrays "the artist as a *poeta doloroso*, a poet whose torments become the source and substance of his work. But Agnon's most conscious poetic manifesto associates his creativity with a specifically nostalgic sorrow ... a longing for the lost ancestral home as the wellspring of his work."[7]

7. Shaked, "After the Fall," 88–89.

Agnon's stories, particularly those of childhood—for example, "The Kerchief"—feature the element of the father going away to the fair and the mother waiting in anxious anticipation for his return. Intensely multivalent, these stories brilliantly succeed in conveying that one single thing means a multiplicity of things. In this light, we are ready to ask: When Agnon stood on the stage in Stockholm and announced, "As a result of the historic catastrophe that Jerusalem was taken and we were sent into exile and I always imagined myself as if I was Jerusalem born," what, precisely, does he wish his audience to understand?

Agnon is making a subtle move, an almost intertextual one. In a kind of understated thematic intertextuality, I submit that he is drawing our attention to a different time that a Jew talked about singing a song, namely Psalm 137, "By the waters of Babylon." Ruth R. Wisse points out in her important book, *Jews in Power*, that the ambiguous relation between Judaism and power can be traced to this very psalm, which conveys the predicament of the captives in Babylon following the sack of Jerusalem.[8] The Babylonian captors taunt the Jews, ordering them to perform songs of Zion, "You Jews, you captive Jews with your harps. Give us a song, one of those old ditties you used to sing in that burnt Temple of yours." The Jews refused, uttering instead the pledge that would echo through the ages, "If I forget you, O Jerusalem, let my right hand forget its cunning." The captive Jews sing about their longing for Jerusalem. When the Jews finally do sing out in that Psalm, the tune is far from the dirge that their captors demanded. "Remember, O Lord, against the Edomites the day of Jerusalem's fall how they cried, strip her, strip her to the very foundations. Fair Babylon, you predator, a blessing on him who repays you in kind what you inflicted on us." "You want a song?" we imagine them saying. "We'll sing you a song. We'll sing you a song about what happens to people who oppress the Jews."

Wisse elaborates:

> "Edomites" are the generic enemies of Israel, Babylon the immediate aggressor. Rather than crushing the Jews' morale, the scorn of their captors has spiked Jewish anger and stiffened national resolve . . . Yet for all its rhetorical severity, Psalm 137 does not exhort Jews to take up arms on their own behalf. Assuming full moral responsibility for the violence that war requires, it calls on the Lord to avenge the Jews' defeat and on other nations to repay Babylon "in kind." This reflects the historical record: It was the Persians,

---

8. Wisse, *Jews and Power*, 15–18.

not the Jews who defeated the Babylonians, and King Cyrus who allowed the Jews to return to Jerusalem to rebuild their Temple, thereby inspiring Isaiah's reference to him as "the Lord's anointed," the messenger of God's will, God's hand. God's hand, not the soldiering of Israel is credited with the Jews' political recovery.[9]

We conclude with a return to 1966, with Agnon receiving the Nobel Prize. The Swedish Academy has finally recognized the Jewish people, the Hebrew language, the nation, the State of Israel—and Agnon stands in Europe and is asked to give a song (or speech) of Zion. This request is far from the evil-minded one made by the bloodthirsty Babylonians; nonetheless, Agnon is indeed standing there in the shadow of the Holocaust. "You want me to sing a song?" Perhaps he thought. "I'll sing you a song. Let me tell you what we do in the face of suffering and exile: we do not respond, we do not wage war," and if we waged war in 1948, and six months after the Prize ceremony in 1967, it is only out of defensive necessity. Instead, what is the authentic Jewish response to suffering? Jews know what it means to live in exile. In her book, Wisse notes that the first Babylonian exile proved that the Jewish nation could survive outside the Land of Israel, leaving open the question of when and how they would regain it. At this point, Agnon might ask: Jews knew how to survive and now they've returned; do you know how Jews still survive? They survive in the text. But the texts become transformed in modernity through a renewed cultural production in our own language, in an authentic way, the kind of writing which Rav Kook years earlier had recognized that Agnon was writing.[10] Creativity is the authentic Jewish response to pain and catastrophe. From the catastrophe of history they will write modern literature; that was Agnon's message, delivered between the lines, standing there fifty years ago in Stockholm.

Bibliography

Agnon, S.Y. *Forevermore & Other Stories*. Edited by Jeffrey Saks. New Milford, CT: Toby, 2017.

———. *MeAtzmi el Atzmi*. Tel Aviv: Schocken, 1976.

———. "The Sense of Smell." *A Book That Was Lost*. Edited by Alan Mintz and Anne Golumb Hoffman. Tel Aviv: Schocken, 1996.

9. Wisse, *Jews and Power*, 16–18.

10. Saks, "A Portrait of Two Artists at the Crossroads: Between Rav Kook and S.Y. Agnon," 32–52.

Saks, Jeffrey. "A Portrait of Two Artists at the Crossroads: Between Rav Kook and S.Y. Agnon." *Tradition* 49/2 (2016) 32–52.

Shaked, Gershon. "After the Fall: Nostalgia and the Treatment of Authority in the Works of Kafka and Agnon, Two Habsburgian Writers." *Partial Answers* 2/1 (2004) 88–89.

Wisse, Ruth R. *Jews and Power*. New York: Schocken, 2007.

8

The Land of Israel for Its Own Sake
Agnon's "The Covenant of Love"

MOSHE SIMKOVICH

S.Y. AGNON'S "THE COVENANT of Love" was first published in Hebrew in 1925, shortly after his return to the Land of Israel after his long German sojourn from 1912–1924.[1] Aside from its aesthetic value as a lyrical short story, the story is an interesting reflection of Agnon's mindset at this key juncture of his life. It leads to an artistic statement about Aliyah and Zionism at a critical point of the Fourth Aliyah, when Jewish life in Palestine was undergoing changes.

The plot of "The Covenant of Love" is straightforward. After having lived full and busy lives in Exile, three elderly religious Jews come to settle in the Holy Land for their retirements. They do not necessarily know each other from before (the story does not make this clear), but their motivations

---

1. Agnon's *Brit Ahavah* was originally published in the very first issue of the newspaper *Davar* (June 1, 1925) and collected in his anthology *Elu veElu*. The English version, prepared by an anonymous translator, appeared in the *Canadian Jewish Chronicle* (April 26, 1935), was revised and anthologized in *Forevermore and Other Stories*, 212–14. Quotations from "The Covenant of Love" are based on the version as it appears in *Forevermore*, but have been revised by me as needed in light of certain liberties the translator took in producing his lyrical rendering (which omitted certain brief passages).

in coming are similar—to live out their final days in the longed-for land. After touring the major sites of the country in the scorching Middle Eastern sun, visiting all the storied places that Jews in Europe identified with living in *Eretz Yisrael*, the three take a break to relax at a hotel on the Mediterranean shore in Jaffa. The story finds them on the beach in the evening, watching the sun set and having tea and biscuits. The first of the three describes his frustration with being in Israel[2]—it was not what he thought it would be. Being in Israel was not religiously uplifting. Indeed, he reminisces that in Exile he felt spiritually inspired, but that inspiration is lacking now that he has arrived in the Holy Land. The candle that gave light in Exile merely flickers in Israel. The second old man responds that this is wrongheaded—the reason the candle seems dim is because the blinding spiritual light of Israel has melted the little candle of Exile spirituality. The third old man says that he has experienced the impressions of the first man,[3] has heard out the response of the second man, but now looks at life in Israel differently. To expect to be automatically spiritually moved by being in Israel is folly, a desire which cannot be fulfilled. Rather, God graciously gives man the opportunity to live in Israel for its own sake. It is up to us, unworthy as we are, to become worthy of the covenant of love that is the covenant of the land.

In the depiction of the three old men, Agnon shows his craft. The men are religious Jews from Europe, and their statements resonate with references to Biblical and Rabbinic passages. Each of the first two men exemplifies a mindset of Jews coming to the land later in their lives. Their positions reflect how European Jews envisioned the Holy Land, and how they responded to the frustration of discovering that the reality did not match their dreams. Each of the first two old men is a symbol of a mindset, and the candle parable that they both use becomes a foil for the third old man as he resolves the frustration of living in Israel. His resolution: Dealing with the land's reality directly is superior to seeing Israel through a parable.

The story starts with a setting by the sea, the old men sitting on the Jaffa shore watching the sun set. Yet the setting sun is peculiar in that it has lost its midday heat, so instead of scorching them it warms them and plays upon their lips, turning their expressions (and possibly their words)

---

2. I use the term "Israel" throughout, as shorthand for *Eretz Yisrael* or the Land of Israel, mindful that Israel as a State and political entity is an anachronism in a story published in 1925.

3. This statement of the third man is omitted in the English translation.

to gold. The three have sat together on this shore for a number of evenings, and are at home with one another. Together, they share the reflections playing on the sea, its evening colors, and the flow of its waves to the shore. Those reflections help them (and us) enter into their reflections on their experiences of Exile and Israel. As the sun of their own lives set, it provides sufficient warmth to enable deeper reflection without scorching them.

It is this comfortable seashore scene that leads the first elder to comment on the peculiar *Eretz Yisrael* sun, which "is already going down, yet it still warms the body and enfolds the limbs like a robe." As his hands play through the sands, he doubts whether this is really the Land of Israel.[4]

This of course is not a real question of fact. It is a playful statement that will lead into the real issue—is this *Eretz Yisrael*, the land we envisioned as a spiritually inspired home? But one of the other two, noting the disappointment in the tone of the first speaker, is willing to play with the statement at face value just to lighten things up. This motivation is not clear in the translation, but in the original Hebrew text Agnon wrote: "This older man knew that his friend was not really referring to Jaffa only, so to lighten his sadness he responded." Quoting the Book of Jonah about the prophet's flight from before God to Jaffa, the second old man interprets the text to mean that Jaffa is not "before God"—that is, Jaffa is not in fact within the Land of Israel.[5] On a different level, he may be hinting that the first speaker is like Jonah, in Jaffa wanting to flee the land.

The first old man persists by making his position crystal clear. What used to be a spiritual experience in Exile, the blessing of the Priests[6] offered in awe only as part of special holiday prayers, is a mundane daily experience in Israel, emptied of any trace of the divine presence. In short, whereas in Israel religiosity flickers weakly like a candle in the empty ark whose content is gone, in Exile the candle burned brightly.

---

4. With hesitation, I offer that the hand in the sands may be a reference to playing with the destiny of Abraham's descendants, who are depicted as "numerous as the dust of the earth" in Genesis 13:16.

5. As I point out later, the whole proof is tongue in cheek, as the text is deliberately misinterpreted. The gist of the text is that Jaffa is a port from which Jonah can catch a boat that will take him away from Israel. Jaffa is still Israel.

6. The priestly blessing, *Birkat Kohanim* (Numbers 6:23–27) accompanies the repetition of the central prayer of the Amidah service. The blessing is recited by descendants of Aaron, and is understood to be the transmission of divine blessing. According to Ashkenazi practice, outside of Israel it is recited only on major holidays, whereas in Israel it is performed daily.

To this, the second old man agrees that the Exile candle that seemed to burn with such great spirituality is barely a flicker in Israel. But the reason for the change is the opposite of what the first man proposes. The Land of Israel's spirituality is like the scorching sun that exhausted these travelers in daytime, blinding a person from seeing any other source of light. It is the intensity of the light in Israel that makes all other lights feeble. The spirituality is so inherent in the reality of the land that it dims the meagre spirituality of Exile. The first old man thought the candle he lit to fight the darkness of Exile would count for something in Israel; perhaps here it would shine all the brighter. He did not consider that in Israel where all is spiritual, his candle would melt away in the direct sunlight. No wonder he is frustrated.

What sources is Agnon drawing on to craft this seaside give and take? It is illuminating to see sources that point out the value of spirituality of Exile, yet nevertheless emphasize the superiority of spirituality in Israel. These sources certainly were known to Agnon, indeed were readily at hand. We will consider one Biblical-Talmudic source, and one twentieth-century reference.

The Prophet Ezekiel writes:

> Therefore say, Thus says the Lord God: Although I have cast them far off among the nations, and although I have scattered them among the countries, and I have been to them a little sanctuary in the countries where they have gone. Yet say: Thus said the Lord God: I will gather you from the peoples and assemble you out of the countries where you have been scattered, and I will give you the Land of Israel... I will give them one heart and put a new spirit in them (Ezekiel 11:16–19).

On which the Babylonian Talmud (Megillah 29a) comments:

> It is taught in a *baraita*: Rabbi Shimon ben Yoḥai says: Come and see how beloved the Jewish people are before the Holy One, blessed be He. As every place they were exiled, the Divine Presence went with them. They were exiled to Egypt, and the Divine Presence went with them, as it is stated: "Did I reveal myself to the house of your father when they were in Egypt?" (1 Samuel 2:27).

> They were exiled to Babylonia, and the Divine Presence went with them, as it is stated: "For your sake I have sent to Babylonia" (Isaiah 43:14).

The Land of Israel for Its Own Sake

> So too, when, in the future, they will be redeemed, the Divine Presence will be with them, as it is stated: "Then the Lord your God will return with your captivity" (Deuteronomy 30:3).
>
> It does not state: He will bring back, i.e., He will cause the Jewish people to return, but rather it says: "He will return," which teaches that the Holy One, Blessed be He, will return together with them from among the various exiles . . .
> The verse states: "Yet I have been to them as a little sanctuary in the countries where they have come." (Ezekiel 11:16)
>
> Rabbi Yitzḥak said: This is referring to the synagogues and study halls in Babylonia.
> And Rabbi Elazar said: This is referring to the house of our master, i.e., Rav, in Babylonia, from which Torah issues forth to the entire world.

Both the text in Ezekiel, and the Talmudic text based in part on Ezekiel, clearly emphasize that life in Exile is capable of spirituality, Babylonia being a prime example. God even accompanies the people in Exile. Yet, God will return with the people from Exile as well, and the people will come alive spiritually in Israel in a way they could not in Exile. This was, in fact, a text well known to Agnon, and one which becomes the central intertextual axis around which the conclusion of his greatest novel, *A Guest for the Night*, revolves. That book, singled out for particular praise by the Nobel committee, is Agnon's most extended meditation on the tension and transference between Jewish life in the Exile and its promise of renewal in *Eretz Yisrael*.

To fully illustrate the contrast of Exile and Israel in terms that would have been familiar to Agnon, let us examine some of the writings of his great contemporary Rabbi Abraham Isaac Kook. The two were fellow members of the Second Aliyah and lived for a while in close proximity in the Neveh Tzedek neighborhood in Jaffa.[7] Agnon maintained a lifelong reverence for Rav Kook, and the Rav showed a pronounced interest in the young writer's stories, seeing in them the type of literary production that he hoped would mark the cultural revival of the Jewish people's return to its land and language. Although other Torah scholars may have expressed

---

7. See Saks, "A Portrait of Two Artists at the Crossroads," pp. 32–52. It is not inconceivable that Rav Kook and Agnon went down to the beach in Jaffa together!

similar perspectives, Agnon would have been most profoundly affected by Rav Kook, who wrote:

> In the Land of Israel which is the spiritual wellspring of inner holiness, which is the vital light of the soul of the holy community of Israel, the spirit strengthens itself on its own. But it requires assistance via active and intellectual divine service, and is perfected by humanity's physical and spiritual work. But in Exile acquiring it comes only by great effort, investigation, research, experiment and in-depth involvement. Divine enlightenment, strengthened by the spiritual aspirations of the soul, comes as a subsidiary support, filling out the spiritual treasury. This comes and is empowered by its battle against the dark forces that rule the darkened lands; lands of the darkness of Exile. As soon as the nation is restored to the land it loves, all the treasures will be revalued to their appropriate worth, incorporating the influx of the great spiritual wealth that had accumulated in Exile. Their [the treasures] values will be inverted, finally revealing their divine impetus in its aspiration to the higher life; and their secondary natures through their human aspects, the work of man and its fruits, intellectuality and aesthetics, in all its aspects.[8]

This somewhat recondite passage in Rav Kook's writing makes clear that the "lights lit outside the Land of Israel" are experienced differently once one has returned to Israel. What once seemed valuable is reevaluated. What is or is not part of the divine finally becomes clear.

This text sets the framework for the first two old men. The first misses his role in the fight against the dark but is blind to the possibilities presented in the intense light of Israel. The second old man argues that holy spirituality is there for the taking if only Old Man 1 can overcome his blindness, can reset his exilic mindset, and see from the perspective of the light of Israel. The stage is now set for the third old man to set things straight.

THE THIRD OLD MAN

The first old man found the candlelight of the divine presence in Exile. The second old man found the divine presence in its dominant glory in Israel.

---

8. *Orot Hakodesh* 117. This volume was not published until after Rav Kook's passing (beginning 1938), more than a decade after Agnon's story was written. Nevertheless, its content reflects Rav Kook's thinking before Agnon's story was published in *Davar* in 1925.

But the third old man sides with neither of them. As the preface to his rejection of their perspectives is not included in the English translation, I bring it with my own translation here:

> The third one then began to speak. "Bless you, my friend, for not withholding your worries from us; pain shared is halfway to consolation. I too had your pain. But oh! We don't want your sort of consolation. For months I sit here, and I am gloomy, sad, and depressed by my pangs of misery. Not only haven't I merited the joy of settling (in Israel), but there are times that settling seems to have embittered me, it shouldn't happen to you." While he spoke he took out some snuff tobacco. He shook two fingers free from the tobacco and scattered some to the wind. And even though typically he spoke slowly and deliberately, now the words came tumbling out.

The third old man has experienced the pains of the first old man; they are real pains. But he has gone beyond those pains and has a resolution for them that is superior to grumbling about Exile lost! It is important to transcend that sensation that his colleagues experience, because if one becomes stuck in frustration, he loses his connection to God, and ends up having lost both Exile and Israel.

But note that at first there is not a single word about the second old man's position. The second man's position is one that does not apply to the third. Perhaps the third man even rejects it, finding it delusional. This becomes clear after we carefully examine the third man's position. At that point, we will be able to reconsider whether Agnon's perspective aligns with that of Rav Kook. As for now, let us consider the web of sources that support the insights of the third old man.

Two Biblical texts and one Rabbinic text provide the underpinning for the third man's approach. He himself provides those sources. But before he produces those texts, he criticizes the first two men for the very presentation of their relationship to Israel, because "there is no need for parables." He is emphatically telling them that by living in an indirect symbolic relationship to the land, a relationship that rejects the reality of the land for a dreamland, they undo all prospects of being satisfied there. By living for a parable, by looking to receive light, they will be frustrated. Even the second man's use of parable, one that justifies the great light in Israel, can bring only frustration to the first man and may itself be a delusion.

The Rabbinic text contains an idea found in multiple sources, but the one that Agnon seems to be quoting from is found in Tosefta Avodah Zarah 4:3—"A person must stay in *Eretz Yisrael*, even in a town that is majority gentile, and not outside the Land, even in a town that is all Jews. Thus, life in *Eretz Yisrael* has equal weight to all the commandments of the Torah."[9]

This statement is used by the third man to give force to his argument that commitment to living in Israel is tantamount to commitment to a life of spiritual connection through the commandments—even if one is unworthy of such a degree of holiness, and in fact does not feel any holier through it. This commitment is such that it gives life in Israel meaning, whether or not it is accompanied by spiritual or other benefits. In fact, other benefits might get in the way.

But how does one frame the nature of this commitment, explain it to the first two old men who are interested more in what they get out of the relationship to Israel, the feeling of satisfaction of enlightenment? To accomplish this, the third old man resorts to Biblical sources. In Genesis 17:1–10 the covenant that the title of Agnon's story refers to is made with Abraham:[10]

> When Abram was ninety-nine years old, the Lord appeared to Abram and said to him, "I am El Shaddai. *Walk in My ways and be perfect (blameless). And I will make My covenant between Me and you, and I will make you exceedingly numerous.*" Abram threw himself on his face; and God spoke to him further, "As for Me, this is My covenant with you: You shall be the father of a multitude of nations. And you shall no longer be called Abram, but your name shall be Abraham, for I make you the father of a multitude of nations. I will make you exceedingly fertile, and make nations of you; and kings shall come forth from you. *I will maintain My covenant between Me and you, and your offspring to come, as an everlasting covenant throughout the ages, to be God to you and to your offspring to come. I assign the land you sojourn in to you and your offspring to come, all the land of Canaan, as an everlasting holding. I will be their God.*" God further said to Abraham, "As for you, you and your offspring to come throughout the ages shall keep My covenant. Such shall be the covenant between Me and you and your offspring to follow which you shall keep: every male among you shall be circumcised.

---

9. Ed. Zuckermandel, 466.
10. The Revised Standard Version of the Bible cited throughout this article.

The Land of Israel for Its Own Sake

There is of course so much to analyze in this passage. We will limit our remarks to what is directly pertinent to our story.

The covenant that Agnon refers to is in the second, italicized verse. You will notice that there is no mention of love there, nor of the Land of Israel. Assuming that the covenant is the same covenant mentioned later in the last italicized verse, it is clear how the Land of Israel becomes part of the covenant. But what's love got to do with it? Rashi comments on the verse, and unlike Agnon I will cite it here in full:

> *And be perfect*—This, too, is a command following upon the previous command: be perfect in all the trials I impose upon you. *According to the Midrash (Genesis Rabbah 46:4), however, it means: walk before Me by observing the precept of circumcision and through this you will become perfect, for so long as you are uncircumcised I regard you as having a blemish. Another explanation of "Be thou perfect"—at present you lack the power of controlling morally five organs, viz., two eyes, two ears and the membrum. Therefore will I add a letter (i.e., the letter* ה*, the numerical value of which is five) to your name (Avram which equals 243) so that the total of the letters of your name (Avraham) will become 248, corresponding to the number of limbs of your body (cf. BT Nedarim 32b).*
>
> *And I will make my covenant*—A covenant of love and a covenant regarding the land—to give it to you as an inheritance *through your observance of this precept.*

Agnon quotes Rashi as follows: "Be perfect in all my trial of you. Then I will give you my covenant—the covenant of love and the covenant of the land." Note how Agnon takes what he wants from Rashi and leaves the rest. I have italicized the parts he omits. It is clear that he does not want "Midrash," just as above the third man did not want parable. To Agnon, the Midrash about circumcision is beside the point. What is his approach?

If you consider the last two verses quoted from Genesis, "God further said . . ." as part of the same passage, it is indeed about circumcision. But Agnon chooses what appears to be *pshat*, the plain meaning of the text—and that separates the second verse from the verse that mentions circumcision; this reorients the quoted text, pointing it in the direction of a new, different covenant. But still, why not *just* land, why another covenant of love as well? Rabbi Judah Loew ben Bezalel (d. 1609), known as the *Maharal*, commenting on a statement by Rashi observes:

> It simply writes 'My covenant,' to say that the covenant is given for a number of purposes, for if it meant only one covenant the

verse should have said which covenant, thus it simply writes 'My covenant' to include it all—the covenant of love and the covenant of the land." There is room for covenant to refer to love.[11]

But still, why love? Why not a different extra covenant? Mishnah Avot (5:3) records the following: "With ten tests Abraham, our father, was tested and he withstood them all; in order to show how great was the love of Abraham, our father, peace be upon him." Now we can see the precision with which Agnon chooses his words from Rashi: "Walk before Me and be perfect.' Our master Rashi adds: 'Be perfect in all my trial of you. Then I will give you my covenant—the covenant of love and the covenant of the land.'" He is following the Mishnaic formulation that links the trials Abraham successfully underwent to the love Abraham gave. That love results in a covenant of love, an eternal commitment, and is accompanied by and concretized by the covenant of the land. Agnon concludes the story with a quote from the second biblical text, Proverbs 2:21, "For the upright shall dwell in the land and the blameless (perfect) shall be left in it." This quote spells out what makes a person deserve security on the land. It is being blameless (perfect)—exactly the quality mentioned in reference to Abraham's qualifications—*temimut*.
Here, he makes clear that it is this blamelessness, or perfection, that is essential.

Yet, these translations may not do justice to *tamim* as a concept. In other places, it has been translated as whole, or simple, or complete. What Agnon means here is multifaceted. First, it must be a quality that understands acceptance of trials as the very fabric of a relationship of value. Also, Agnon himself emphasizes that it connotes *lishmah*—"for its own sake." Settling Israel while undergoing challenges is "an extra grace of Providence, if we do not enjoy it, for so are we accorded the merit of fulfilling this holiest of ordinances for its own sake."

LISHMAH—FOR ITS OWN SAKE

What does "for its own sake" mean here? Is it doing something—in this case settling the land—without enjoyment, reward, or some ulterior motive? If so, is it not strange that such a concept should be linked to love?

---

11. Maharal, *Gur Aryeh* on Genesis 17:2.

The Land of Israel for Its Own Sake

In Agnon's time, as part and parcel of his upbringing in Eastern Europe the term *lishmah* would have been hard to avoid and would have conveyed a very specific concept. It was a basic element in a very live debate about why Torah was inherently valuable, and with what motivation Torah should be learned. Scholars and students wanted to know what the highly sought-after goal of study of Torah "for its own sake" meant. This was not a new debate,[12] but in the nineteenth century it took off in new directions. I will use this discussion to enter into what *lishmah* might mean in our story.

Norman Lamm reviews three primary ways that the concept of *lishmah* has been defined: functional, devotional, and cognitive.[13] In terms of Torah learning, functional connotes learning in order to know what to do, devotional in order to come close to God, and cognitive in order to know the content of Torah. Can any of these definitions fit with what the third man in our story is saying: that one is fulfilling the ordinance for its own sake, without getting anything out of it? Neither the functional nor the cognitive definitions lend themselves to what Agnon's third man presents. Perhaps only the devotional definition fits. Yet, the devotion shown by overcoming trials sounds like an unsettling devotion, not the closeness and love devotion through study would connote.

A further, and more helpful explanation of *lishmah* is suggested by Rabbi Abraham of Sochaczew (1838–1910):

> I have heard that there are people who have a mistaken notion concerning the study of the Torah. They hold that one whose method of study consists of creating *hiddushim* (innovative insights) and who revels therein is not properly engaged in the study of Torah *lishmah*. Instead he should study the plain meaning of the text, deriving no pleasure from it and doing it solely for the sake of the mitzvah . . . But this is an obvious error. To the contrary, the main purpose of Torah study is to rejoice and derive pleasure from it. Only then are the words of the Torah absorbed into one's being. By enjoying the study of Torah, one will cleave to it.[14]

This definition, a version of the devotional approach, leaves room for total involvement to the exclusion of other motivations, yet provides an entry point to love and joy. Involvement in the flow of learning provides its

---

12. See, e.g., M. Avot 4:11, 5:17, and 6:1.

13. Lamm, *Torah Lishmah*.

14. Introduction to *Eglei Tal* (Piotrkow, 1905), translation here from Lamm, *Torah Lishmah*, 37.

own pleasures, pleasures inherent in learning itself. Perhaps involvement in living in Israel, with all its trials and challenges, but just for its own sake, allows one to feel graced by the relationship with the divine, a relationship inherently meaningful, even without spiritual highs.

Agnon himself had written about Torah "for its own sake." It is actually the title of one of his short stories, anthologized immediately prior "The Covenant of Love" in his collection *Elu veElu*.[15] In this story, a scholar Rabbi Yosef denies himself any benefit from his devoted Torah learning. He is oblivious to the demise of the family business and refuses an opportunity to a respected and salaried position as a Torah leader.[16] He prefers learning for its own sake and ignores (perhaps hardly notices) poverty. At the end of the story he is rewarded with a substantial inheritance. In the meantime, learning is all that is meaningful, the object of his only desire.

In this story, it is clear that "for its own sake" is also a denial of all ulterior motives or benefits. Yet, as R. Abraham of Sochaczew would have said, there may be a lot of joy in the person's learning of Torah, and it is a joy that gets side benefits at the end of the story only because God wants to give it, not because Rabbi Yosef expects it. Perhaps by not aiming at the joy, one gets it and more. And that may be the case for our third old man as well. He has come to love Israel as it is, inadequate as he may be to fully benefit from its holiness (as a scholar may feel about his studies), but that love begins to be rewarding by its very nature, and frustration is eventually not a problem.

A teaching in Mishnah Avot 6:1 is consistent with this perspective: "Rabbi Meir says: Any person involved in Torah for its own sake merits many things. Not only that, but the whole world becomes worthwhile. He is called friend, beloved, loves God, loves creations, pleases God, pleases people, etc." Love follows on the heels of doing what you should be doing for its own sake, and this is being a *tamim*. It culminates in, and is the very substance of, a covenant of love.

THE PLAYFUL USE OF SOURCES

It is characteristic of Agnon to use sources in Jewish tradition, sometimes explicitly, sometimes through veiled reference, and often tongue in cheek.

---

15. "Ma'aseh Rabbi Yosef, o Torah Lishmah" was also originally published in *Davar*, on July 10, 1925, about one month after "Covenant of Love," and was collected in *Elu veElu* as part of the same cycle of "Stories of the Land of Israel."

16. For Rabbinic model of such devotion, see Mishnah Avot 4:7.

I would like to highlight three texts which he weaves into the fabric of "Covenant of Love" whose intertextual role contributes to the depth of his storytelling, and—if properly understood—to the insight we can gain from our reading of the story.

Jonah

Early in the story, the first old man wonders aloud, "Is this really the Land of Israel?" He did not mean to doubt whether Jaffa beach was indeed within the traditional borders of Israel, but rather to express his disillusionment with the character of spiritual life as he found it in Israel. The second old man's response poked fun at his *kvetchy* question by taking it literally and making the case that it was conceivably true—perhaps Jaffa is not part of the Holy Land! In order to make the case for it, he took liberty with the text in Jonah. He paraphrased or misquotes a few words of the verse: "Jonah sought to flee from the presence of the Lord—so he went down to Jaffa" However, these words do not make the same point as the real verse: "Jonah started out to flee to Tarshish from before the Lord. He went down to Jaffa and found a ship going to Tarshish" (1:3). In short, the second old man misrepresents the verse, intentionally or not, to mean that as soon as he got to Jaffa, Jonah had already left Israel. This is a subversion of the Biblical text. The second old man plays with the text, and Agnon may be playing with whether we are paying attention—but this seems to be lost on the first old man.

Rashi on Genesis

Above, we explained how Agnon carefully selected the parts of Rashi he needed to make his point about the covenants of love and Israel being tied to living life in Israel for its own sake, and left out the other parts (the Midrash and any mention of circumcision). But we must note that Rashi, at least according to the editions commonly used, blended the two covenants with the act of circumcision in his commentary. For Agnon to have followed Rashi in this blended path would have weakened Agnon's point about receiving love for overcoming the trials of living in Israel, for he would have had to redirect the emphasis of the trials to circumcision.

It may indeed be that Rashi himself saw two optional ways to understand the verses. It is plausible that when the text reads "God further said

..." that a new discussion was opening between God and Abraham, and a new third covenant was being introduced, that of circumcision. However, it is far from clear whether this is a new separate covenant, or a continuation of the previous verses bearing an explanation of the covenant mentioned above. The exact relationship between verses 1–8 and verses 9–10 is unclear, which gives Agnon room to play out the third man's point of view.

Proverbs

In order to make the point that dwelling in the Land of Israel depends upon acting according to Abraham's model, entailing overcoming trials with *temimut*, Agnon brings a clinching argument through citation of Proverbs 2:21. It does seem to be a powerful ending. However, it is worth thinking about the larger context of that verse:

> So follow the way of the good and keep to the paths of the just. For the upright will inhabit the earth, the blameless will remain in it. While the wicked will vanish from the land, and the treacherous will be rooted out of it. (Proverbs 2:20–22)

Note that there is no mention of the Land of Israel at all in this passage. Indeed, the only mention of Israel at all through the initial chapters of Proverbs is in the opening verse which identifies Solomon as the author of Proverbs. The third old man appropriates the verse to make his point resound with the other men, that only the person who lives in Israel for its own sake will persevere in Israel despite frustrations. But the verse itself may not be talking about Israel at all. It may instead be talking about any person's destiny in any land on earth. And so, one could argue that Agnon took liberties with this text.

Now that we have considered the third man's argument, it is clear that the second man's argument is ignored. The third man suffered like the first man. He didn't see the light; he was far from "holy enough to enjoy the meanest part of it." But what did the third man think of the second man's point of view, beyond it being a parable?

The question is, was it not possible for the third man, or for anyone, to see the brilliant light of the second man? That is, the second man's position is essentially that of Rav Kook—the light of Israel shines so brightly that all other sources of light are dimmed. Did the third man reject that position,

The Land of Israel for Its Own Sake

or was he simply incapable of experiencing it personally? Here, Rav Kook himself may shed some light:

> For the Jewish people to fulfill their national destiny, God's seal must be placed on the people as a whole. The nation must recognize its special mission as God's people living in His land. When the Jewish people as a whole abandoned God, even though many individuals still kept some of the *mitzvot*, the nation had lost their distinctive mark. The land was no longer recognizable as God's land, and the nation was no longer recognizable as God's nation. They saw themselves as a people like all other. At that point, the Jewish people required exile. They needed to wander among the nations, stripped of all national assets. During this exile, they discovered that they are different and distinct from all other peoples. They realized that the essence of their nationhood contains a special quality; and that special quality is God's name that is associated with them . . . Only when the Jewish people fully assimilate this lesson will the exile have fulfilled its purpose, and the Jewish people will be able to return to their land . . . the object of exile is not to correct the individual, but to correct the nation . . .[17]

In short, the Jewish people will not have the full enlightenment that comes with being in the Land of Israel until they learn that they are distinct in their mission. Perhaps the third old man realizes that they are not yet at that point of evolution as a nation, and thus the light that the second old man sees is a delusion. Or perhaps it is a dream for the future. Or perhaps the second man is ahead of his time, an aberration who is ready and living in enlightenment without anyone else joining him as a nation. But certainly, the third man will not join him yet. Perhaps someday . . .

IS AGNON'S INSIGHT CONTEMPORANEOUS?

Whether Agnon injected himself and his personal worldview into this story as one of the old men or not, the positions they take resonate into our day. There are those who see going on Aliyah as fraught with difficulty and miss the ease of where they grew up and had a greater spiritual presence in their communities. There are others who are forever overwhelmed by being in Israel and cannot see spirituality of note anywhere else. Yet, nearly a century

---

17. Based on *Eyn Ayah* to Shabbat 41a, chapter 3, #2, as translated in Morrison, *Gold from the Land of Israel*, 218–220.

after Agnon composed this story, the extremes of frustration have lessened, and the expectation of messianic light has weakened.

The third position—land for its own sake—has, if anything, been reinforced. With the trials of existence in Israel, the attitude that our satisfaction in living in Israel depends on being swept away by its atmosphere of holiness and the pleasure gained in contact with divine immanence seems naïve. Although it would be misleading to say that many people feel it to be providential grace to be challenged, still many people frame living in Israel in covenantal terms. That sense of a covenant of love somewhere in the air seems to make the trials of living in Israel negotiable, and sometimes lends living in Israel a sense of satisfaction and even love. Agnon may have at an early stage understood the heart of our relationship to the land better than we who still live today.

Bibliography

Agnon, S.Y. "Brit Ahavah." In *Elu veElu*, Tel Aviv: Schocken, 1941.

———. "The Covenant of Love." *Canadian Jewish Chronicle* (April 26, 1935), rev. and rpt. *Forevermore and Other Stories*, 212–14. New Milford, CT: Toby, 2016.

———. "Ma'aseh Rabbi Yosef, o Torah Lishmah." *Davar* (July 10, 1925).

———. *A Guest for the Night*. Edited by Jeffrey Saks. New Milford, CT: Toby, 2014.

Agnon, S.Y., and Jeffrey Saks. *Forevermore & Other Stories*. New Milford, CT: Toby, 2017.

Kook, Abraham Isaac. *Orot Hakodesh*. Jerusalem, Rav Kook Institute, 1963.

Lamm, Norman. *Torah Lishmah: Torah for Torah's Sake*. Hoboken, NJ: Ktav, 1989.

Morrison, Chanan. *Gold from the Land of Israel*. Jerusalem: Urim, 2006.

Saks, Jeffrey. "A Portrait of Two Artists at the Crossroads: Between Rav Kook and S.Y. Agnon." *Tradition* 49/2 (2016) 32–52.

Zuckermandel, M., ed. *The Tosefta*. Jerusalem: Wahrman, 1970.

9

Agnon's "Orange Peel"

Word on the Street in the State Book Satires

Laura Wiseman

S.Y. Agnon's "Kelipat Tapuah Zahav," "The Orange Peel," first appeared in *Haaretz* on the Tenth of Tevet corresponding to December 22, 1939. The Hebrew story is subtitled: *Feuilleton leMa'aseh o Ma'aseh she-lo Hayah—*"*Feuilleton* of an Incident *or* An Incident That Never Occurred." The French term refers to a printed page or leaf of a newspaper and was commonly used for light-hearted tongue-in-cheek compositions or serials. Despite the self-effacing subtitle, suggestive of an entertaining fluff piece, this story demonstrates that sometimes the harshest truths are delivered in jest. Through the ironic account of the storyteller, "The Orange Peel" levels some of the author's criticism of emergent Israel's politics, bureaucratic committees and public works, and its society's herd instinct enacted at the expense of individual autonomy and at times, that of collective welfare. In effect, "The State is [both] the context and the object of the ironic criticism."[1] The spoof also delivers Agnon's views on the development of modern Hebrew as a

---

1. Hever, "Mitiv'i Ayni Medini," 121.

communicative-heritage language, specifically at the hands of people who purport to own and regulate its growth.

In "The Metaphysics of Agnon's Political Satire" that serves as a foreword to the annotated translations of the stories gathered in *The Orange Peel and Other Satires*, Jeffrey Saks conveys a literary dispute about the scope of the social satires of "The Book of State" (henceforth, State Book)—"The Orange Peel" among them—to carry Agnon's characteristically multivalent writing. In the past, Gershon Shaked had expressed his doubts about whether such allegorical pieces could give rise to an array of understandings: could they in fact generate multiple or multidimensional interpretations? More recently, Ariel Hirschfeld has asked, "Do we truly understand what our [. . .] orange peel littering the public domain truly represents? Might it not be a symbol pointing in multiple directions, and isn't this a clever enough story to keep multiple ideas in play?"[2] It is in response to Hirschfeld's question that I situate my analysis of "The Orange Peel." Despite the fact that there is decidedly less to mine textually in this story than in some of its companion pieces, I propose a strong reading—in combination with the common threads running through the State Book satires—that presents one interpretation for an enriched understanding of the parable.

Israel has long been a site of productive tension between individual and collective needs, desires and actualities. From the plural and public *anu ba'nu* (collective foundational) accounts of the *aliyot* (waves of immigration) and the communal ethos of early formative State-building stories, to the introspective *ani* (first-person singular voices) of late twentieth- and early twenty-first century Israeli novels, and lyrical poetry for that matter, we see varying degrees of torque between personal interest and group concerns. Agnon, an acute observer of human nature, makes an art of this very tension in his idiosyncratic constellation of four stories written between 1939 (eight years before the establishment of the State) and 1950, that he grouped with an introduction as *Sefer HaMedinah*.[3] Set in the pre-Statehood *yishuv*, the State Book satires pit public pressure, sometimes in the form of collective inertia, against individual initiative, and vested personal interests of the elite few against the collective good.[4]

2. Saks, "The Metaphysics of Agnon's Political Satire," viii.
3. All in Agnon, *Samukh veNir'eh*.
4. The *yishuv* refers to the Jewish settlement in Palestine during the period spanning late Ottoman Turkish rule and the British Mandate.

Agnon's "Orange Peel"

First this essay takes a look at the threads that unite the satires and surveys the stories with a wide-angle lens. It then homes in on "The Orange Peel" and filters it through the lens of cultural theory to interpret it as a parable that makes use of "literary mediation in the transmission of cultural values," in this case those of the emergent State of Israel.[5] In the process, the analysis draws on the approach of Maimonides to the expression of wisdom in language, set out in his introduction to *The Guide of the Perplexed*.[6] On its basis, the analysis presents a strong allegorical reading of the text.

First and foremost among the shared threads in the compilation is the projection of too much talk and too little decisive action: specifically, a preponderance of public pontification, and a paucity of individual initiative. The tension between word and deed, or lack thereof, becomes apparent as early as the introduction, added in 1950, in which *Ba'al Sefer HaMedinah* (the collection's narrator; in his playful way Agnon may have wished for his readers to see this character as an autobiographical projection of the author himself) sets out to chronicle the *ma'asim*—occurrences, accomplishments and exploits of the State. For various reasons this task eludes him. Among them, he finds language resistant to his attempts to capture the fluctuating essence he wishes to convey.[7]

> For the State is not like other living entities that inspire the writer, [. . .] Neither is the State a random gathering of people, a fraternity or group of groups that happen to be in a single place, so that the competent scribe can sketch them out with a single flourish of his quill. Rather the State is a metaphysical concept rendered into something physical which feigns meta-physicality. When you attempt to approach it as a metaphysical entity it slips back into physicality; if one considers it in physical terms, it suddenly reverts into meta-physicality. [. . .] Yet the idea of recording the deeds of the State continued to haunt me; though I despaired of ever writing the book, the book never despaired of being written. Many a time I was struck by a vision of blank pages rustling in the wind, each page crying like a soul stripped bare—"Have you no Hebrew words to clothe us in?"[8]

---

5. Locatelli, "Literature's Versions of Its Own Transmission of Values," 20.
6. Maimonides, *The Guide of the Perplexed*, tr. Pines, 1:5–20.
7. Saks, "Metaphysics," viii–ix.
8. Agnon, "Introduction [to the State Book Satires]," tr. Sara Daniel, *Orange Peel*, 125–26.

The capacity of language, among additional language-related issues, preoccupies the storyteller and constitutes a central focus of most of the stories, forming another prominent thread that runs through the State Book, one to which this essay will return in due course. Owing to the perceived resistance of language to convey the shifting entity of the State, the narrator manages to sketch only a handful of vignettes about the escapades of the leaders: statesmen, businessmen, doyens of *Va'ad haLashon* (The Hebrew Language Committee) and other self-important impresarios.[9] Although few in number, the vignettes are highly charged, culturally speaking, and they function in concert as a collection.

Yet another shared thread is a marked lack of respect for individual enterprise, and collective attempts by the general populace or agents of the State to restrict it when it does occur. This phenomenon is pronounced in "Peace Everlasting" and "The Orange Peel" in which individuals operate independently and proactively for the good of society. They are eschewed, nevertheless, in vociferously enunciated public opinion and by State law. The threads identified are discernible, in varying measure, in all episodes of the State Book, loosely yoking them as a compendium.

In the first story, "The Kidnappers," published in 1942, the narrator conveys a lethargic populace. There is a scarcity of deed and a profusion of speechmaking by politicians such as Schreiholtz—Yiddish for "Screaming Tree" or "Screaming Block of Wood"—an uncomplimentary reference to a certain budding statesman. Agnon installs his criticism of the lack of productive activity in the parable, from its inception, in the ratio of speech to deed that he entrenches in the wording. The story opens on an auditorium overflowing with people waiting to hear a discourse:

> The meeting hall was full to capacity. Not a person in town failed to come, because the State was in the grip of major crises and no one knew what to do about them. Since Mr. Schreiholtz was to be the speaker, the city's entire population turned out. For the custom of this State is that nothing is done without first deliberating upon it, and deliberation means speakers and orators. Once the speeches have been made and the orations delivered, the citizens of the State believe they have done something. If the crisis passes, well and good, if it does not pass another speech is made. Until a

---

9. *Va'ad haLashon* was established in 1890 as the authoritative body in matters of Hebrew language. It was the forerunner of Israel's Hebrew Language Academy, formally authorized by the Knesset in 1953.

more serious crisis arises and a different orator is called upon. If the crisis passes, well and good, and if it does not pass, etc., etc.[10]

The sheer number of words that Agnon embeds in the original Hebrew text related to speech, discussion, expounding, declaiming and oration—such as *lin'om* (to speak, make a speech), *lidrosh* (to expound), and *ladun* (to deliberate)—far outweighs the number connected to deed or supposed accomplishment. In fact, the latter, mainly from *la'asot* (to do), are couched in the negative and accrue throughout the State Book, forming a negative leitmotif that reinforces the noted inertia.

Michael Keren comments specifically on Agnon's personal preference for decisive action over public political discourse, in particular over State speeches that foray into the realm of metaphysical thought.[11] In an article that theorizes Agnon's relationship to the State based on the State Book satires, Keren builds a conceptual framework on the back of his identification of the author's intellectual integrity: that is, integrity expressed in Agnon's insistence on maintaining a differentiation between the metaphysical and instrumental domains. Agnon himself cleaved to the realm of deed.

Keren's assessment also rests on indicators of Agnon's view of the establishment of the modern State of Israel as a rational construct of history, rather than a link in the messianic vision, as certain early statesmen were fond of framing it in public speeches. Keren positions Agnon's view as counter to that expressed in the speeches of his contemporary, David Ben-Gurion. Ben-Gurion tended to project the birth of the modern State as a messianic development, and the nation as *am segulah* and *or lagoyim*—the chosen people and a light unto the nations, standpoints that Agnon studiously avoided.

Keren notes that despite the author's attitude, his storyteller persona refrains from direct attacks on the State itself. Keren cites excerpts from Agnon's notes in *MeAtzmi el Atzmi* that illustrate the author's grateful stance to the State for its physical protection, supplied in the form of "young men of Israel" who saved his life during the 1929 riots near his home in isolated Talpiot.[12] Agnon deliberately refrains from rebuffing the entity that protects

10. Agnon, "The Kidnappers," Isaac Frank, trans., *Orange Peel*, 129.

11. Keren, "Teguvato shel Agnon," 446–54.

12. In a letter to his publisher, Sh. Z. Schocken, following the riots of 1929, Agnon tells of the soldiers who rescued the residents of Talpiot, himself among them, carrying two satchels of manuscripts; those who helped him return to his ransacked home to save additional documents from his extensive archive of *Eretz Yisrael*; and all "the young men

him, life and limb. Security and defense on the part of the Jewish nation-state, rather than messianic salvation, is precisely the kind of endeavor that the author supports. Further, Keren points out, the storyteller is cognizant that the nascent State has no need for internal opposition: it has more than enough external enemies, particularly in the years of Hitler's influence, when the State Book stories are written.

That he chooses to depict the foibles of the State and its leading lights in ironic sketches with a quill rather than a rapier is, according to the gestalt set out by Keren, a backhanded expression of gratitude, but a critique nevertheless. The fact that the storyteller manages to sketch only a handful of the escapades of the State and its leading citizens conveys, to my mind, a conscious and related choice. That he is not convinced of his success in capturing, in that handful, the shifting essence of the State is, I suggest, a literary conceit: the apologia serves to legitimate his initiative to express criticism of individuals. From the apologia he derives license to paint the tensions of the era over the nature of the emergent State, whether actual, historical or yearned for.

In sum, writes Keren, "The State Book attests that Agnon, to a greater extent than other intellectuals, steadfastly maintained a separation between the metaphysical realm and the instrumental realm" and favored the latter. And if Agnon cannot shoulder the obligation for decisive action all on his own, I suggest that he bids his characters to assist him. We encounter just such individuals who demonstrate initiative in the State Book satires.

In "The Kidnappers," a spate of clandestine abductions by opposing political interest groups takes place to keep the leaders of the respective oppositions from dominating the auditoria and influencing the public with their words. This underhanded phenomenon ultimately leads to diminished attendance in public venues, fewer political speeches, and enhancement of the quality of family life, with family members opting to remain at home and learn together. In addition to the increase in learning of classical texts, this turn of events signals a shift in priorities from an attraction to the fleeting spoken word, to an attraction to the written word and its longevity.

In the second story, "Peace Everlasting," also published in 1942, the author encodes a drought through an intertextual conversation with Deuteronomy 11:13–21, the biblical passage which serves as the second section of *Shema*, and underscores the direct link between allegiance to God, enacted through fulfillment of the commandments, and timely,

---

of Israel who fought like lions"; *MeAtzmi el Atzmi*, 423–31.

divine precipitation to cultivate the earth's produce for sustenance. The story depicts a consequent food shortage leading to illness, starvation, and death among the general populace. At the same time, entrepreneurial food storage magnates manage to produce groaning boards sagging under the weight of all the hoarded victuals.[13] These keep their bellies full and profits rising. Two opposing factions—those who cover their heads and those who do not, and splinter groups of each—pull together by default against a maverick who takes it upon himself to actually *do* something—pray for rain—without first seeking the sanction of *any* group. The guilds of the opposing factions eventually work together, against their own best interests, to weave a textile covering or canopy to keep any rain that *might* result from the rogue's petitions from reaching the earth. In the planning phases of this misguided enterprise, the amount of talk-talk-talking reaches new heights when all the bigwigs troop off for a summit at a place dubbed *Siftotayim* (Lippery) conjuring up images of pairs of jabbering lips or talking heads.

The fourth satire, to jump ahead briefly, published in 1950, is "*Al HaMisim*" ("On Taxes"), a title that riffs on the supplementary holiday prayer *Al HaNisim* (On Miracles) through assonance.[14] In it the bureaucrats muster all the collective wisdom we would usually ascribe to the wise men of Chelm, and decide to tax walking sticks in order to make up the mounting deficit of the fledgling State.[15]

Kelipat Tapuaḥ Zahav ("The Orange Peel"), the third satire, shares the most prominent threads running through the four-story compilation.[16] The third satire opens on an orange peel that has been cast into a public thoroughfare. Observers react variously to its presence. Some are hotheads, jealous of its languor, just lying about attracting attention and causing harm without remorse. Some are moderates who pin the blame for its presence on whichever ravenous glutton gobbled the fruit and tossed the rind aside. Some denigrate the municipality for being lax in its street-cleaning duties. After all, the municipality collects taxes for this very purpose. Some onlookers reason that at least the consumer of the orange made a point of

---

13. Agnon, "Peace Everlasting," Jules Harlow, trans., 137–46. For a reading that proposes the title "Eternal Peace" based on literary analysis of the Hebrew text, see Wiseman, "Shelom 'Olamim," 163–85.

14. Agnon, "On Taxes," Sara Daniel, trans. *Orange Peel*, 147–64.

15. On the holidays of Hanukkah and Purim, the text of *Al HaNisim* is inserted into the *Amidah* prayer as well as the Grace after Meals, as a form of thanks and recognition of divine miracles and salvation.

16. Agnon, "The Orange Peel," *Orange Peel*, 147–52.

eating locally grown fruit, and not the competing imports! One pedantic soul ponders the spelling of *kelipah* (peel) and is adamant that spelling it *plene*, with the letter *yod*, is an egregious error that ought to be addressed *posthaste*. Some stare at it, some slip on it, still others debate responsibility for its removal. Another individual interprets the discarded peel as a symbol of autonomy, showing that people feel the liberty to do the same in public as they do at home. One woman, the wife of a State clerk—an anonymous *jobnik*, to use the vernacular—starts broadcasting to anyone who will listen, the story of her mother-in-law who broke her leg by slipping on a fruit peel, and all the woes that ensued: for *herself*, that is! This woman and her outspokenness are Agnon's equivalent of a YouTube clip that makes the matter of the orange peel "go viral."

The perfectly lovely peel goes on lying in the street. People see it. People talk about it. Nobody lifts a finger to pick it up. The peel is buffeted by the breezes, scorched by the sun, and bypassed by the masses. It remains in the public eye, day by day losing its luster. At the height of the drama, the storyteller interpolates himself in the plot by daring to shatter both authorial propriety and public stasis. He boldly steps into the narrative and into the street and prepares to remove the deteriorating peel, lest quarrels escalate and imperil the community.

His unusual undertaking evokes strong feelings among the bystanders. One woman takes pity on all the other poor peels and papers in the street and implores the narrator to pick them up as well. Along comes a man who adjures *her* to calm down. He relates rumors of a partition plan, and suggests that the peel could very well fall outside *our* jurisdiction, implying "Why bother?!" *Ba'al Sefer HaMedinah*—the storyteller himself—decides, nevertheless, to do a little extra tidying up of the public square. Along comes a series of people to dispense their unsolicited and oh-so-sage advice: how to push the peels aside, how to remove them, and where to throw them; first to pick up the grapefruit peels; no—first the banana peels; no, no—first some *other* kind of peel. In order to fulfill, or perhaps avoid, all this very good advice, the narrator starts scooping up everything in sight using both hands. "However," writes Agnon, "advice-givers are many, and a person's hands are few." Ultimately, heated arguments erupt among the dispensers of advice, threatening danger, the very outcome the storyteller had sought to prevent. His audacious move precipitates a *ḥad gadya* type of chain of events that concludes with a police officer issuing tickets to the storyteller for being *makhil kehalot,* and initiating a public *ambouha* (illegally assembling crowds, in effect demonstrating in public—practices which can lead to a community brouhaha), and for practising a trade without a license, rubbish removal in this instance.

In "Orange Peel" the narrator *performs* his message, literally: when it comes to public hygiene, safety, and waste management, individuals like himself need to counter public inertia and to dare to intervene; but Agnon's writing is far more complex than the performance of a singular mimetic message. In fact, in modern literature, any attempt, writes Locatelli, "to extract a univocal "moral of the fable," or single-minded intention, would be an unacceptable hermeneutic constraint."[17] And when it comes to Agnon's writing, all the more so. Figuratively, the storyteller is performing another message altogether. The question is where to look for textual cues in order to decrypt it.

As indicated, "The Orange Peel" is not as densely encoded with rhetorical devices, allusions, and intertextual conversations as most of Agnon's stories. At bare minimum, we can look to his story title, as Agnon excels at intimating associations in cleverly naming his works.[18] On the surface, the Hebrew title of this story refers to the early modern Hebrew epithet for orange—*tapuaḥ zahav*, later to coalesce as *tapuz*. On a deeper level, *Kelipat Tapuaḥ Zahav* (literally, the peel of a golden apple) presents readers with a clue in the form of an allusion to the golden apples of *Ketuvim* (Writings). In Proverbs 25:11 we read, *tapuḥei zahav bemaskiyot kasef, davar davur al ofenav* ("Golden apples in silver filigree display-pieces, are [as] phrases well-turned"). The golden apples of Proverbs, displayed in silver coverings with apertures through which the golden fruit remains visible, may be likened figuratively to the finely crafted essence of belletristic writing.

In the introduction to *The Guide of the Perplexed*, Maimonides makes amplified use of the biblical metaphor of the golden apples in silver showpieces in relation to the expression of wisdom, particularly the oracles of the biblical prophets. There he writes:

> See how beautifully the conditions of a good metaphor are described in this good figure! It shows that in every word that has a double sense, a literal one and a figurative one, the plain meaning must be as valuable as silver, and the hidden meaning still more

---

17. Locatelli, "Literature's Versions of its Own Transmission of Values," 20.

18. Consider, for example, the title "Tallit Aḥeret" for its double entendre: "Another Tallit" or "An Other Tallit." Additionally, consider the Hebrew title "BaYa'ar uva'Ir" ("In the Forest and in the City") for the reflective traces embedded in its metathesis.

precious; so that the figurative meaning bears the same relation to the literal one as gold to silver... The same is the case with the figures employed by the prophets. Taken literally, such expressions contain wisdom useful for many purposes, among others, for the amelioration of the condition of society... Their hidden meaning, however, is profound wisdom, conducive to the recognition of real truth.[19]

With the analogy of Maimonides in mind, I return first to the State Book satires in general, and then to the specific story of the orange peel, to discern their allegorical messages. In examining their allusions and rhetorical devices, I find that what piques the narrator's ire most, and keeps his satire streaming, is any and every matter related to language in the emergent State: the way Hebrew is perpetuated, innovated, spelled and pronounced, taught, written, published and handled.

The storyteller spurns the overuse and abuse of language in pompous speechmaking and at the hands of those who purport to own or control the development of modern Hebrew. Consider his treatment of Schreiholtz in "The Kidnappers." The storyteller looks askance at high-level meetings with expressions of low-level thinking. Consider the summit at *Siftotayim* (Lippery) in "Peace Everlasting." He cannot abide by the nonsense he overhears as snatches of conversation on the street in "The Orange Peel." He is derisive of the pandering to punditry that occurs in terms of spellings, neologisms, and misspellings. Consider the spelling of *Protestyah*[20] in "Peace Everlasting" with one *tet* and one *tav* to cater to those among the members of the Hebrew Language Committee partial to one or the other. Consider the debates over whether to employ *plene* spelling or retain "deficient" spelling in strict accordance with *torat hanikkud* (rules of Hebrew vocalization). Consider the pedantic figure Agnon presents in "The Orange Peel" who is so focused on the *plene* spelling of the word "peel" in the news, incorrect in his view, that he sidetracks people from discussing the fact quite literally on the ground: an orange peel littering the street. In "Peace Everlasting" the narrator practically jeers at the diminishing prowess of writers in composing rhyme: why else, he muses, would the Hebrew Language Committee generate dozens of new words by tacking the syllables *yah* and *yot / iyah*

---

19. "Introduction," *The Guide of the Perplexed*, tr. S. Pines, 1:12.

20. The syllable *-yah* functions as a theophoric suffix, ironically rendering *Protestyah*, "protest of God."

and iyot onto loan words rather than reviving and reinvesting words drawn from classical Hebrew texts with nuanced meanings?!

Many readers are willing to hear the voice of the narrator and his pronounced language predilections in the State Book satires, and in other stories by the author, as the voice of Agnon *in propria persona*. Consider, for example, the storyteller of *Ḥush HaReaḥ* ("The Sense of Smell"), a story outside of the State Book. In it, the speaker spends countless sleepless nights scouring Talmud, collections of Midrash, and exegetical commentaries for the source that justifies a turn of phrase he has used through his own keen language knowledge, that has caused some raised eyebrows about his linguistic competence among less erudite writers.[21] Only an artist and language perfectionist like Agnon would have been so perturbed and so persistent in finding a solid proof text. In such instances the narrator's voice and the author's voice overlap.

Agnon was a proponent of Hebrew language use in the public arena. He was an advocate of Hebrew, rather than Yiddish or other languages, as the language of instruction for students, especially students preparing to teach. He was contemptuous of those who purported to have extensive linguistic knowledge in their languages of origin but resisted the use of Hebrew in their pedagogy for Hebrew language and its bodies of literatures.[22] In "Peace Everlasting" the storyteller, channeling Agnon, deploys scathing wit to disparage the committee of linguistic experts and wordsmiths assembled to confer a name on the textile cover that the guilds have woven to keep rain from reaching the earth: "They finally decided to give the naming into the hands of the Society Linguistia, the Linguistia being in charge of all linguistic matters, all of whose members are linguists and verbally verbal, experts in all languages, among them even members who are expert in in the language of our State."[23]

There came a point at which Agnon felt compelled to part company with the Hebrew Language Committee over language-related tensions and

---

21. Agnon, "Ḥush HaReaḥ" in *Elu veElu*; in English as "The Sense of Smell," in *A Book That Was Lost*, 149–56.

22. Bar-Adon identifies several educators who fit this description in the *yishuv*, upon whom Agnon modeled certain of his characters. See Bar-Adon, "S.Y. Agnon and the Revival of Modern Hebrew," 150–55.

23. Agnon, "Peace Everlasting," Jules Harlow, trans., *Orange Peel*, 143. In the original Hebrew text, the linguistic society is dubbed *Leshon-yah* (God's language). With the theophoric suffix, I suggest that Agnon delivers a facetious moniker for the organization, akin to "The Almighty Language Association."

politics.[24] Whether or not that body or subsequently the Hebrew Language Academy ever publicly or sufficiently recognized Agnon's language contributions, in truth Agnon was every bit as responsible for the revival of Hebrew as a communicative-heritage language as those who are more often publicly credited: Bialik literarily, and Ben-Yehuda whose recognition is linked popularly to his lexicon and historical dictionary.

With specific attention to "The Orange Peel," Hannan Hever views the approach of the high and mighty language pedants, who pontificate in this particular story and its companion pieces, as the artificial sanctification of modern Hebrew by elevating the status of its rules and regulations for syntax, lexicon, spelling and so forth, to a pseudo-halakhic level. To illustrate, he highlights the wording of the sophist in "The Orange Peel" who laments the *plene* spelling of *kelipah* (peel) in the press: "For years I've been crying that peel shouldn't be spelled with a double e. Yet the world insists on doing so, and it's an error we ought to rend our garments over." So egregious is this violation in his eyes that it mandates the legally prescribed grief practice of tearing one's clothing in mourning over communal calamity or death. Agnon, himself, was less than pleased with any issues that signaled the demise of Hebrew which he preserved and developed with respect for both its communicative and heritage dimensions. At the same time, he had very little patience for the inflated ego battles over minutia, such as whether the use of *matres lectionis* (the use of certain consonants in spelling to represent vowels) compromised the principles of grammar; nevertheless, the hairsplitting irony and struggles of pomposity did not escape him, and he harnessed them in hyperbolic sketches and scathing satire.

Hever's interpretation extends the charge of artificial sanctification of language to that of public space as well, pointing out the story's allusion to the talmudic laws of damages. They warn that no *ashpatot* (dunghills; heaps of rubbish) are to be made in Jerusalem.[25] Hever notes that the storyteller refrains from commenting on the rumored partition plan, and instead focuses single-mindedly on the sanctity of cleanliness for the *yishuv*. We are to understand that the holiness of Jerusalem is in jeopardy on account of an orange peel. Hever observes that "Agnon satirically presents the intrusive State that does not permit its civilian population to exist or function

---

24. Regarding Agnon's eventual departure from the Hebrew Language Committee, see Bar-Adon, "Lehitpatruto shel Agnon miVa'ad haLashon," 291–302.

25. BT Baba Kamma 82b.

without its oversight."[26] The veneration of State-controlled public works, such as street cleaning, is so entrenched that a private citizen is restricted from stooping to extract rubbish from the road. Ultimately, Hever observes, the artificially constructed sanctity inhibits the ability of the storyteller "to fulfill the national, unifying obligation of an author."[27] In this way the writer "points out his inability to act in the best interests of a state that prevents literature from improving national space."[28]

To return to the allusion built into the orange peel, connected to *tapuhei zahav bemaskiyot kasef* (golden apples in silver filigree display-pieces) in Proverbs, as well as to the Maimonidean extension of the metaphor, we have the opportunity to reread "The Orange Peel" with fresh eyes. In retrospect the title is indeed the first clue that in this story too, Agnon is exercised about the Hebrew language and the way it is handled. If the lack-luster item lying in the street is indeed *kelipat tapuaḥ zahav*—a lattice silver showpiece, metaphorically speaking, and a fine phrase, allegorically speaking—then the golden apple that it must have originally contained is long gone. The silver casing is becoming tarnished and bent out of shape as people trample it: words are being defaced and devalued. Based on the metaphors outlined, my strong reading proposes that in *this* story, Agnon levels his criticism of word pollution in the burgeoning State. With so much speechmaking and rhetoric in the State Book satires, people have absorbed the essence of the golden apples, or not, and subsequently carried the silver slogans of the politicians and societal leaders out of the meeting halls and into the streets. In our day people would tweet them on Twitter, post them on Facebook, and incorporate them in the banners of their blogs. The citizens of the State have used and abused the phrases, then discarded them like so much detritus. The narrator, so aware of and sensitive to language use, cannot stand the situation any longer. He sets out to address the word pollution by rescuing the words. In this regard there is good news and bad.

The bad news is that words can and do become devalued over time. In his essay "Revealment and Concealment in Language," Bialik expresses this thought in contemplating the power of words in their naissance and noting that over time and through use, words are susceptible to a loss of impact: they become empty husks, or abandoned orange peels, as in our

---

26. Hever, "MiTiv'i Ayni Medini," 123.
27. Hever, "MiTiv'i Ayni Medini," 122.
28. Hever, "MiTiv'i Ayni Medini," 123.

story.²⁹ The good news, according to Bialik, is that the husks are durable: in the vernacular of this day and age, we would say "sustainable." To mix metaphors, the husks can be retrieved and refilled with new and precious golden apples. With a little polish, the husks can be made to shine like *maskiyot kesef,* silver display-pieces, to draw the eye to the fruit gleaming within. In the proposed strong reading of Agnon's "The Orange Peel," I suggest that refilling the peel would have been the storyteller's next step. Like Agnon, who frequently breathed new life into ancient words, so would he have done.

If only the author were still with us today. Picture Agnon, about fifty years after receiving the Nobel Prize for literature, with a new laptop perched atop the *shtender* (lectern) in his upstairs study on Klausner Street. I speculate that the author would want writers to be mindful of the value of the words they cast into the public domain, and readers to be ethical in the treatment of those words, even after consuming the golden apples they once held. And for our part, when those words inevitably lose their potency, we can still gather them with care so that knowledgeable and inventive artists like Agnon, familiar with all layers of our communicative-heritage language, can refill them with new and precious golden apples to use in our speech and writing.

To be sure, the strong reading that this article offers is but one understanding of the story among potential responses to Hirschfeld's musing about the capacity of "The Orange Peel" for complex symbolism. In that context I'll close with the words of Locatelli: "good literature always is political and philosophical in a broad sense, rather than doctrinaire in a narrow sense. This is what makes it intrinsically ethical," that is " perpetually imbricated with the question of being variously and perfectibly human."³⁰ The word on the street is that Agnon's writing is very much this good kind of literature.

Bibliography

Agnon, S.Y. "Al HaMisim." *Haaretz* (February 17, 1950).
———. "Ḥush haReaḥ." In *Elu veElu*, 296–302. Tel Aviv: Schocken, 1974.
———. "Introduction [to the Statebook Satires]." Translated by Sara Daniel. In *The Orange Peel and Other Satires.* New Milford, CT: Toby, 2015.

29. Bialik, "Giluy veKhisuy baLashon," 251–58; in English in *Revealment and Concealment: Five Essays.*

30. Locatelli, "Literature's Versions of its Own Transmission of Values," 31.

———. "Kelipat Tapuah Zahav." *Haaretz* (December 22, 1939).

———. "The Kidnappers." Translated by Isaac Frank. In *The Orange Peel and Other Satires*, 129–36. New Milford, CT: Toby, 2015.

———. "Letter to Sh. Z. Schocken." In *MeAtzmi el Atzmi*, 423–31. Tel Aviv: Schocken, 1972.

———. "On Taxes." Translated by Sara Daniel. In *The Orange Peel and Other Satires*, 153–64. New Milford: Toby, 2015.

———. "The Orange Peel." Translated by Sara Daniel. In *The Orange Peel and Other Satires*, 147–52. New Milford, CT: Toby, 2015.

———. "Peace Everlasting." Translated by Jules Harlow. In *The Orange Peel and Other Satires*, 137–46. New Milford, CT: Toby, 2015.

———. *Samukh veNir'eh*. Tel Aviv: Schocken, 1950.

———. "The Sense of Smell." Translated by Arthur Green. In *A Book That Was Lost*. Edited by Alan Mintz, and Anne Golomb Hoffman, 149–56. Tel Aviv: Schocken, 1996.

Bar-Adon, Aharon. "Lehitpatruto Shel Agnon miVa'ad haLashon." In *Shai Agnon: Meḥkarim uTe'udot*, edited by Gershon Shaked and Refael Weiser, 291–302. Jerusalem: Mosad Bialik, 1978.

Bar-Adon, Aaron. "S.Y. Agnon and the Revival of Modern Hebrew." *Texas Studies in Literature and Language* 14/1 (1972) 150–55.

Bialik, Hayyim Nahman. "Giluy veKhisuy baLashon." In *Knesset: Divrei Sifrut*, 251–58. Bezarna: Moriya, 1915.

———. *Revealment and Concealment: Five Essays.* Jerusalem: Ibis, 2000.

Hever, Hannan. "Mitiv'i Ayni Medini: Te'ologiyah uPolitikah bi"*Ferakim shel Sefer HaMedinah* me'et Shemuel Yosef Agnon." In *Bikoaḥ Ha'El: Te'ologiyah uPolitikah B/BeSifrut Ha'Ivrit HaModernit*. Jerusalem: Van Leer Institute, 2013.

Keren, Michael. "Teguvato shel Agnon liMedinat-haLe'om haYehudit al pi *Sefer HaMedinah*." *Iyyunim biTekumat Yisrael* 5 (1995) 446–54.

Locatelli, Angela. "Literature's Versions of Its Own Transmission of Values." In *Ethics in Culture: The Dissemination of Values through Literature and Other Media*, edited by Astrid Erll, Herbert Grabes, and Ansgar Nünning, 19–34. Berlin: de Gruyter, 2008.

Maimonides, Moses. *The Guide of the Perplexed*. Translated by Shlomo Pines. Chicago: University of Chicago, 1963.

Saks, Jeffrey. "The Metaphysics of Agnon's Political Satire." In *The Orange Peel and Other Satires*, vii–xvii. New Milford, CT: Toby, 2015.

Wiseman, Laura. "*Shelom 'Olamim*—Eternal Peace by S.Y. Agnon: Yishuv-Era Society on the Brink of Statehood." *Journal of Modern Judaism* 36/2 (2016) 163–85.

10

From Hanye to Tehilla
The Righteous "Grandmother" as Personification of the Shtetl and Jerusalem in Baron and Agnon

WENDY ZIERLER

How Israeli readers have interpreted Agnon's "Tehilla" (1950)—the story of a modern writer's encounter in pre-State Jerusalem with a righteous, long-suffering old woman, who asks him to pen a letter to her long-dead former fiancé that she intends to take to her own grave—is a story in its own right. Indeed, to write or speak about Agnon's "Tehilla" at this point in Hebrew and Israeli literary history is akin to walking into a crowded room where two opposing groups have been busy hollering at one another for years and trying in the midst of it all to get a word in edgewise. I refer here to the critical argument of those such as Baruch Kurzweil, Eli Schweid, Leah Goldberg and more recently Hillel Weiss and Rut Ben-Pinḥas.[1] These scholars tend to read the character of Tehilla as an apotheosis of faith, a woman who manages by dint of her extraordinary righteousness and

---

1. Kurzweil, *Massot 'al Sippurei Shai Agnon*, 130–35; Goldberg, "Agnon biSheloshah Kolot," 194–95; Weiss, "Silluk haShekhinah," 131–49; Ben-Pinḥas, *U-Tehilato biYerushalayim*. "Tehilla" can be found in Hebrew in Agnon's *Ad Henah*, 138–60; in revised and annotated English translation in *Two Scholars Who Were in Our Town and Other Novellas*, 223–58.

forbearance to transcend her many sorrows and die at an extraordinary old age at a time which she herself appoints, thereby personifying and embodying the virtues of traditional piety and of Old Jerusalem. Those on the other side of the argument, including Amos Oz, A. B. Yehoshua, Ada Shossheim and Aryeh Naveh see "Tehilla" as the story of a once pious woman whose encounter with the modern skeptical writer/narrator provokes her to reevaluate her life and question her faith and who dies in a condition of madness, anger, and skepticism.[2]

I do not intend to rehearse the various arguments on either side. To borrow from Agnon's own comments about Hebrew secular poetry in the Middle Ages, I believe that a careful reading of "Tehilla" reveals aspects "in which the sacred and the secular work together in the story in suggestive ways."[3] That is to say, the story is best understood as embodying both modernity and fidelity to tradition rather than as lodged in one or the other of these poles. I refer again to Agnon's own remarks, this time on the occasion of receiving the Israel Prize in 1954, four years after the publication of "Tehilla":

With regard to my lack of modernity and so forth, I must concede that I do not follow their statutes. But even I, ladies and gentlemen, have not been scrubbed clean of all traces of **modernity**. Even if I do not wish to **modernize, modernity** rises up against me and places its **rod** over me.	וענין חוסר המודרניות שבי, על כגון זה חייב אני להודות שאיני הולך בחוקותיהם. אבל אף אני מורי ורבותי איני מנוקה מכל שמץ מודרניות, ואפילו איני רוצה להתמדרן המודרניות מתמרדת ורודה בי.

Note the word play that Agnon enacts in this passage with such words as *moderniyut, lehitmadren, mitmaredet,* and *rodeh.* Agnon couples the foreign word *moderniyut* together with a novel *hitpa'el* usage of the root *m-r-d* (*mitmaredet,* rise up against me) along with the verb *rodeh,* which means "to rule," but which I have translated as "to place a rod over" in order to

---

2. Oz, *Shetikat HaShamayim,* 19–28 [in English as *The Silence of Heaven*]; Yehoshua, *HaKallah haMeshuḥreret* [*The Liberated Bride*]; Naveh, "Tehillah haMoredet haKedoshah," 7–33; Shossheim, "Tilei Tilim shel Parshanut al Tilli (Tehillah)," 26–29.

3. Agnon, "Otiyot u-Sefarim," 76.

capture the play of similar sounds. Agnon even goes so far as to create a neologism—*lehitmadren*, to modernize oneself—itself an act of linguistic modernization. On the one hand Agnon claims that he is loath to modernize, that modernism is happening to him willy-nilly; on the other hand, his word choices themselves clearly demonstrate a conscious intent to bring the experience of modernity to his writing, both on the micro-level of linguistic inventiveness and the macro-level of the depiction of modern social and existential reality.

In the case of "Tehilla," I would suggest, a similar dialectic operates, with Agnon lauding and reveling in traditional modes and sources, and yet playfully, slyly and inventively engaging with contemporary issues and modes in terms of specific word choices and in the broader realm of ideas and literary history. One of these ideas is the role of women in Jewish tradition and contemporary Jewish life. Indeed, Agnon's story both eulogizes and upends the model of the Old World Jewish woman.

With this in mind, I turn my attention to an aspect of "Tehilla" that has not received sufficient attention, namely the possibility, first raised by scholar Nurit Govrin,[4] that Agnon may have been inspired in the creation of the character and plot of Tehilla by a 1909 story entitled "HaSavta Hanye" by Agnon's literary contemporary Devorah Baron (1887–1956); Baron was one of the first women to publish fiction in Hebrew and the only Hebrew woman prose writer of her generation to achieve canonical status, with Israeli children to this day studying her stories for their matriculation exams. The tale of a righteous woman in an Eastern European village, which evokes

---

4 Govrin, *HaMaḥatzit haRishonah/Parshiyot Mukdamot*, 174. Baron's "HaSavta Hanye" has was originally published in *HaOlam* 3:33 (29 Elul 5669 / September 15, 1909), 8–9. Baron also published the story in a Yiddish version as *"Di Bubbe Henye" Yugend: A Literarische Samlung* 1 (1910) 27–32. The Hebrew version of story is found on 465–70 of the Govrin-Holtzman volume, while the Yiddish version can be found on 657–63. My translation of this story, the first in English, can be found in the appendix to this essay. A translation of the Yiddish version appears in *The First Day and Other Stories*, trans. Kronfeld and Seidman, 162–71. Citations from the Hebrew story follow the Govrin-Holtzman edition. There are a number of thematic and stylistic differences between the Hebrew and the Yiddish versions of this story. The Yiddish includes more dialogue and a greater vernacular quality, with Hanye being addressed as "Bubinke" and other such loving diminutives. The Hebrew has a more formal style, including overt liturgical and midrashic references, such as in the introductory paragraph, which refers to Hanye reciting *tefiloteha vetaḥanuneha*, something which is completely absent in the Yiddish. As Naomi Seidman observes, the Yiddish also takes a more macabre and punitive turn, with Henye's pride in her husband and sons' Torah study, seen as "threatening the social and hierarchical social order." Seidman, *A Marriage Made in Heaven*, 98.

folktale traditions of Old World Jewish women's piety, but also includes some surprising, counter-traditional, modern elements, Baron's "HaSavta Hanye" adduces many parallels with Agnon's "Tehilla." In creating "Tehilla" Agnon may have intentionally resurrected and expanded upon the story of Baron's Savta Hanye (a metonym or female personification of the shtetl) and repurposed her in "Tehilla" as a personification of the Old City of Jerusalem. With Baron's story in mind, the burying, or as Hillel Weiss contends, the *genizah*[5] of Tehilla that occurs at the end of Agnon's story becomes a means not just of paying tribute to the Old World and mode that Tehilla represents, especially after the fall of the Old City in 1948, but also of honoring and rewriting Baron's proto-feminist story (in the way that *genizah* functions as a means of honoring worn and tattered sacred Jewish texts).[6] All of this becomes particularly suggestive when one considers that Baron herself did not re-publish her 1909 story in her own lifetime, dubbing this and other explicitly feminist, early stories *smartutim*[7] (rags) and excluding them from her later, published story collections. Might Agnon have specifically set out to rehabilitate and improve upon a story that had, in later years, been shunned by its own author? Might he have been motivated in "Tehilla," which itself refers to the tattered and worn aspects of Jerusalem, to mend the tatters of Baron's early story and lend it renewed glory?

We do have some indication that Baron's story was remembered by close friends and readers of Agnon's own work. For example, upon the occasion of Baron's death, Agnon scholar Meshulam Tochner read "HaSavta Hanye" has out loud to his Hebrew literature class as a tribute to her.[8] We also know that the practice of using the work of another contemporary Hebrew writer as a template for his own work was not foreign to Agnon. Hillel Halkin refers, for example, to Agnon's use of Y.H. Brenner's *Shekhol*

---

5. Weiss, *Parshanut leḤamishah miSippurei Shai Agnon*, 75–93.

6. Unfortunately, because Agnon left Palestine and all of his books from this early stage were destroyed in a fire in his house in Germany in 1924, we cannot point to Agnon's own copy of the story. His library, however, does include several, signed copies of works by Baron. And Agnon certainly could have re-accessed the story from a library copy of *HaOlam* and may also have known the story from its Yiddish version.

7. For a discussion of this, see Baron, *Agav Orḥa*, 9–10. Notably included among Baron's *smartutim* was a 1908 Hebrew story entitled "Genizah" that deals with a young girl's frustration over the exclusion of her mother's worn *tkhine* book, deemed a mere *smartut*, from category of sacred texts buried in the town *genizah* ceremony. See Baron, *Parshiyot Mukdamot*, 421–26.

8. Personal recollection of Tochner's former student, Benzi Cohen (October 30, 2016).

veKishalon (*Breakdown and Bereavement*) as a model for his own treatment of Second Aliyah Zionist disappointment in *T'mol Shilshom*. As Halkin writes, "Borrowing the outlines of *Breakdown and Bereavement*'s plot certainly seems a back-handed literary tribute, a way of saying, 'Good idea, and now let me show you how to do it.'"[9] It is my contention, therefore, that in "Tehilla," Agnon may have set out to offer his own expanded and more subtle treatment of the themes raised in Baron's early story, shifting the focus of the Old World model from the Diaspora to Jerusalem, and adding greater depth and ambiguity to the story.

AGNON AND BARON

To make this argument, I must first establish connection between Agnon and Baron, in general, and the two stories, in particular.

In S.Y. Agnon's 1919 story, "Aggadat HaSofer," a visitor comes to the home of the protagonist, Raphael the Scribe, and brings him word of new trends in the realm of Jewish scribal arts:

What should we say and what should we relate, Reb Raphael? If I told you, you wouldn't believe me. In the house of So-and-So the Sofer, I saw with my own eyes a number of young men sitting by day and night writing scrolls, phylacteries and *mezuzot*, thus making factory work out of the holy Torah. *Not only this, but I have heard that in the house of another even girls sit and write.*"	מה נאמר ומה נדבר רבי רפאל. לא יאומן כי יסופר. בעיני ממש ראיתי אצל פלוני הסופר יושבים כמה בחורים יומם ולילה וכותבים ספרים תפילין ומזוזות ועושים מן התורה הקדושה מעשה פבריקאות. ולא עוד אלא שמעתי אומרים אצל אלמוני אפילו נערות יושבות וכותבות.

The ostensible purpose of this this passage is to contrast Raphael's rigorously pious practice of his craft with the permissive practices of other modern scribes. But insofar as the word *sofer* also means writer—the same term is used in "Tehilla" to refer to the narrator of the story, who is called upon by Tehilla to write that famous letter to long-dead Shraga—this passage also hints at secular Hebrew prose writing and the modern emergence of women's writing in Hebrew. The expression used at the beginning of the passage to express incredulity, "If I told you, you wouldn't believe me," only

---

9. Halkin, "The Disappointments," 30.

serves to underscore the conflation here of sacred scribal arts and modern writing or storytelling, insofar as the word for "told," *yesuppar*, comes from the same root as *sofer* (scribe or writer) and *le-sapper* (to tell). What does it mean, then, when women writers begin to enter into a Hebrew literary/storytelling tradition where women's voices and writings were so glaringly absent for so many centuries? What does it mean when women, the eternal object of male fascination and imagination, who commonly appear in Hebrew literary tradition as personifications of the abject or redeemed land, but rarely as speaking or writing subjects in their own right, suddenly begin telling their own stories? How did the first women writers alter the script, so to speak, and how did a modern prose writer such as Agnon register or respond to these modern alterations?

When "Aggadat HaSofer" was published, Agnon was already well-acquainted with one such pioneering woman writer/storyteller, namely, Devorah Baron, a rabbi's daughter from Ouzda in the Pale of Settlement, who began publishing fiction in Yiddish and Hebrew while still a teenager, left home to pursue a secular education and immigrated to Palestine in December 1910, settling, as Agnon did in 1908, in Neve Tzedek, where she immediately joined the editorial staff of the Jaffa-based, influential weekly, *HaPo'el HaTza'ir*. During Baron's time as literary editor, Agnon published several landmark works in the paper, including *Tishre* (serialized October–December 1911; later reworked as *Givat HaḤol* or in English as "Hill of Sand") and his famous novella, *VeHaya he'Akov leMishor* (serialized January–May 1912; in English as *And the Crooked Shall Be Made Straight*), while several of Baron's own stories and literary reviews appeared in the publication during this same period. We know that during his first sojourn in Palestine, Agnon was in daily communication with Baron's husband, *HaPo'el HaTza'ir*'s editor Yosef Aharonovitz (1877–1937);[10] two of the reminiscences about Baron that appear in the book *Agav Orḥa*, edited by Baron's daughter Tzippora Aharonovitz, refer to Agnon as a regular visitor to their household.[11] Agnon himself mentions that he gifted to Baron the curtains that he used to protect his clothes from dust upon leaving Palestine for Germany in 1912.[12] In several of Agnon's letters to his wife Esther, written when he was already back in Palestine and Esther and children were still in Germany, Agnon recalls visiting with Baron and having literary

10. Band, *Nostalgia and Nightmare*, 18.
11. Baron, *Agav Orḥa*, 225, 233.
12. Agnon, *MeAtzmi el Atzmi*, 133.

discussions with her.¹³ Agnon's library, preserved in Beit Agnon, includes a copy of Baron's 1932 translation of Flaubert's *Madame Bovary*, as well as an autographed copy of Baron's prize-winning 1933 book *Ketanot*. And the Baron archives at Genazim includes at least two letters of congratulations and admiration to Baron on the occasion of her publishing various story collections.¹⁴

"HASAVTA HANYE" AS A TEMPLATE FOR "TEHILLA"

But the connection between "HaSavta Hanye," and "Tehilla" runs much deeper than the mere acquaintance and contact between these writers. A comparison of these stories reveals that they include many common elements including similar motifs, word choices, and most importantly, almost identical elderly female protagonists, women whom both stories depict as extraordinarily pious but also unconventional in certain specific ways. Baron published her Hebrew story in the Elul 5669 (September 15, 1909) issue of *HaOlam*, over a year after Agnon immigrated to Palestine, as well as a Yiddish version of the story in *Yugend* in 1910, the same year she arrived in the country. As Naomi Seidman sketches out, between the years 1908 and 1910, Baron's last years in Europe, she published several stories that explicitly treat feminist themes, and "HaSavta Hanye" is part of this series. "These stories," Seidman explains, "argue for women's participation in Torah study, expose the mistreatment of women's texts, insist on women's entitlement in ritually memorializing the dead, and explore the place of daughters in the patriarchal family."¹⁵ As I mentioned, I believe that in "Tehilla" Agnon may very well have been directly responding to and furthering some of the themes and messages of Baron's early story.¹⁶

Agnon himself registers the argument for women's ritual and literary inclusion in "Tehilla," and has Tehilla herself make the case. Toward the end of the story, as Tehilla begins to dictate her letter in Yiddish to the narrator (after giving him a piece of sugar, like an old time *melamed*!), she makes

---

13. Agnon, *Esterlein Yakirati*, 280, 286.

14. These two letters from Agnon to Baron, from 1927 and 1934, from the Baron archives, were published in *Genazim* 99:8, 16.

15. Seidman, *A Marriage Made in Heaven*, 95.

16. We also have evidence of the reverse, namely Baron revising structures and themes from Agnon in her fiction. For a discussion of Baron's revision of Agnon's "Agunot" in her early story "Agunah," see Bernstein, "On the Story 'Agunah,'" 117–44.

FROM HANYE TO TEHILLA

the following remarks, reminiscent of the passage from "Aggadat HaSofer" quoted above, that call attention to new forms of Hebrew/Jewish education for women, deeming it a recent divine improvement of the world:

| Take up the quill and write. I shall speak in Yiddish, but you will write in the holy tongue. I have heard that now they teach the girls both to write and speak the Holy Language: you see, my son, how the good Lord is constantly improving His world from age to age. When I was a child, this was not their way. | טול את הנוצה וטבול אותה בדיו וכתוב. אני אומר לך באידית ואתה תכתוב בלשון הקודש. שמעתי שמ־למדין את הבנות לדבר ולכתוב בל־שון הקודש. רואה אתה בני, הקדוש ברוך הוא בחסדו מנהג את עולמו בכל דור ודור יפה יותר. כשהייתי אני ילדה לא היו נוהגין כך. |

If one accepts the premise that Baron's "HaSavta Hanye" may have inspired and influenced the shape and details of Agnon's story; if one takes seriously the idea that Agnon's Tehilla may have been derived from the product of the pen of a woman whose own rabbinic father, Shabbetai Eliezer Baron, had taught her to read and write in the Holy Tongue and had encouraged her own literary education and ambitions, how doubly resonant Tehilla's statement about God's improving the world from age to age becomes! Is the implication, perhaps, that if Tehilla had been given the same education as Baron—if the new ways that informed Baron's education that allowed her to become a writer of Hebrew fiction had been adopted by Tehilla's father—she may not have found herself in the tragic situation that she did? The plot of the story within the story, namely, the breaking off of Tehilla's engagement to Shraga, whose very name means light or enlightenment, suggests that on some level, Tehilla's father robbed her of the "light." Insofar as Tehilla is presented throughout the novella as an extension or personification of Old Jerusalem, does this mean that Old Jerusalem, as admirable and religiously authentic as "she" may seem, can no longer afford to shun or lose the light?

To get to this larger question, however, one needs to traverse several interpretive stations and sketch out the many significant parallels and connections between Hanye and Tehilla, beginning with their names.

The name Hanye, evokes the idea of *ḥen-yah* (the grace of God) together with Anya, the Russian version of Hannah, the biblical mother of Samuel, who, in praying for a child in silence with only her lips moving, furnishes the basis of rabbinic silent prayer. Throughout Baron's story, Hanye is seen as reciting prayers and psalms of praise, linking her with the female Jewish tradition of reciting *tkhines* as well as chapters from the biblical book of Tehillim (Psalms). In keeping with her own name, of course, Agnon's Tehilla also has a daily practice of reciting Psalms. In the very first paragraph of "Tehilla," Agnon's protagonist is described as ḥinanit (gracious or affable), a designation that recurs later in the story and that etymologically associates Tehilla with Baron's Hanye. What we have in these two stories, then, are two women whose dignity, kindness, and daily devotions render them walking, talking prayers, if you will: one of the European shtetl, named Hanye-*tkhine*, a Yiddish women's prayer; the other, of Jerusalem, named Tehilla, a biblical Hebrew prayer.

At the beginning of Baron's story, Hanye is shown carrying a copper jug that she uses to collect food for the poor;[17] Agnon's "Tehilla" is similarly identified at the beginning of his story as carrying a pail of water on behalf of a housebound person, which the narrator repeatedly offers to carry for her, but which Tehilla insists on carrying on her own so as to attain full merit for her good deed. With respect to Hanye's copper jug, it is worth noting that copper vessels also appear at the end of Agnon's story in the description of the various light-giving lamps in Tehilla's synagogue-like flat.

The Old City scholar in Agnon's story catalogues the various charitable activities that keep Tehilla out of her flat during the day, making it difficult to find her at home:

> What is there to say? She is a righteous woman: yes, righteous in the simplest sense of the term. And if you have the opportunity to see her, you should go. But I doubt you will find her at home, for typically, she is out either visiting the sick, or taking care of incurables or doing some other unsolicited *mitzvah*. Still you may find her at home, since between one *mitzvah* and the next she goes home to mend garments or stockings for poor orphans. In the days when she was rich, she spent her wealth upon deeds of charity, and now that nothing is left her but a meager pittance to pay for her own slender needs, she does her charities with her own body.[18]

---

17. In the Yiddish version the pitcher seems to be an earthenware vessel, that one might link with the clay jar in which Tehilla places the letter to Shraga at the end of "Tehilla."

18. Translation adapted from "Tehilla," 240.

All this seems to be anticipated by Baron's description of Savta Hanye, who similarly spends her days and nights giving food to the poor, medicine to the sick, sweets to the young, and loving care to orphans. When she first arrives one sultry summer night (the time of year bringing to mind the summertime mourning period for the destruction of the Jerusalem Temple), the people of the *shefeilah* or low-lying village, a topographical marker that suggests downtrodden status, do not know at first what to make of her. Immediately Hanye sets to work doing her fairy godmother-like good deeds, the results of which become evident to all in the morning, such that all of them become quickly aware and appreciative of her beneficent presence:

> By morning, however, by the time the residents of the lowland had awakened from their sleep, they discovered that some mysterious hand had affected their lives for the good: the weak babies had red threads tied around their hands, and their faces no longer looked infirm. The sick old folks had full bottles of water next to them; they were sipping water and recuperating. And the children of the poor had what they needed in the corners of their homes.[19]

And, as in the above description of Tehilla, the people in the plain wonder how it is that Hanye has the means to give so much to others:

> Surely she gives out more than she collects. Clearly she gives from her own pocket as well... But how is it that she can afford to spend so much of her own? From whence and by what means does she sustain herself?

Early on in the story, Savta Hanye is described as lingering or being delayed in performing *mitzvot*, such as giving out of nuts and sweets to the children:

> If she came upon a band of schoolboys she would tarry (*mit'akevet*) with them for a while, pulling out handfuls of nuts and candies from the small, apron pocket to dole out to the tiny hands. Crack them open, and may you show great strength in Torah, [she would say].

Later in the section that describes her arrival in the unnamed village, Baron describes a wagon that tarries in the middle of the road, suggesting a blocking or diverting of the regular mores and byways of the shtetl with Savta Hanye's arrival in town.

---

19. All translations of "HaSavta Hanye" are from my translation, appended to this essay, the first translation of the story to English.

Agnon's narrator (who like the children in Baron's story receives sugar from Tehilla) repeats the same Hebrew verb for tarry or detain ('e-k-v) several times in "Tehilla." When the narrator fails to recognize Tehilla the second time he meets her, he expresses regret for *detaining* her, an occasion that Tehilla uses to praise the narrator for his good deed of having sent a portable heater to a common acquaintance of theirs, the cantankerous and sickly *Rabbanit*. The same verb appears again later when the narrator attempts to reassure a guilt-ridden Tehilla that she ought not be concerned that she has not gotten around yet to finish reciting her chapter of Tehillim for the day: "Yes, I said, the *delay* is from heaven, that one more day be added to your sum of days."

It is worth noting as well that the same verb appears in a later speech that Agnon gives at the Schocken Library on the occasion of his seventieth birthday, eight years after the original publication of "Tehilla." In this speech, Agnon tells the audience that twenty years earlier, around the time of his fiftieth birthday, he had planned to evade the marking and celebration of the day by retreating to the Old City, relying on the righteous Tehilla, whom he depicts in the speech as a real-life person, to find him a place to stay for a few days within the Old City walls. However, the righteous Tehilla stays the plan and convinces Agnon to accept the blessings of his family and friends:

> The next day I got up early and came to the city while it was still daytime and found Tehilla. But Tehilla, whom I had depended upon, *detained me*, and said, "My son, go home and let your friends and acquaintances bless you on your birthday. The blessings of Israel are becoming, and it is becoming for the blessed to be blessed by such blessings.[20]

All of these uses of the verb 'e-k-v (together with the repetitions of bless and blessings) signal a beneficent detainment, wherein Tehilla and, by extension, Hanye on whom she seems to be modeled, are seen as figures who manage to slow down, even reverse the regular run of time.

Indeed, both Savta Hanye and Tehilla are repeatedly singled out for their grace and youthfulness despite their advanced age. Baron's narrator calls specific attention to Hanye's enduring youthfulness even though she is wrinkled and stooped over: "And her glance—a young girl's eyes, radiating softness and love—strayed and sought in every corner of the houses, lingering upon the faces of babies, surveying the withered faces of the elderly." Tehilla is similarly described throughout the story as evincing a kind of

20. Agnon, *MeAtzmi el Atzmi*, p 49.

extraordinary youthfulness despite her extreme old age: "Moreover, she had within her the alacrity of youth. If not for her old woman's clothes, no trace of old age would be discerned."

Both women appear at various points in their respective stories carrying a walking stick or cane, but just as often are shown hurrying about without it. In Baron's story, for example, when the righteous Hanye is seen in the evening carrying two orphan children in her arms, the narrator specifically remarks that "there would be no cane in her hand at these times."

Similarly, at the end of the story when Hanye donates a Torah scroll to the community in preparation for her own death, an extension of her supposed donation of her remaining years to the ailing rabbi of the town, she is seen as setting aside her walking sticks so she can dance unencumbered with the Torah.

A similar dynamic of using and then setting aside a cane occurs in Agnon's story, with Tehilla walking without a cane in some instances but leaning on one when she tells the story of her broken engagement with Shraga and her subsequent travails. When the writing of the letter is complete, Tehilla takes up her cane for her last walk, but nevertheless, is portrayed as walking with uncharacteristic alacrity for one who relies on a walking stick to get around.

Both Hanye and Tehilla are praised from the outset for their constant affability and good cheer. Baron's Savta Hanye is described as walking about the village, "her two kindly eyes caressing each face she happens upon along her way, the light smile on her lips never straying from her lips." Similarly, when Agnon's narrator first meets Tehilla and offers to carry her water can while she shows him the way to the unnamed scholar's house, she refuses his offer with a smile. Recalling Savta Hanye's affable eyes and demeanor as she strolls through the lowlands, Agnon writes about Tehilla's last walk through the streets of the old city of Jerusalem: "As she walked, she looked kindly upon every place that she passed and every person that she met."

The use in both of these stories of the word *tovot* and the folktale nature of their protagonists recall the antecedent, historical/legendary figure of Sore bas Toyvim, an eighteenth-century author of *tkhines*. In one of her works, Sore bas Toyvim refers to herself as "I, the renowned woman Sore bas Toyvim, of distinguished ancestry"[21] and tells the story of her own fall

---

21. Sore bas Toyvim is mentioned directly in Agnon, "In Search of a Rabbi, or The Governor's Whim," 293. See Weissler, *YIVO Encyclopedia*, s.v. Sore bas Toyim; and also Weissler, *Voices of the Matriarchs*, 131.

from a wealthy youth to an old age of poverty and wandering, attributing her fate to the sin of talking in synagogue—a narrative that matches the purported backstories of both Hanye and Tehilla. Sore bas Tovim figures in modern Yiddish literature, such as in S.Y. Abramovitsch's fictional autobiography, *Shloyme Reb Khayims* (1899), where women are seen reciting her *tkhine* for *kneytlakh leygn* (laying wicks) and making candles for Yom Kippur.[22] In Y. L. Peretz's Yiddish story, "Der ziveg oder Sore bas Toyvim" (The Match; or, Sore bas Toyvim), Sore bas Toyvim appears as a kindly fairy godmother, who flits back and forth between Jews living in far flung places, helping secure matches for those who faithfully recite her *tkhines*. Traces of this kindly fairytale character can be discerned in the extraordinary matchmaking activities undertaken by Savta Hanye in helping to marry off fifteen orphan girls; in fact, Sore bas Toyvim's *tkhine* and the *kneytlakh leygn* ritual are directly evoked when Hanye is summoned back to the shtetl after marrying off several orphans to intercede on behalf of a woman struggling in childbirth. Here Hanye is seen heading to the cemetery to lay wicks on the graves of the pious people, a ritual intercession that proves successful in turning the tide of the woman's birthing process.

Agnon's "Tehilla" similarly includes references to female folk practices such as visiting Rachel's Tomb; one might go so far as to say that the entire story is a metaphorical laying-of-a-wick on the grave of Tehilla so as to absorb her merit and cull its lesson. Note as well that as in the Peretz and Baron stories, matchmaking occupies a prominent place in "Tehilla," albeit in a failed form. When Tehilla's father breaks off her engagement with Shraga on account of his family's hasidic "apostasy," Tehilla's mother is described as "beseeching" (*mithanenet*) her father to make peace with Shraga," the use of the verb *mithanenet* perhaps alluding to the women's *tkhines* tradition and to Hanye, who is described at the very outset of Baron's story as having a habit at various points during her days of engaging in prayers and *tahanunim*. One might connect her women's spirituality, more broadly speaking, to the world of non-mainstream Hasidic spirituality that Shraga's father refuses to conscience, with Tehilla bearing the consequences of this refusal. Undeniably, Tehilla's father behaves badly in summarily rejecting Shraga and breaking off the marriage. That Shraga eventually renounces Hasidism, and Tehilla's husband eventually adopts hasidic ways, ironically underscores this point. At the same time, it is perverse to imagine God

---

22. For more on this ritual and the related *tkhines* see Weissler, *Voices of the Matriarchs*, 132–146.

visiting harsh punishment upon Tehilla or Tehilla acquiescing to such punishment for a wrong that she herself did not commit and before she was of an age to assume responsibility for her actions. It is even more perverse to assume that living a life of faith and goodness entails accepting that view of God as so petty and arbitrary in meting out punishment. In this sense, I would concur with Amos Oz who argues that "to find in 'Tehilla' an apotheosis of the world of faith is to violate the story and perhaps also the world of faith."[23] Put differently, it is at this juncture of the story that the unnamed Jerusalem scholar's description of Tehilla as a "a righteous woman, pure and simple" seems a tad too simplistic.

This latter point is crucial, as it is one of many clues that point away from the purely pious reading of both of these central characters and their stories that has characterized my comparative reading thus far. Agnon's narrator himself signals a desire to veer away from the happily-ever-after tenor of Peretz's evocation of Sore bas Toyvim as well, as from the view that Tehilla simply accepts her punishment as good and well and befitting God, in the following passage where the narrator waits for Tehilla to dictate the letter: "She was in the habit of saying she had seen good things, and yet better things. From what I had been told, these things could not have been so good. The adage was true of her that the righteous mourned in their hearts and joy was upon their faces."

If author Sore Bas Toyvim gives voice in her *tkhine* to the notion that God actively metes out terrible, incommensurate punishments for minor infractions (such as talking in synagogue), both Baron and Agnon's stories dramatize and challenge this premise.

The challenge emerges from the origin stories that circulate around both of these figures. Because of their outsized goodness and kindness, both Savta Hanye and Tehilla become subjects of speculation as to how and why they arrived at their current, reduced station. According to the first origin tale that is related in Baron's story, Savta Hanye, who was never actually privileged to become a grandmother, was once a rich city woman and new mother, whose husband suddenly and tragically died. And then, even more tragically, after putting her baby to sleep in her own bed and going to sleep next to him, Hanye accidentally smothers the baby to death, too.[24]

23. Oz, *Shetikat HaShamayim*, 29.

24. As Naomi Seidman notes, the Yiddish version of the story, published a year after the Hebrew, adds an element of perverse culpability to this tale and "hints darkly at a connection between the father's death and the mother's taking near-incestuous comfort in her son." See Seidman, 97.

In response to this tragedy, Hanye gives all of her money away to charity, grabs her cane and moves to the lowland shtetl where the story takes place, signifying an acceptance of her newly lowly, humbled state.

According to a second more macabre origin story that also circulates in the shtetl, Hanye had previously lived in the neighboring village and was the mother of seven sons, the number seven linking Hanye with the Hannah of 2 Maccabees 7, whose seven sons were martyred by the Greeks. Hanye toils mightily to support her husband and sons, who learn Torah together day and all night; the one small pleasure this otherwise self-abnegating woman allows herself is to sneak into the women's section of the Beit Midrash at nighttime to watch her husband and sons as they study. According to this version of her backstory, God does not look kindly on Hanye's habit of observing their learning and her tendency to swell with pride as she watches and listens to them.[25] Implied in this story is a strict prohibition against women entering into the masculine sphere of Torah study. Echoing the punishment of Nadav and Avihu for sacrificing an alien fire (Leviticus 10), God sends out a fire from heaven that consumes the study house along with her husband and seven sons. Though Savta Hanye ages instantly as a result of this cataclysmic punishment, she maintains her equanimity and good cheer and levels no complaint against heaven. On the contrary: she piously sits *shiva* and when the days of mourning are complete, donates her house and worldly goods to the cause of Torah study.

Remarkably, following the recounting of this horrifically humbling origin story, Baron's tale shifts to another mode, one of outsized feminine power and agency. From this point on in the story, there is no decree from God that Savta Hanye cannot counter with her prayers. The folk in the shtetl begin to pray that this old woman's *Shekhinah*-like providence never depart from their midst. Savta Hanye is thus transformed from a woman to a feminine, providential principle. Though they dwell in the *shefeilah*, the people nevertheless believe that with Savta Hanye as their intercessor, they occupy a higher plain, dwelling under the protective wings of a band of angels.

---

25. The Hebrew expression used here, *da'atah zaḥah 'aleha*, comes from a rabbinic commentary on the creation of Adam. Why was Adam created last, ask the rabbis. So that he [would be humble] and not swell with pride (see Tosefta Sanhedrin 8:8, ed. Zuckermandel). What is so ingenious about the selection of this expression and this source is that they link Hanye with notions of enforced humility as well as with the first woman's reaching for forbidden knowledge.

If the idea of the people of the shtetl praying for the ongoing providence of Savta Hanye were not subversive enough, the concluding scenes of the story raise the feminist volume of the story several notches. First, the rabbi falls ill, and sixty-five year-old Savta Hanye, elevated in terms of her spiritual powers above the rabbi himself, altruistically volunteers to donate her remaining five years to the rabbi so that he can live on, suggesting a godlike power to set the limits of her own life as well as others. Tehilla makes a similar offer to donate her remaining years to the clerks of the burial society. To mark and seemingly to celebrate the end of her life, Savta Hanye announces a plan to donate a Torah scroll to the Beit Midrash. If, according to the second version of her origin story, her entire family was consumed by punishing fire because of her excessive pride in their Torah study, Hanye's decision to commission the writing of a new Torah scroll and then to participate so centrally in the bringing of the new Torah into the sanctuary proves more than a little surprising. After such a divinely instigated tragedy one might have expected Hanye to stay far away from the Beit Midrash.[26] That Hanye does not stay away but rather inserts herself prominently and proudly into the ritual of bringing the Torah into the synagogue, a trail of women following her, suggests an outright rejection of the very idea that God would punish a woman and put her whole family to death for her wanting to be involved in some way in the study and love of Torah. Hanye's Torah scroll dedication includes a scene in which she herself dances on the *bimah* with the Torah (like King David in II Samuel 6) and then invites all the folk from the poor man's alley to join with her, modeling a radical egalitarianism and inclusiveness that undermine the very elitist, patriarchal tenets that undergird the rumored story of the death of her husband and seven sons.

The problem, of course, is that immediately following this, Hanye dies, and with her departure from this world the people of the low-lying shtetl are left without her protective presence. As a benevolent personification of the enduring virtue and integrity of shtetl life, she ceases to be an active agent.

The townspeople who come back from the cemetery after burying her are thus described as struggling to find a foothold as they descend from the cemetery, their faces as pale as the parchment of the Torah she donated, as if

---

26. Earlier in the story we also see her bringing two orphaned children to and from *ḥeder*, also suggesting an ongoing commitment to Torah study, despite the supposed trauma that led her to move to this shtetl.

that scroll and nothing more were all that was left of Hanye. The story ends with the specter of the huge white Catholic church looming in the high ground and with the menacing sound of dogs wailing. The publication date of the story—the year before Baron herself moved to Palestine—signals the impending end of the Diasporic, shtetl way of life for the characters, the author, and the readers.

Hanye is praised and lionized throughout the story, but her piety and goodness in her lifetime are not enough to sustain and protect her low-lying community after her death. And before she dies, she departs significantly from traditional protocol both in terms of her flouting of notions of divine punishment and her participating so blatantly in a public religious ceremony. A similar disruption of the veneer of communal continuity and traditional piety also emerges toward the end of Agnon's "Tehilla." I refer to that moment in the dictation of Tehilla's letter where her face suddenly takes on an aspect not just of sorrow but of rage. Additionally, her final request of the narrator is that he write in the letter that she forgives and by implication, blames Shraga, "the light," for all of her suffering. Insofar as Shraga had declared that he will never forgive Tehilla's family for the insult inflicted upon him in breaking off the engagement, and insofar as Tehilla interprets her suffering as the consequence of Shraga's determination never to forgive, implying a kind of curse, Tehilla might be seen here as impugning the unfairness of her suffering. If Tehilla is meant to stand for something larger than herself—the Old City and an Old World way of life—the post-Holocaust, post-1948 War composition of the story certainly reinforces a sense of tragedy and protest.

I would like to suggest, then, that to whatever degree Agnon might have incorporated aspects of Savta Hanye in his Tehilla—her association with angels,[27] her superhuman equanimity, her positive outlook and joy—he also seems to have included some of her subversive, oppositional elements. To be sure, Tehilla is a far longer, more complex and psychologically resonant story. Agnon allows his female protagonist to relay much if not all of her life story in her own words, with the *Rabbanit* supplying some additional painful details (as opposed to Hanye whose story is told entirely via shtetl rumor and lore). All of this has deep emotional effect. More than that: the frame structure of "Tehilla," which relays the story through the first person narrative perspective of the modern *sofer*, also places greater

---

27. In the very first paragraph for the story, the narrator says, "I know that women are not be likened to angels: yet her I would liken to an angel of God."

significance on the role of the modern writer in dramatizing and forwarding such stories and issues.

I will also note in this context that whereas Baron's Hanye as personification of the best of shtetl life has to die off and become a folk memory so as to justify and undergird the Zionist socialist project, Agnon's Tehilla both dies and lives on, serving as a model of what necessarily dies off in tradition as well as what ought somehow, through creative adaptation, to endure. Readers of "Tehilla" often note the ways in which the figure of Tehilla is frequently elided or equated with the femininely personified Jerusalem.

The second paragraph of the novella, which refers simultaneously to Tehilla and Jerusalem is a prominent case in point:

Until I had left Jerusalem she was quite unknown to me; only upon my return did I come to know her. How is that I did not know her earlier? How is it that you still do not know her now? Rather everyone is fated to know whomever he knows at a particular time and for a specific reason.	עד שלא יצאתי מירושלים לא הכרתי אותה, משחזרתי לירושלים הכרתי אותה. והיאך לא היכרתיה קודם? היאך אתם לא הכרתם אותה עכשיו? אלא כל אדם נועד לו להכיר את מי שיכיר אותו ובאיזו סיבה יכיר אותו.

The almost obsessive repetition here of the verb *le-hakir*[28] (to know, to recognize) suggests that part of the story's trajectory is of the writer-narrator's coming to learn and know the many facets of the character of Tehilla as Jerusalem, including those that are not immediately evident, such as her connection with Baron's Hanye, and by extension, her simmering anger and protest over what has happened to her despite her goodness and surface equanimity.

All this is reflected, I would argue, in the relationship between Tehilla and the widowed and sick *Rabbanit* whom the narrator visits, and purchases a heater, but never satisfies or provokes gratitude from her. The *Rabbanit* seems to embody everything that Tehilla is not, except that at various points, the *Rabbanit*, too, is elided with Jerusalem.

Unlike Tehilla who embodies the celestial aspirations for the Holy City, the *Rabbanit* represents the terrestrial, broken reality. She serves as

---

28. Hillel Weiss includes a discussion of this word repetition; see Weiss, 78–82. On the elision of Tehilla and the Old City of Jerusalem see Shmuel Werses, *Shai Agnon Kifshuto*, 292–93.

the alter ego of the city, its bent, decrepit, and terminally ill aspects. All this is clearly evident when one considers the unflattering descriptions of Jewish Jerusalem that precede the narrator's visit with the sick *Rabbanit*: "Huddled in their tattered rags sat the beggars, not caring even to reach a hand from their cloaks and glowering sullenly at each man who passed without giving them money." Angry, disgruntled Jerusalem seems to be an extension of the *Rabbanit*, whom the narrator finds buried under a heap of blankets and pillows, an agitated and irritated old woman. The *Rabbanit* is everything we'd expect Tehilla to be, based on what she has suffered, but somehow is not. The narrator disingenuously claims that in telling about the old *Rabbanit*, his "aim is not to praise one woman to the detriment of the other; nor indeed do I aspire to tell the story of all of Jerusalem and its inhabitants." I say disingenuously, because this is precisely what the narrator sets out to do. Tehilla and the old *Rabbanit* are both clearly represented in the story as stand-ins or personified extensions of aspects of the city. As such, the narrator clearly *does* intend to praise one woman to the detriment of the other. At the same time, the story pairs and in some sense blurs the distinction between these two women; they are after all both old widows, currently reduced in status, both nearing the end of their lives.[29] The old *Rabbanit* actually dies during the process of dictating Tehilla's letter to Shraga, which suggests something about Tehilla's own need, perhaps, to put to death certain aspects of her angry past, before she moves on to the next life.

Significantly, it is the *Rabbanit* who introduces the nickname Tilly into the story, a diasporic secular sobriquet (short form for Mathilda), as well as a diminutive for Tehillim that appears in talmudic and liturgical literature. The nickname "Tilly" might also be seen as an intertextual reference to Menahot 29b, where Moses ascends to heavens and sees God, as author, busily affixing crowns onto the letters of the Torah. When Moses asks about the purpose of these crowns, he is told by God that these crowns are there so that one day Rabbi Akiva can derive *"tilei tilim shel halakhot"* ("heaps upon heaps of laws") from each calligraphic crown. In this regard, the name Tilly points to the notion that within a certain revelatory, sacred context, words can give rise to mountains of meanings. Recall the obsessive referencing in Baron's story to the people's geographical placement in the lowlands (rather than the mountains), as well as the ending of the story,

---

29. The old *Rabbanit* notes that here in Jerusalem "people do not know me and the kind of respect I used to be steeped in," and one page later, makes the same observation about Tilly, that "everyone used to know her, that she used to be a rich widow, then a prominent widow, and now she is just an old woman."

where following her death, the people are described as pale as parchment. The meaning of Baron's story is stark, straightforward and simple. Life for Jews in the Diaspora, despite the piety of its best leaders, is unsustainable. Tehilla's life story, however, as rendered into text by the narrating *sofer*, is the very antithesis of the " plain meaning." It is the kind of text that gives rise to *tilei tilim*, heaps upon heaps of interpretations.

DEVORAH BARON AS CANTANKEROUS RABBANIT?

I'll add one more layer to the heap, that is, the possibility not just that Baron's "HaSavta Hanye" may have informed the creation of "Tehilla," both character and story, but that the old, sick *Rabbanit*, whose many traits and tendencies that Tehilla struggles valiantly throughout her life to keep at bay, may have been inspired in part by the image of the widowed, reclusive, sickly, and occasionally cantankerous Devorah Baron.[30] The volume of reminiscences of Baron, edited by Baron's daughter Tzippora, includes one essay that refers at once to Baron's extraordinary love for the shtetl of her youth, but also her hatred. "She knew how to hate powerfully in the same way that she knew how to love, both in life and in her stories. She did not cover over her hatred."[31] Another reminiscence refers to the experience of coming into Baron's sick room in language that eerily echoes the description of Tehilla's Jerusalem flat:

> The entryway to the Aharonovitz-Baron residence marked a change not just in light and air but also in atmosphere. Silence, as if all were in the midst of standing for the silent prayer. And dimness, as if the entire room were sketched in soft pencil.[32]

I do not mean to suggest, in some crass, reductive way that the *Rabbanit* or Tehilla are stand-ins for Devorah Baron, merely that Agnon's acquaintance with Baron in her mysterious, long reclusive stage may have been stored away in his mind. I similarly do not mean to reduce the old *Rabbanit* and Tehilla to mere extensions or flip sides of one another. Proof of this is that the *Rabbanit*'s death is mentioned in barely one sentence, whereas the preparation for Tehilla's death unfolds over several pages, insofar as the telling of the story of Shraga is what enables Tehilla finally to die at the impressive

---

30. Yosef Aharonovitz died in 1937.
31. Zakkai, "Kefi Shere'itihah," 228.
32. Twersky, "Beveitah," 235–36.

age of 104. The *Rabbanit*'s death is the logical, realistic outcome of her long illness; the story of Tehilla's death has a distinctively miraculous aspect that allies it with the biblical story of Elijah's ascent to heaven in a chariot of fire.

TEHILLA AS ELIJAH AND THE *SOFER* AS ELISHA

Indeed, the allusion in "Tehilla," in the scenes following the writing of the letter to Shraga, to the biblical episode of Elijah's "death" (see 2 Kings 2) constitutes a significant departure from the model of "HaSavta Hanye." Implied in the Elijah-Elisha-like scene, where Tehilla repeatedly attempts to send away the narrator so that she can go to her self-appointed death, is a kind of immortality—a means of redemptively transcending regular life and human time with its limits and vicissitudes that has been traditionally associated with Elijah's unconventional "death" and his later role in prophetic and rabbinic literature as harbinger of the Messiah. Additionally implied in these scenes is the potential role of the *sofer*-narrator as an Elisha-like successor to Tehilla/Elijah. Before Elijah is taken away from this world in a whirlwind, he says to Elisha: "Ask what I shall do for thee, before I am taken from thee. And Elisha said: I pray thee, let a double portion of thy spirit be upon me" (2 Kings 2:9). Elijah stipulates that this request will be fulfilled so long as Elisha actually sees Elijah as he is being taken from him, which Elisha does. Agnon's narrator does not in fact witness Tehilla's death; on the contrary: he, like the clerks in the burial society office, all dismiss Tehilla's assertions concerning her imminent passing. In this sense, Agnon's story frankly acknowledges the gap between tradition and modernity, between the role and worldview of Tehilla and the modern narrator-writer. Given his modern, skeptical subject location, the *sofer* cannot actually inherit in any straightforward way a double portion of Tehilla's spirit. Still, the narrator's insistence on accompanying Tehilla as far as he does underscores the role that he can still play in shaping and relaying her story and maintaining its ongoing relevance. Add to this the role the narrator plays in intertextually carrying on the model of Baron's Savta Hanye. As Nitza Ben-Dov notes about Agnon's habits of intertextuality, "through a complex of interconnected allusions which simultaneously invoke numerous antecedent texts, sometimes with contradictory meanings, Agnon created a versatile, consistent genre, which both draws upon and transforms tradition."[33] It is my contention that the ending of "Tehilla," where the biblical story of Elisha

---

33. Ben-Dov, *Agnon's Art of Indirection*, 3.

and Elijah comes together with Baron's "HaSavta Hanye," is precisely one such transformative, intertextual occasion.

It is important again to call attention to the significant ways in which the end of Tehilla departs from the ending of Baron's "HaSavta Hanye." When Diaspora-based Hanye dies, all that is left is pale-faced Jews, fear of gentiles, and wailing dogs. No narrative voice endures beyond the frame of the actual story to take up and maintain Savta Hanye's legacy. Baron's own real-life, authorial/editorial decision to bury this story along with her other earlier feminist tales by omitting it from all of her book-length collections, only serves to add a literary-historical element to the sad plot of Hanye's death and burial.

In taking up Baron's heroine, however, Agnon in effect revivifies and restores Hanye as a protagonist. As a female personification of Old World Jerusalem, perched on a hill instead of lodged in the precarious lowlands, Tehilla dies like Elijah, which is to say she does not quite die. In so far as she is a completely fictional creation, one that continues to generate *tilei tilim* of interpretations, she very much lives on. (Agnon's resurrection of her in his birthday speech is merely one illustration of Tehilla's immortality). Given the biblical tradition of feminine personifications of Jerusalem, particularly in the biblical book of Lamentations,[34] where the city, once a former princess among the nations, is likened after the destruction of the Temple to a captive, despoiled, ruined daughter, utterly humiliated, vulnerable and powerless like a widow, Tehilla emerges as an alternative, grandmotherly personification of Jerusalem, a counter-traditional feminine figure of agency, dignity, longevity and valiance, who has the additional insight to recognize the flaws of the past including the practice of arranged marriage, the fanning of baseless hatred, and the secondary status of women. She also has the good sense and perspicacity to enlist the offices of a modern *sofer* to write the Torah of her life so as to carry the past forward in all of its complexity, bringing to it ever-new interpretations and echoes, including the voice of Devorah Baron, an important, path-breaking woman writer.[35] Agnon's story thus resurrects and mobilizes Baron's figure of holy

---

34. Agnon frequently refers to these female personifications of Jerusalem as in the opening of "Agunot" and in "The Kerchief" (both in *A Book That Was Lost*) and in his novel, *A Guest for the Night*, the title of which derives from Jeremiah 14:8. For more on this see Halevi-Wise, "Agnon's Conversation with Jeremiah," 395–416. For more on the biblical habit of female personifications of Jerusalem, see Boase, *The Fulfillment of Doom?*

35. Leah Goldberg refers to the narrating *sofer*'s role in the story as that of a kind of ritual scribe, who is tasked with writing, in a clean and beautiful script, one more *scroll*

Grandmother to offer a personification of Jerusalem in which tradition and modernity intermingle in suggestive, riddling, and mutually enriching ways, and in which the modern writer plays a crucial role in lamenting, confronting and recasting the pieties of the past.

---

to the other *megillot,* the "Book of Tehilla." See Goldberg, 194.

11

"Savta Hanye"

DEVORAH BARON[*]

Translated by Wendy Zierler

A SOFT WOOL DRESS, a parted wig, and a grey shawl—this was Grandma Hanye's customary outfit. Weekdays she would typically tie a wide apron above her waist, its hems cinched and pinned under her belt; inside she would store various leftovers—food for the poor folk of the lowland.

An hour before noon, after she had completed all of her prayers and supplications, she would take her copper jug, tie and tightly bind a clean rag over its mouth, and leaning upon her thick walking stick, would set out toward the lowland. If she came upon a band of schoolboys, she would tarry with them for a while, pulling out handfuls of nuts and candies from the small apron pocket and doling them out to tiny hands.

—Crack them open, and may you show great strength in Torah, she would say.

If she would come upon a person who was sick or in pain, her gaze would linger upon him:

---

[*] Originally published in Hebrew: Baron, "HaSavta Hanye." This translation, the first to English, by permission of © ACUM.

—Take this medication, she would say. —It will lessen your suffering.

Grandma Hanye had a refreshingly clear voice, always steeped in abundant compassion. As soon as the women residents of the lowland sensed the arrival of Grandma Hanye, they would hurry and leap to greet her with the joy of performing a good deed!

—Grandma, I have these few leftover bagels that I set aside for you.

—I have this plate of grain, where is your jug?

Each one of the women would hurry, so as to preempt her neighbor with her donation.

Grandma Hanye would nod her head thankfully: May it be that none of you ever needs charity from others!

From there would she direct her attention toward the alley of the poor folk, her two kindly eyes caressing each face she happened upon along her way, her easy smile never straying from her lips. The people accompanied her with hesitant whispers: Surely she gives out more than she collects. Clearly, she gives from her own pocket as well. But how is it that she can afford to spend so much of her own? From whence and by what means does she sustain herself?

The neighboring women would tell of Hanye: Each and every night, after she has had but a taste of sleep, she rises like a she-lion, takes up her book of Psalms and begins busying herself with prayerful praises and adorations. By her table she has a sack full of feathers, from which she plucks the down from the quills. From this she ekes out her living and in turn sustains the poor folk of the lowland, and from this too she scrimps and saves for the sake of the rectification of her soul . . .

The women of the lowland would cast a long gaze at the gaunt, stooped-over body making its way into the alley: Such a woman!

Only at ten o'clock at night, when darkness and silence prevailed within the shtetl, could one hear from within the town square of the lowland the muffled echo of heavy, regular footsteps. These were the footsteps of Grandma Hanye, returning from the alley. At this time she would be especially bent over, her shawl dragging behind her, her apron now empty, its hems fluttering in the winds. She clutched two small bodies in her arms, holding them close to her heart, cuddling and encouraging them both with warm words. These two babies, who had been left orphaned after the death of their parents, were ill, with withered legs. Grandma Hanye brought them into her home, lay them to rest on her bed and at long last, nursed them back to health.[1] When they had recovered but their legs were still too weak to carry them, Grandma Hanye would carry them every morning to the schoolroom to study Torah. In the evening she would collect them and bring them home.

And there would be no cane in her hand at these times.

This is what the women of the lowland would tell about Grandma Hanye's arrival in the shtetl: It happened one evening, after a blazing summer day. Most of the women of the lowland were sitting at the time on porches, barefoot and half-naked, cooling themselves down in the gentle breeze that blew in from the meadow. Suddenly they heard the clanging of a bell, and a large wagon, tarrying in the middle of the road, let out from its midst an old, bent over woman. In one hand was a walking stick, and in the other a small handbag. Already that evening they saw her doing rounds at each of the doors of the lowland.

—What is it you'd like, Grandma?

She nodded her head contentedly: —"Grandma" . . . Yes, yes, that fits me.

And her glance—a young girl's eyes, radiating softness and love—strayed and searched in the corners of each house, lingering upon the faces of babies, surveying the withered faces of the elderly.

On the street she was accompanied by a suspicious glance: What was it that she wanted? Where did she come from? Who invited her here?

By morning, however, when the residents of the lowland awakened from their sleep, they discovered that some mysterious hand had affected their lives for the good. The weak babies had red threads tied around their hands, and their faces no longer looked infirm. The sick old folks had full bottles of water next to them; they were sipping and recuperating. And the children of the poor had what they needed in the corner of their homes.

Within a few days the story went around the lowland: The name of this old lady is Hanye, and she comes from the city. Her husband died and left her much wealth and one baby. One night, when her small child was deep in sleep in her bed, his body was smothered under hers. The baby cried out in vain, in vain he struggled and flailed—but the mother was so deep in sleep that she did not sense a thing. The next morning, she found him lying dead next to her, hot red blood flowing out of his mouth. Grandma Hanye neither eulogized him, nor did she weep. She sought to leave that place but her feet would not obey. Only after the seven days of mourning had passed

---

1. Literally, "wholly turned over their bed of suffering." See Psalm 41:4.

did she arise, distribute her assets to various charities, take up her walking stick and come to the shtetl.

Others countered: In truth she is none other than a native of the neighboring shtetl. Once she had a husband and seven young sons, who occupied themselves with Torah day and night. As for her—she sorted legumes[2] and laundered linens and in this way supported her husband and sons. When night arrived, and she was completely exhausted, her limbs fatigued from hard work and craving rest,—still she would not get into bed. Rather she would climb and silently enter the women's gallery, bowing her head and training her ears to the little cracks in the partition to listen in on the learning. Eight invigorating and sad voices joined together in one melody, reverberating against the walls of the study house. Against the eastern wall a lamp shone and illuminated the Holy Ark, its sparkling curtain, and the eight faces—these were the faces of her husband and sons, occupying themselves with Torah. Surveying all of this she would swell with pride, would observe and take pleasure. But this pleasure was not approved by the One who spoke the world into being.[3] A fire went out from heaven and set the study house on fire, just when these eight souls were present inside its walls. A few days later Grandma Hanye accompanied a wagon laden with bones, the charred bones of her husband and sons. But Grandma Hanye did not cast aspersions on the deeds of God, did not hurl a single harsh word toward heaven. When she returned to her home and found it empty—the rows of wretched, closed books peering out at her from the book case, eight prayer shawl and phylactery bags resting sadly and desolately in the corner—she rent her garments, removed her shoes, slipped down and sat on the ground, her ten fingers raised up on high in thanks: Thou art just and Thy justice is just!

Her eyes shed not a single tear. In an instant, however, her face withered and wrinkled, forming creases within the creases. A few days later she donated her house to Torah students and dedicated herself to charity work. From then on there was no decree from the Creator of the World that Grandma Hanye could not overturn with her prayers.

---

2. See Mishnah Beitzah 1:8.

3. *Mi she'amar vehayah ha'olam* as in the "Barukh she'amar" prayer in the daily morning service, which originates in a commentary of the R. Isaac Alfasi (1013–1103) on BT Berakhot 32.

"Savta Hanye"

That night the residents of the lowland went to bed with one prayer on their lips: May it by Thy will that the providence of this elderly woman never disappear from this place.

That night the elderly folk among them saw in their dreams an entire band of pure angels, flying and fluttering in the air over the lowland, flapping their wings and spreading them over the squat houses.

Once again the women recounted: There were fifteen orphan girls in the shtetl and each of them had reached marriageable age. The braids of some of them had grayed and their teeth had fallen out. The faces of some of them had withered and turned ugly, and all of them were abjectly poor.

Grandma Hanye took pains and found each of them a handsome young man and married them off, one by one. When the time came for the last of them to wed her village groom, Grandma Hanye took her leave from the lowland and went to the village to bring the young couple to their bridal canopy. While she was away from the shtetl, the hearts of women of the lowland quaked in fear upon hearing the news: A mother of six small children was struggling in childbirth, and the midwife was giving the relatives discouraging reports.

A cry went out from the lowland. Young women, with frightened faces, rolled up their sleeves, offered care in the form of cold and hot water, dragged basins from place to place, all the while sighing and sopping up the sweat from their faces. Old women wrung their hands, wailed and hollered out to the heavens. The relatives, crowded and crammed into a tight space, banged their heads against the walls and pulled out their hair. A *minyan* of elders assembled in the study house and rent the sky with verses from Psalms. Even so the strength of the birthing mother began to wane ever further and her pains increased in intensity. At which point the residents of the lowland resolved: Call back Grandma Hanye.

Before evening she returned with speedy footsteps, her eyes wide and amazed. When they told her about what was happening, her face turned white and severe and she hurried in the direction of the graveyard. A deep silence prevailed in the lowland. With beating hearts and bated breath, they all waited for the old woman's return. Afterward, they saw her descend from the hilltop, her face quiet and her hand clutching a skein of thread with which she had measured the graves.[4] When she approached the house of

---

4. A reference to the female folk ritual of *kneytlakh leygn* (laying of wicks), wherein a cemetery or particular set of gravestones are measured with thread that is later used to make candles for Yom Kippur.

the woman giving birth, everyone breathed in with relief: Grandma Hanye will do and will prevail.

Two hours later the residents of the lowland told each other the news: A baby boy was born in good fortune.

And eight days later when they brought the boy into the covenant of Abraham, Grandma Hanye sat at the head of those called to the celebration.

Grandma Hanye was worthy of reaching seventy years of age—that was clear to all the residents of the lowland. Nevertheless, she passed away at age sixty-five. This is how it happened: One clear spring day the lowland was engulfed by a great cloud of sorrow. The elderly rabbi of the town had suddenly taken sick and was at death's door. With dark faces and faltering knees, the residents of the lowland assembled in the study house, decreed a fast, read psalms, and with their prayers still fresh on their lips, the rabbi's wife arrived at the study house with her hands on her head, her face was as white as plaster and her words—a lament:

—Already... Already... He sees the grim Old Man wrapped in black standing before him... Come all of you... All of you must come...

Wailing and crying they all hurried to the door but here—the withered and stooped-over body of Grandma Hanye blocked their way out:

—Where to?—she said lifting her two eyes toward them, two oceans of compassion:

—I have only five more years left to my life. I hereby donate them to our rabbi. Anyone who wishes to donate more may add on to them.

A few days later Grandma Hanye went out with two walking sticks in her hands: I am bringing a new Torah scroll into the study house, hurry and join me in my celebration. Evening came and the entire lowland was illuminated with a great light. Lanterns shone, the flames of the candles trembled, and torches flickered in every corner. Grandma Hanye, her face beaming and her eyes sparkling, floating along as she went[5] under the canopy that was strung over her head, a Torah scroll in her arms. In front of her—an orchestra with violins and trumpets, cymbals and drums,[6] and after her elderly women rustling in her silken dresses, young women fluttering in colored raiments, young girls with plaited braids, old folk and children.

And when they placed the Torah scroll in the Holy Ark, its doors having been closed and its curtain pulled shut, Grand Hanye stood, thrust

---

5. *Halkhah vetafefah mitaḥat laḥupah.* Cf. Isaiah 3:16, where the expression *halokh vetafof* is marshaled to depict the haughtiness of the daughters of Zion

6. Evocation of Psalms 150.

her walking sticks aside, straightened her posture, the wrinkles on her face smoothing out and her skin softening. Her eyes radiated sparks of fire and she spread and raised her arms to the heavens: Ay, ay, ay, Father in Heaven . . . Ay, ay, ay, Master of the Universe . . .

And as she danced and did several wild leaps she began encircling the podium, turning her gaze toward the doorway—toward the alley of the poor folk; and all were drawn after her, joining in with her in one circle, dancing and leaping, dancing and leaping.[7] The musicians blasted and trumpeted, elderly men snapped their fingers and women clapped their hands together. In the east dawn began to rise.

The next day the residents of the lowland returned from the graveyard and their faces were like parchment. From one of the hearts a sigh broke out that first trembled in the air and then dissipated and expired. A great darkness prevailed, each person descending from the hilltop on his own, groping in his steps, trying to find the earth below his feet. Upon the hilltop the giant church loomed, threatening everything in its peculiar whiteness.

In the lowland the dogs wailed.

Bibliography

Agnon, S.Y. "Aggadat HaSofer." In *Elu ve'Eilu*. Tel Aviv: Schocken, 1953.
———. "Agunot." Translated by Baruch Hochman. In *A Book That Was Lost*. Edited by Alan Mintz and Anne Golumb Hoffman. Tel Aviv: Schocken, 1996.
———. *Esterlein Yakirati*. Tel Aviv: Schocken, 2000.
———. *A Guest for the Night*. New Milford, CT: Toby, 2014.
———. "In Search of a Rabbi, or The Governor's Whim." In *A City in Its Fullness*. Edited by Alan Mintz and Jeffrey Saks. New Milford, CT: Toby, 2016.
———. "The Kerchief." In *A Book That Was Lost*. Edited by Alan Mintz and Anne Golumb Hoffman. Tel Aviv: Schocken, 1996.
———. "Letters to Devorah Baron." *Genazim* 99:8 (5741) 16.
———. "Otiyot veSefarim." In *MeAtzmi el Atzmi*. Tel Aviv: Schocken, 1976.
———. "Tehilla" In *Ad Henah*, 138–60. Tel Aviv: Schocken, 1952.
———. "Tehilla." In *Two Scholars Who Were in Our Town and Other Novellas*. Edited by Jeffrey Saks. New Milford, CT: Toby, 2014.
Band, Arnold. *Nostalgia and Nightmare: A Study of the Fiction of S.Y. Agnon*. Berkeley: University of California Press, 1968.
Baron, Devorah. *Agav Orḥa*, Tel Aviv: HaPo'el HaTza'ir, 1960.
———. "Bubbe Henye." In *The First Day and Other Stories*, edited by Chana Kronfeld and Naomi Seidman, 162–71. Berkeley: University of California Press, 2001.
———. "Di Bubbe Hanye." *Yugend: A Literarische Samlung* 1 (1910) 27–32.
———. "HaSavta Hanye." *Ha'Olam* 3/33 (29 Elul 5669 / September 15, 1909) 8–9.

---

7. See 2 Samuel 6:16.

———. *Parshiyot Mukdamot*. Jerusalem: Mosad Bialik.
Ben-Dov, Nitza. *Agnon's Art of Indirection*. Leiden: Brill, 1993.
Ben-Pinḥas, Rut. *U-Tehilato biYerushalayim*. Israel: HaDuvdevan, 2014.
Bernstein, Marc "On the Story 'Agunah.'" In *Hebrew, Gender and Modernity: Critical Responses to Dvora Baron's Fiction*, edited by S. Jelen and S. Pinsker, 117–44. College Park: University of Maryland Press, 2007.
Boase, Elizabeth. *The Fulfillment of Doom? The Dialogic Interaction between the Book of Lamentations and the Pre-Exilic/Early Exilic Prophetic Literature*. Maiden Lane, NY: T. & T. Clark, 2006.
Goldberg, Leah. "Agnon biSheloshah Kolot." *HaOmetz leḤulin*, 194–95. Tel Aviv: Sifriyat Po'alim, 1975.
Govrin, Nuri. *HaMaḥatzit haRishonah/Parshiyot Mukdamot*. Edited by Avner Holtzman. Jerusalem: Mossad Bialik, 1988.
Halevi-Wise, Yael. "Agnon's Conversation with Jeremiah in *A Guest for the Night*: 'Aginut in an Age of National Modernization." *AJS Review* 38/2 (2014) 395–416.
Halkin, Hillel. "The Disappointments." *The New Republic*, August 7, 2000, 30.
Kurzweil, Barukh. *Massot al Sippurei Shai Agnon*. Jerusalem: Schocken, 1963.
Naveh, Aryeh. "Tehillah haMoredet haKedoshah." *BaMikhlalah* 9 (5758) 7–33.
Oz, Amos. *Shetikat HaShamayim: Agnon Mishtomem al Elohim*. Jersualem: Keter, 1993, 19–28.
Peretz, Y.L. "Sore bas Toyvim." Translated by Ben-Azriel. *Doar Hayom*, June 13, 1924.
Seidman, Naomi. *A Marriage Made in Heaven*. Berkeley: University of California Press, 1997.
Shossheim, Adah. "Tilei Tilim shel Parshanut al Tilli (Tehillah)—VeOd Parshanut Aḥat." *Mikra Ve'Iyyun* 66 (1994) 26–29.
Twersky, Yoḥanan. "*Beveitah*." In *Agav Orḥa*, 235–36. Tel Aviv: HaPo'el HaTza'ir, 1960.
Weiss, Hillel. *Parshanut leḤamishah miSippurei Shai Agnon*. Tel Aviv: Ekked, 1974, pp. 75–93.
Weiss, Hillel. "Silluk haShekhinah." *Akdamot*, April, 2003, 131–49.
Weissler, Chava. *Voices of the Matriarchs*. Boston: Beacon, 1998.
Weissler, Chava. "Sore bas Toyvim." In *YIVO Encyclopedia of Jews in Eastern Europe*, YIVO, https://yivoencyclopedia. org/article.aspx/Sore_bas_Toyvim.
Werses, Shmuel. *Shai Agnon Kifshuto* Jerusalem: Mossad Bialik, 2000.
Yehoshua, A.B. *HaKallah haMeshuḥreret*, 228. Jerusalem: Mo'ed, 2001.
Zakkai, David. "Kefi Shere'itihah." In *Agav Orḥa*. Tel Aviv: HaPo'el HaTza'ir, 1960.

12

Agnon at Yeshiva University

SHULAMITH Z. BERGER

SHMUEL YOSEF AGNON'S NOBEL Prize was a source of great pride for the Yeshiva University Community. American Modern Orthodoxy of the time greatly appreciated Agnon's blend of traditional Jewish piety and Jewish modernism, his evocation of the lost world from which both Agnon and the Yeshiva community gained sustenance, and their shared commitment to religious Zionism and the State of Israel. The Nobel award ceremony in Stockholm, Sweden, in December 1966 provided an opportunity for Yeshiva University to honor the noted Hebrew author as one of their own.

Agnon's personal connections at Yeshiva were deep. Dr. Esther Appelberg, Agnon's niece, was a professor at YU's Wurzweiler School of Social Work, and Dr. Elazar Hurvitz, professor of Talmud at the Bernard Revel Graduate School of Jewish Studies had been a confidant of Agnon's during the 1950s until Hurwitz left Jerusalem for New York in 1961. Both joined Agnon in Stockholm for the Nobel ceremony. Hurvitz and Appelberg brought a scroll, which they presented to Agnon "in recognition of Mr. Agnon's contributions to the art of writing, to the prestige of Israeli and Jewish culture, and to the Hebrew language."[1] The scroll was signed by Dr. Samuel Belkin, President of Yeshiva University (fig. 1). A year later, in 1967, Agnon was invited to Yeshiva as a graduation speaker and to receive the first

1. Yeshiva University Archives.

honorary Doctor of Hebrew Letters ever awarded by Yeshiva University (fig. 2). Yeshiva had approached Agnon via a number of intermediaries to encourage him to accept the honorary doctorate from Yeshiva University; among the go-betweens were Abba Eban, Yaakov Herzog, Pinchas Peli, and Emanuel Rackman.[2] Elazar Hurvitz also encouraged Agnon to visit Yeshiva to receive the degree.[3]

However, it seems to have been a family connection which won the day for Agnon's agreement to accept Yeshiva's honor. Esther Appelberg (b. Hamburg 1923), Agnon's niece, appears to have been the primary contact between Agnon and Yeshiva (fig. 3). She was particularly close to her uncle. If not for Agnon, Dr. Appelberg may well have perished in the Holocaust. *The New York Post* reported:[4]

> Dr. Appelberg, a professor at Yeshiva University's Wurzweiler School of Social Work, remembers Uncle Samuel Joseph ('We usually use both names') with special warmth because he arranged for her entire family to leave Nazi Germany in 1939. "At that time only a certain number were able to go to Palestine every year' she said. 'He did everything that was humanly possible to get us the certificates to come and live with him. It took a lot of effort and devotion, and probably money too. But he never talked about that. He would be the last person to ask for gratitude . . .". . . "If he had not done this probably we would all have been destroyed by the Nazis.". . . After their arrival in Jerusalem, for a while the family moved in with Uncle Samuel Joseph, who lived in a suburb. "He wanted us to get acclimated quicker and to learn the Hebrew language." And she stayed in his home for a full year.

At first Agnon refused Yeshiva's invitation to speak at graduation. In a letter that Agnon sent to his niece, dated May 4, 1966, he explained in Hebrew his inability to go to America:

> . . . the hustle and bustle around my home from the honks of the automobiles which keep multiplying and racing has sapped my strength and it is only with difficulty that I do my work. If I had energy I would go to America to honor Yeshiva University and for

---

2. Yeshiva University Archives, Box 12, Folder 35/3–51 "P" correspondence, exchange of letters between Pinchas Peli and Emanuel Rackman.

3. Author's interview with Dr. Elazar Hurvitz, April 4, 2019.

4. October 21, 1966, 36.

the sake of the honor they want to bestow on me and for your sake, dear Esther, and for our brethren the children of Israel there . . .[5]

Appelberg forwarded Agnon's response to Sam Hartstein, YU's Director of Public Relations. There matters rested until it became publicly known that Agnon planned a trip to New York under the auspices of the American Friends of Hebrew University. Belkin formally wrote to Agnon, in Hebrew, on April 12, 1967, inviting Agnon to Yeshiva to accept an honorary degree at the Commencement exercises scheduled for June 12, 1967. Belkin explained that Yeshiva University is the largest traditional Jewish institution in the United States; Agnon's acceptance of a degree would offer Agnon an opportunity to honor the Torah. Telegrams and letters flew back and forth between Agnon, Belkin, and the Israeli consulate in New York regarding the date of the event, and Agnon finally agreed to visit Yeshiva for the presentation of the honorary doctorate on June 12, 1967. The doctorate was to be awarded at the graduation on June 12, however the outbreak of what would become known as the Six-Day War on June 5 changed the plans. Agnon wanted to return to Israel as soon as possible, so Yeshiva rushed to organize a special convocation on June 7 to bestow the honorary degree. The last-minute invitation stated that "the ceremony, honoring one of Israel's most distinguished citizens, represents a unique opportunity for the entire University family to express its support and solidarity for the State of Israel in its hour of crisis."[6]

Hartstein reflected on the time he spent with Agnon in a letter he wrote to Dr. Joshua Fishman, former Academic Vice-President in 1983:

> In June 1967, preceding the outbreak of the Six Day War, Agnon was in America. Among his multi-faceted chores on these shores, in common with Israeli dignitaries, was the honorary degree at YU's Commencement. The heightened tensions preceding the War were counterbalanced by an excessive exhilaration which burst forth when the results were in. Finally the big day came. The upbeat scenario prevailed as we walked along Amsterdam Avenue past Morgenstern Dorm heading for the Nathan Lamport Auditorium. As is my practice, I was bringing up the rear and chatting with Agnon in Yiddish no less. Put to the test. In his inimitable poetic manner with twinkling eyes he took in our newly built buildings on both sides of the street. These new edifices, fresh and clean, projected that period's aura of enthusiastic expansionism. I

---

5. Yeshiva University Archives, Public Relations Events, Box 5.
6. Yeshiva University Archives, Public Relations Events Collection, Box 69.

turned to Agnon to respond to his queries, particularly explaining our Blueprint for the Sixties. To which he responded, "Of course I've heard of YU; I thought of it as a Yeshiva but I visualized it as a place of batlanim in the traditional Yeshiva mold" (figs. 4–5).[7]

Agnon's walk on Amsterdam Avenue with Belkin and Hartstein took him past groups of students, and from YU's modern vision for the 1960s, including the construction of the Mendel Gottesman Library, to its iconic Main Building, completed in 1928 (fig. 6–7). One thousand people attended the convocation in Lamport Auditorium, despite the last-minute announcement of the event. The date on the Hebrew calendar was 28 Iyar, and the charged atmosphere of the war and the battle for Jerusalem are evident in the audio recordings of the convocation, held by Yeshiva University Archives. The twenty-eighth of Iyar is now celebrated as Jerusalem Day, *Yom Yerushalayim*. When Agnon spoke at the Nobel award ceremony in Stockholm, he famously introduced himself in Hebrew: "As a result of the historic catastrophe in which Titus of Rome destroyed Jerusalem and Israel was exiled from its land, I was born in one of the cities of the Exile. But always I regarded myself as one who was born in Jerusalem."[8] Little could Agnon have known in Stockholm that only half a year later, while in exile in New York to receive an honorary degree from YU, he would be able to return home to Israel and re-visit the Old City of Jerusalem. On June 7, 1967, 28 Iyar, Agnon and YU celebrated the reunification of Jerusalem together. The convocation opened with expressions of solidarity between YU and Israel: the master of ceremonies proudly announced that students had just recently gathered in the same auditorium to recite Psalms for the welfare of Israel; Yeshiva and Stern College students were collecting funds for Israel, and a hundred students had traveled to Israel to volunteer during the war. He prophesied that "today's students will tell their children and grandchildren of the miracles that occurred during this war." The consciousness of the state of war in Israel was palpable throughout the ceremony.

Belkin gave an impassioned speech prior to the formal citation and conferral of the degree. His remarks were punctuated by loud and extended applause. He noted that this was the most unusual convocation in Yeshiva's history; an academic convocation which dispensed with academic rituals. The gathering honors "one of the great literary figures of our age . . . Reb Shmuel Agnon," who wants to return, as quickly as possible, back to the

---

7. Yeshiva University Archives, Public Relations People Collection, Box 2.
8. See the article by Jeffrey Saks in this volume.

Holy Land, to Israel. Belkin proclaimed that we rejoice with Agnon. "Until nineteen years ago Agnon prayed at the *keysel ha-ma'arovi* [the Western Wall, as pronounced in Dr. Belkin's Lithuanian accent], every Friday night. For nineteen years that privilege was denied to him, and we hope that this Shabbos, and on those to come, he will pray there . . . and deliver our prayers for the State of Israel." The audience gave an extended ovation when Dr. Belkin expressed the hope that "that this city of peace, the ancient Yerushalayim will never be taken again by Arabs." After Belkin's impassioned oratory, he intoned the formal citation for Agnon's degree: "We salute you as a trail blazer and pioneer in interpreting our ancient Hebraic spiritual literature to the contemporary world in modern Hebrew terminology. Through you we also convey our prayers and good wishes for the welfare of our brethren in the Holy Land." In response to the conferral of the degree, or the *ketubah*, as he dubbed it, Agnon remarked that he is not a speechmaker, he is a storyteller, and he will tell a story relevant to *inyana de-yoma*, the current situation (fig. 8). He spoke in Hebrew in a soft voice, apologized for being hoarse, and explained that he had a cold and it was difficult for him to speak. Agnon told a story which had occurred during his first days in the Land of Israel, sixty years earlier, when Jews were few, troubles were many, and defenders of the Land were scarce. A man went to synagogue and prayed as usual on Friday night, although he knew that his son, a border guard, had just been killed by Arabs. Agnon commented that as difficult as it is to imagine, the power of the Land of Israel, the holiness and sanctity of the Land, enabled the father to distract himself from his personal loss and grief for a time. Agnon then related a medley of stories and historical anecdotes, selected because the students at YU study Torah and general studies. The convocation closed with a stirring rendering of *Hatikvah*. In addition to the ceremony itself, Agnon attended a reception in his honor at YU. Students presented Agnon with a copy of the 1967 *Nir*, the yearbook of the *Beit Midrash le-Morim shel Yeshivat Rabenu Yitshak Elhanan*, the Teachers Institute for Men (fig. 9). The issue included an article about Agnon by Meir Havazelet entitled "Agnon bein Shene Olamot," "Agnon Between Two Worlds," a fitting title for that day, when Agnon was suspended between two Jewish worlds, the world of Yeshiva University in New York, and the climactic events in the State of Israel. Agnon was unable to distance himself from the Land of Israel, even when he was in New York, and was anxious to return.

A YU press release of June 7, 1967 stated:

> Speaking to reporters later, Mr. Agnon said he was returning to Israel in the midst of its conflict with the Arab nations because, 'it is my home, it is my country, I want to be with my people, I would return even if I knew I would be greeted by all the cannon fire in the world.' He added that although he was 'too old to fight,' he would do whatever his nation asked of him in order to help his people 'fight for our lives.'[9]

A few weeks later (July 6, 1967), Agnon wrote a letter in Hebrew from his home in Jerusalem to thank Belkin for the doctorate and described his impressions of Yeshiva: "At that event I saw your home. All I had heard about it did not express even half of its greatness and glory" (fig. 10).[10]

S.Y. Agnon died in Israel on February 17, 1970, and is buried on the Mount of Olives, an appropriate final resting place for a person who had adopted Tisha be-Av as his birthday and Jerusalem as his birthplace. Yeshiva University's obituary for Agnon in the *New York Times*[11] offered the traditional condolence message: "May the bereaved family be comforted among the mourners of Zion and Jerusalem," a particularly apt tribute for Agnon, a champion and chronicler of Zion and Jerusalem. Yeshiva University continued to honor its honorary alumnus, Agnon, and his legacy with a conference in 1986 entitled "S.Y. Agnon; Nobel Laureate, Twenty Years After—A Promise Fulfilled," and a conference held on October 31, 2016, sponsored by YU's Center for Israel Studies, "on the works and influence of Nobel Prize-winning Israeli author S.Y. Agnon in commemoration of the 50th anniversary of his award."

---

9. Yeshiva University Archives, Public Relations Events Collection, Box 69.

10. Yeshiva University Archives, Samuel Belkin Records, Cabinet A30, Drawer 4.

11. Yeshiva University Archives, Public Relations Events Collection, Box 5. Actual notice appeared in the "Deaths" column in the *New York Times*, February 18, 1970.

Agnon at Yeshiva University

בס״ד

ישיבה אוניברסיטה

לגדול בישראל

ר׳ שמואל יוסף עגנון שליט״א

שלומך ישגה ושמך ינון בכרם תרבותנו, שהאבת בו יד ושם לדורות.
על ידך נתגלגלה זכות שהחזרת כבוד לישראל אחר שגלה ממנו. יצירותיך
קושרות קשרים ועטרות לספרותנו, שנצרה על ידך בצרור תרבות העולם.

פרס נובל, המוכתר את גאון עבודתך בתחומי מקדש הספרות העברית,
הוא הפרס לכל ישראל שבכל אתר ואתר.

אתה פתחת לרווחה אופקי חיים חדשים להמוני ישראל באמריקה
ועוררת את לבבותיהם לראות את מאור היהדות וגאון ספרותה.

ישיבה אוניברסיטה מברכת אותך ליום הגדול הזה בו הכיר העולם
מחדש ברוח ישראל היוצרת באותך שתתן הקדושה.

השוכן בציון והבוחר בירושלים יאריך ימיך ותראה את עולמך
בחייך. בימיך ובימינו יבוא שלום על ישראל ועל כל באי עולם.

כ״ב כסלו תשכ״ז

שמואל בלקין
נשיא הישיבה אוניברסיטה

Figure 12.1: Certificate Presented to Agnon on the Occasion of His Nobel Prize Ceremony, Stockholm, Sweden, December 1966 (Yeshiva University Archives, Public Relations Events Collection, Box 5, Folder "Advertising—Obituary—S.Y. Agnon").

Figure 12.2: Agnon and Belkin at Yeshiva University convocation in Lamport Auditorium, June 7, 1967 (Yeshiva University Archives, Public Relations People Photo Collection, Box 1, Folder "Agnon, Shmuel Y").

Figure 12.3: Esther Appelberg, Agnon's Niece (Yeshiva University Archives, Public Relations People Collection, Box 4, Folder "Appelberg, Esther").

Figure 12.4: *"Yearning to breathe free," Yeshiva University 75th Anniversary.* Advertisement, Supplement to *The New York Times*, September 10, 1961, Section 11, p. 8 (Copy in Yeshiva University Archives, Public Relations Events Collection, Box 32, Folder "Blueprint for the Sixties.").

Figure 12.5: Agnon and Belkin Walking to Lamport Auditorium. (Yeshiva University Archives, Public Relations Photo Collection, CPA Negatives, 22212_K19).

Figure 12.6: Yeshiva College Students of 1967 Watch Agnon's Academic Procession (Yeshiva University Archives, Public Relations Photo Collection, CPA Negatives, 22212_K21).

Figure 12.7: Agnon, Belkin, and Hartstein Walking on Amsterdam Avenue (Yeshiva University Archives, Public Relations Photo Collection, CPA Negatives, 22212_I3).

Figure 12.8: Agnon at the Podium Holding his Degree (Yeshiva University Archives, Public Relations People Photos, Box 1, Folder, "Agnon, Shmuel Y.").

Figure 12.9: Article on Agnon in the 1967 issue of the *Nir* (Yeshiva University Archives).

Agnon at Yeshiva University

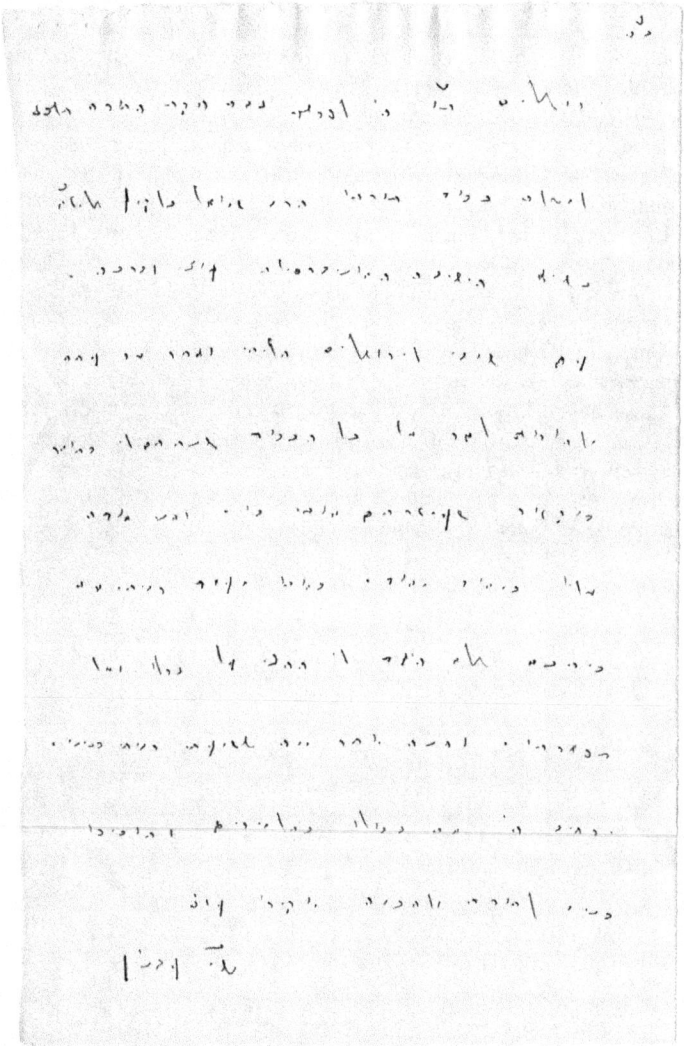

Figure 12.10: Letter of Thanks from Agnon to Belkin, July 6, 1967 (Yeshiva University Archives, Samuel Belkin Records, Cabinet A30, Drawer 4, Folder "Honorary Degrees to 1970.").

Bibliography

Invitation to Special Convocation. Yeshiva University Archives, Public Relations Events Collection, Box 69, Folder "Convocation—Agnon, 1967."

The New York Post (October 21, 1966), 36.

Press release, Dec. 16,1966, Yeshiva University Archives, Public Relations Events Collection, Box 5, Folder "Advertising—Obituary, S.Y. Agnon."

"S.Y. Agnon, Israeli Nobel Winner in Literature, Dies." *New York Times,* February 18, 1970.

Yeshiva University Archives, Public Relations People Collection, Box 2, Folder "Agnon, Shmuel Y."

Yeshiva University Archives, Public Relations Events Collection, Box 69, Folder "Convocation—Agnon, 1967."

Yeshiva University Archives, Samuel Belkin Records, Cabinet A30, Drawer 4, Folder "Honorary Degrees to 1970."

Yeshiva University Archives, Emanuel Rackman Records, Box 12, Folder 35/3–51 "P" correspondence, exchange of letters between Pinchas Peli and Emanuel Rackman, dated between March 29, 1967 and April 24, 1967.

Yeshiva University Archives, Public Relations Events, Box 5, Folder "Advertising—Obituary—S.Y. Agnon." Translation by author.

Contributors

Shulamith Z. Berger is the Curator of Special Collections and Hebraica-Judaica at the Mendel Gottesman Library of Yeshiva University. She blogs at https://blogs.yu.edu/library. Her English translation of a Yiddish novel, *Hibru*, by Joseph Opatoshu is forthcoming from Ben Yehuda Press.

Shalom Carmy teaches Jewish Studies and Philosophy at Yeshiva University and writes the "Litvak at Large" feature in *First Things*. He has published widely on Jewish thought, Bible, and contemporary religious intellectual problems. He edited two volumes on prayer by his teacher R. Joseph B. Soloveitchik and two volumes in the Orthodox Forum series, *Modern Scholarship in the Study of Torah* and *Jewish Perspectives on the Experience of Suffering*.

Zafrira Lidovsky Cohen is the Rabbi Arthur Kahn Professor of Hebrew and the director of the Hebrew Language and Literature Department at Stern College for Women of Yeshiva University, where her teaching and research focus on Hebrew as a second language and Hebrew literary texts to nonnative Hebrew speakers. She has published books in Hebrew and English on the poetry of Yona Wallach and numerous articles on women's poetry and prose.

Steven Fine is the Dean Pinchos Churgin Professor of Jewish History at Yeshiva University and director of the YU Center for Israel Studies. Fine specializes in Jewish history in the Greco-Roman period. He focuses upon the literature, art, and archaeology of ancient Judaism, and the ways that modern scholars have interpreted Jewish antiquity.

Contributors

Hillel Halkin is an American-born translator, author, and literary critic who has lived in Israel since 1970. Among his many translations of contemporary and classical Hebrew and Yiddish literature are Agnon's novels *A Simple Story* and *To This Day*.

Avraham Holtz is Professor Emeritus of Hebrew Literature at the Jewish Theological Seminary of America. In addition to many scholarly articles in the fields of Hebrew literature and Jewish liturgy, he is the author of *Mar'ot uMekorot*, an annotated and illustrated edition of S.Y. Agnon's novel about early nineteenth-century Galicia, *Hakhnasat Kallah*. He is currently at work on a similar edition of Agnon's novel *T'mol Shilshom*, about the Second Aliyah period in the Land of Israel.

Alan Mintz (1947–2017) was the Chana Kekst Professor of Hebrew Literature at the Jewish Theological Seminary, and one of the preeminent scholars of Hebrew Literature in America. Prior to his untimely passing, he had co-edited the English edition of S.Y. Agnon's *A City in Its Fullness* and had authored a companion volume of literary criticism, *Ancestral Tales: Reading the Buczacz Stories of S.Y. Agnon*.

Jeffrey Saks is the founding director of ATID—The Academy for Torah Initiatives and Directions in Jewish Education, in Jerusalem, and its WebYeshiva.org program. He is editor of the journal *Tradition*, series editor of The S.Y. Agnon Library at The Toby Press, and director of research at the Agnon House in Jerusalem.

Moshe Simkovich has been an educator in the United States and Israel and has been instrumental in the founding of several successful synagogues and schools. He holds degrees from the University of Chicago and was founding Head of Stern (now Kohelet) Yeshiva High School in Philadelphia. Presently, he is the Educational Consultant for the Associated Talmud Torahs, in Chicago.

Laura Wiseman is a member of faculty in Humanities and Education at York University in Toronto. Professor Wiseman's research is in layers of Hebrew of Hebrew language and literature, and the influence and effects of intertextual echoes.

CONTRIBUTORS

Wendy Zierler is Sigmund Falk Professor of Modern Jewish Literature and Feminist Studies at HUC-JIR in New York. She is the author of *And Rachel Stole the Idols: The Emergence of Modern Hebrew Women's Writing*, and most recently of *Movies and Midrash: Popular Film and Jewish Religious Conversation*, which was a finalist for the National Jewish Book Award in Jewish Thought. She is co-editor of *Prooftexts: A Journal of Jewish Literary History* and of two forthcoming books, *These Truths We Hold: Judaism in the Age of Truthiness* and *Building a City: Writings on Agnon's Buczacz in Memory of Alan Mintz*.

Index

Ahad Ha'am (Asher Ginzberg), 13, 37–39, 98
Another Tallit, 8, 159n18
Auden, Wystan Hugh, 2, 4

Bahya ibn Paquda, 15
Balak (Biblical), 68, 79
Balak (dog), 6, 8, 9n4, 68, 79–83, 87–89, 92–93, 97–98, 105, 108–10
Baron, Devorah, 34, 166, 168–88
Ben-Avi, Itamar, 24
Ben Dov, Yakov, 49
Ben-Dov, Nitza, 70, 186
Ben-Gurion, David, 118, 123, 155
Ben-Yehudah, Eliezer, 63, 74–75, 85, 102
Bezalel ben Uri ben Hur, 30
Bezalel School of Art, 30, 39, 55, 63, 74–75, 77, 85
Bezalel Museum, 52–53
Bialik, Hayim Nahman, 5, 34, 98, 125, 162–64
Bnai Brith Lodges, 55
Brehm's *Life of Animals*, 110
Brenner, Yosef Hayim, 6, 20, 24, 28, 62–66, 72, 75, 85–86, 96, 98, 169
The Bridal Canopy, 3, 74, 100, 116
Buczacz, xvii, 16, 44–48, 50, 52–56, 58, 102, 115–24, 127, 131

Chelm, 157

Council of the Four Lands, 122
The Covenant of Love, 135–39, 140–46, 150

Dina (Biblical), 33–34
Double Headed Eagle (Hapsburg Eagle), 47, 48, 50–53, 58
Dreidels, 47–48, 50
Dubno, Great Synagogue Menorah, 50–52, 55

Eban, Abba, 128, 198
Eliot, Thomas Sterns, 2, 4
Elkan, Benno, 56–57
    See Knesset Menorah
Exile, xvii–xviii, 2, 18–19, 26–29, 36, 40, 65, 80, 95–96, 98, 122–23, 129, 130–33, 135–41, 149, 200
Ezekiel (Prophet), 11, 35n44, 53, 138–39

Fable of the Goat, 22–25, 33
Faulkner, William, 127

Get (Jewish Bill of Divorce), 26
Ge'ulah (redemption), 18–19, 25, 27, 37–40
A Guest for the Night, 3, 7, 13, 139
Gordon, Yehuda Leib, 34, 73, 75
Green, Graham, 1, 2
Gustav of Sweden, 126, 128

Index

Ḥalutzim (Zionist pioneers), 19, 20–21, 66, 76, 94–95
Hasiman, 15
Hanukkah, 42–43, 47, 63
HaSavta Hanye, 168–69, 172–83, 185–88
Herzog, Isaac Halevy, 56–58

ibn Gabirol, Shlomo, 15–16
Ir uMelo'ah, 115, 117–19, 122, 126

Jaffa, xv–xviii, 20, 24–25, 30n34, 38, 61, 64, 66, 69, 70, 73–76, 79, 84–85, 94–96, 98, 105, 136–37
Jerusalem, xv–xviii, 6, 15–16, 21, 24–30, 32–33, 35–38, 39n49, 40, 49–50, 61, 63–64, 66–67, 74–76, 77, 79, 84–84, 94, 96–97, 105, 108, 121, 128–30, 132–33, 162, 166–67, 169–70, 173, 183–84, 187, 188
Jonah (Biblical), 14n10, 137, 147
Joseph (Biblical), 23, 45

Kierkegaard, Soren, 2
Khmelnytskyi Uprising, 115
Knesset Menorah, 56–57
Kotzo Shel Yod, 34
Kook, Abraham Isaac HaKoen, 133, 139–41, 148–49

Lamm, Norman, 145
Levites, 129–30
Lewis, Clive Staples, 2, 9
Lewy, Yohanan (Hans), 49
Lowe, Rabbi Judah (Maharal), 143–44

Ma'aseh ha-Menorah, 42–48, 50–51, 53–56, 58–59
Maimonides, Moses, 55n41, 56, 130, 153, 159–60
Margaliot, Hayyim Zeev, 50, 52
 Dubno Rabbati, 50, 51–52

Meah She'arim, 67–68, 79–81, 87, 91, 94, 96, 109
Menorah, Arch of Titus, 43, 49–50, 56
Menorah, Jerusalem Temple, 43, 49–50, 54–55
Menorah, film company, 49
Menorah, Hammath Tiberias synagogue, 49
Menorah, of the Tabernacle, 47, 55
Menorah, national emblem of Israel, 43, 50
Mendele Mokher Sforim, 97
Midrash, 26, 32, 34, 36, 83–84, 107, 129, 143, 147, 161

Neveh Shalom, 66, 71, 139
Nazis, 15, 44, 50, 53, 198
New Yishuv, 25, 73, 96
Nobel Prize Acceptance Speech, xviii, 21, 125–26, 128–33

O'Conner, Flannery, 1
Old Yishuv, 6, 25–26, 30, 32, 67, 73, 78–79, 96
Only Yesterday (Tmol Shilshom), xv–xviii, 3, 6–7, 20, 55, 61–99, 100–106, 108–12
The Orange Peel, 151–64
Oz, Amos, 71–72, 94–96, 98, 167, 179

Petaḥ Tikvah, 59, 104
Political satire, 152–157, 160–64
Polish Eagle, 47, 51

Rabies, 92, 98, 108, 110

Sa'adia Gaon, 15
Sachs, Nelly, 126–27
Satan, 8, 29, 33
Second Aliyah, xv–xviii, 19–20, 22, 24–25, 28, 30–31, 38, 66, 68, 74, 94–95, 105, 139, 170
 See also Halutzim, New Yishuv
Sefer HaMa'asim, 2, 8, 15
Schatz, Boris, 30, 38n47, 63, 74, 85

Index

Scholem, Gershom, 24
Schocken, Salman, 104, 118
Shtetl, 19, 44, 68, 76, 94, 108, 169, 174–75, 178, 180–83, 185, 190–93
Slouschz, Nahum, 49
Soloveitchik, Joseph Baer, 10–11
Strypa River, 46–47, 49, 52
Sukenik, Eleazar Lippa, 50

Tabernacle, 27, 30, 48
Tehilla, 12, 108, 115, 166–70, 172–79, 181–88
Tel Aviv, 56, 105
Temple of Jerusalem, 43, 45, 48, 53–55, 123, 129–30, 132–33, 175, 187

Tiber River, 49–50
Tisha BeAv
    Adopted birthday, 202; in Nobel speech, 128–29
Titus
    Emperor, 129, 200; Menorah 43, 49–50, 56; Arch of 3, 49–50, 56

Wisse, Ruth, 132–33
A Whole Loaf (story), 8–9, 11 12

Yadin, Yigael, 56
Yaron, Emunah, 110, 115
Yom Kippur, 8, 130, 178, 193n4

Zweig, Stefan, 49

www.ingramcontent.com/pod-product-compliance
Lightning Source LLC
Chambersburg PA
CBHW051642230426
43669CB00013B/2401